Praise for
Bring Work to Life by Bringing Your Life to Work
and Tracy Brower

"This book captures one of the most important challenges facing companies today. No matter the size of the company, the engagement of the employee base is critical to success. Tracy Brower expertly explores how leaders can look at all aspects of the work/life conundrum and how they can create solutions that have great impact on people, the workplace, and the ultimate positive return that can be produced. This should be recommended reading for anyone who is truly interested in having an engaged employee population."　　　　　　　—Lisa Brummel, chief people officer, Microsoft

"As the industrial corporate ladder gives way to a digital-age lattice, resetting the career-life fit agenda is essential. Brower sharpens our grasp of this elusive though vital topic, offering pragmatic, accessible solutions."
　　　　　　　—Cathy Benko, vice chairman and managing principal,
Deloitte LLP, and best-selling author of *Mass Career Customization*
and *The Corporate Lattice*

"Tracy Bower asks us the most important question we can imagine about our work: Can our work be brought to life? The simple answer, of course, is yes, and we do it by bringing our life to work and honoring both. But simple is never easy. Know that by applying the lessons in her book, you are contemplating one of the most arduous journeys, and perhaps the most rewarding."
　　　　　　　—Richard Sheridan, CEO and chief storyteller, Menlo Innovations,
and author of *Joy, Inc.: How We Built a Workplace People Love*

"Brower has nailed it with very clear ideas, compelling stories, and a wonderful combination of theory, research, and practice. Brower brings together unique knowledge and experience for great impact. This is a must-read."
　　　　　　　—Xavier Unkovic, global president, Mars Drinks

"Everyone experiences blurring boundaries of work and life. Brower cleverly and clearly shows that integration of work and life through abundance, alignment, and adaptation will be good for people, organizations, and communities. Her ideas are fresh and recommendations grounded. Her work helps leaders lead, architects design, and employees work in the integrated organization of the future."

—Dave Ulrich, PhD, Rensis Likert professor, Ross School of Business, University of Michigan, member of the board of directors of Herman Miller Inc., and author of twenty-five books on human resources

"This is the next great advance in management: work-life integration. Tracy Brower's powerful insights provide a clear and implementable guide managers can use to put employees first and improve organizational performance."

—Paul J. Zak, PhD, professor of economics, psychology and management, Claremont Graduate University and author of *The Moral Molecule: The Source of Love and Prosperity*

"Tracy Brower's new book is a tour de force of inspiring, yet practical ideas for bringing humanity to your workplace. It is guaranteed to make you rethink the way that life and work can be integrated. Hint: If you are a CEO or HR leader, you ignore this book at your peril! You probably won't survive the decade without adding these ideas to your repertoire."

—Dan Denison, PhD, professor of organization and management, IMD Business School, Lausanne, Switzerland, and co-author of *Leading Culture Change in Global Organizations*

"Tracy has an amazing wealth of knowledge and experience that she has captured and synthesized into a highly readable and thought provoking book. This is not just another book that inspires you but leaves you wondering how to apply what you have learned. It is the perfect blend of theory and practical strategies to help you cope with the changing world of work."

—Cynthia Kay, author of *Small Business for Big Thinkers: Unconventional Strategies to Connect With and Win Big Business*, and owner of Cynthia Kay and Company

"Tracy has the rare ability to deliver profound uncommon sense in an increasingly hectic world full of supposed quick fixes and silver bullets. We don't so much have a work life and a personal life...we have a life. And Tracy clearly shows how to add as much value to our lives and by extension, the lives of the people we're fortunate to work with. Tracy's book should be required reading for everyone entering the business world."

—Kevin Knebl, international speaker, author,
trainer, and coach

"Tracy has provided a clear roadmap and makes the business case for a new way of managing that will help leaders bring a more civilized environment to the workplace. Her book isn't just a philosophical treatise on today's work-life demands, but is based on extensive research with hundreds of executives. In the clutter of new wave business books, this is one to read and use."

—Karen Bates Kress, president, Yellowstone Park Foundation

"Work-life integration and time poverty are global challenges. Brower's clear ideas and compelling stories provide both direction and inspiration for companies across the globe. Her pragmatic recommendations allow you to tap into energy, enthusiasm, and abundance to transform your organization and drive performance. This is a pioneering book that delivers."

—K. H. Moon, president, New Paradigm Institute of Korea,
member of the Drucker Institute advisory board,
former member of the Korean National Assembly,
and past chairman and CEO of Yuhan-Kimberly

"This is a great playbook for leaders that want to build high performing organizations through cultures leveraging work life supports and driving exceptional employee engagement. This is not just theory. We put into action many of the ideas outlined in this wonderful guide during a significant office tower makeover. Our results were outstanding and we succeeded in bringing work to life."

—Sue Ortenstone, SVP and chief human resources officer
at CenterPoint Energy and previously EVP and
chief administrative officer at El Paso Corporation

"The way we work is constantly changing. And as we look at the role Design plays in creating productive environments that promote health, engagement, and well-being, evidence must be central to the decisions we make. Tracy's research is helping ASID to showcase the impact and value of those decisions. This book helps to tell that story."

—Randy Fiser, president and CEO of ASID,
American Society of Interior Designers

"Bring Work to Life by Bringing Life to Work shows how work-life integration is not some touchy-feely concept or a nice add-on to have once a company attends to the more nitty-gritty parts of its business. Rather, work-life integration is absolutely essential if organizations are to get the most from the key resource in our knowledge age—their people—and thrive in today's fast-changing corporate world. Tracy Brower has managed to make all of this abundantly clear by deftly balancing serious scholarship with elegant simplicity, historical context with practical insights, and deep research with telling anecdotes."

—Rick Wartzman, executive director, Drucker Institute,
and author of *What Would Drucker Do Now?*

Bring Work
to Life

by

Bringing Life
to Work

Bring Work
to Life
by
Bringing Life
to Work

**A GUIDE FOR LEADERS
AND ORGANIZATIONS**

TRACY BROWER

First published by Bibliomotion, Inc.
39 Harvard Street
Brookline, MA 02445
Tel: 617-934-2427
www.bibliomotion.com

Printed in the United States of America

Library of Congress Cataloging-in-Publication Data

Brower, Tracy.
  Bring work to life by bringing life to work : a guide for leaders and organizations / Tracy Brower.
     pages cm
  Summary: "Bring Work to Life by Bringing Life to Work is your go-to guide to work-life support, providing easy-to-read strategies for building and implementing your organization's strategies to harness work-life supports, increasing positive impact to your bottom line"— Provided by publisher.
  ISBN 978-1-62956-003-8 (hardback) — ISBN 978-1-62956-004-5 (ebook) — ISBN 978-1-62956-005-2 (enhanced ebook)
  1. Quality of work life. 2. Work environment. 3. Personnel management. I. Title.
  HD6955.B738 2014
  658.3'12—dc23
                    2014020199

Dedicated with love to my family.
You are abundance and the life in my work-life.

Contents

PART III

Leading for Adaptation:
Implementing Work-Life Supports

Foreword

Brian C. Walker
President and CEO, Herman Miller, Inc.

In 1927, just four years after he bought Michigan Star Furniture Company and renamed it The Herman Miller Furniture Company after his father-in-law, D.J. De Pree had an epiphany. This event has shaped attitudes at the company I work for ever since, the first expression of what's now an inclusive and welcoming organization.

One day the company millwright died, the guy who kept all the woodworking machines in good order. D.J., like the good man he was, went to visit Hermann Rummelt's widow at home, where he learned that Rummelt was a poet, an expert craftsman, a good family man, and a counselor to veterans of the Great War worried because they had killed so many people. A deeply religious man, D.J. pondered all these dimensions of Rummelt's life he had not known about.

The result: D.J. came to the conclusion that he had missed many parts of the people he worked with, that each person "was extraordinary," and that Herman Miller would be much better off if everyone felt free to bring all of themselves to work. This was the beginning for us of what Tracy Brower in her new book calls "bringing life to work." This aspiration has shaped our company and the people in it for decades.

The book you're about to read will prove to you that in the second decade of the twenty-first century, encouraging people to bring their lives to work results in happier people and more productive organizations. The experience and evidence Tracy brings to this proposition are impressive. Not only will you hear what organizations from all over the world have learned about engaging people at work, but you will see how "work-life supports" have been realized to great effect. For the foreseeable future, organizations will be ever more dependent on the creativity, engagement, and enthusiasm of their employees. With global competition as a given, what some writers have called the "war for talent" has already become international. Tracy has examined a real tool for attracting and keeping committed, creative people.

Work-life supports should be on every leader's list of things to understand and realize.

The increasing diversity around the world presents us all with unlimited possibilities for improvement and performance—but only if we understand it and welcome it. Tracy is right to point to many kinds of diversity—in age, education, and simply in the ways we choose to live our lives. Diversity can become a wonderful engine for creativity and community. Though he wouldn't have used the word, D.J. felt the potential in diversity on his way home from the millwright's house that day.

D.J. De Pree was the first of many wonderful leaders at Herman Miller. He began a tradition of holding leaders—himself included—to a high standard. One of my favorite ideas from D.J., who lived to be 99 and showed up at the office into his late eighties: businesses must "face scrutiny as to their humanity." Tracy, I, and everyone working here now are the beneficiaries. The commitment to work-life supports begins with leaders, and Tracy's experience with and observations about leaders form the proper context for what you will learn about bringing work to life.

The combination of personal experience, a range of examples, and ways of actually bringing work to life makes this book part inspiration and part how to.

The humanity of organizations begins with leaders. For me, a large part of being human is working for a purpose, something larger than ourselves. At Herman Miller our work includes the many volunteer and service activities we participate in. We don't pretend to dictate a purpose to everyone, and we give two days a year to every employee to spend as a volunteer for a purpose they believe in. To a large extent, employees also decide where we direct our financial contributions as a corporation.

The realities of organizational life today make bringing work to life an imperative. Without it, I'm certain that you will have no employees, and thus no customers and no business. Leaders of all sorts—and I mean both hierarchical leaders and what we call at Herman Miller "roving leaders," the people who rise to leadership ad hoc—must make the choice to acknowledge and provide for the humanity of their followers. And followers must feel free to be engaged in life and work simultaneously. Whether you're acting as a leader or a follower, this is the real secret for more and more talented, creative people around the world: work is part of life, not the other way round.[1]

Introduction

This is a book about how to bring work to life. It's about both work and life, and how to leverage work-life supports to bring vitality, vigor, and verve to the experience of work—and thus to life. Bringing work to life means that employees are able to bring their talents and passions to a career that fulfills them and in turn produces better results for organizations. Bringing work to life also means that work and life are part of a connected whole. When the demands of life can be a part of work, and when work can appropriately integrate with life, employees benefit and organizations benefit. I will explain, but first, it is important to start with a sense of the demands that organizations, leaders, and employees are facing.

A BLURRED WORLD

Most of us work for a living, and most of us face significant demands from both life and from work. We need to work. We need to achieve a level of fulfillment in our careers. We must foster good relationships with our partners, spouses, children, and other family members. We want to make a contribution to our communities. We need to quench our spirits with our own hobbies or activities. We are required to be at work early for the monthly staff meeting. We must retrieve the kids from dance class. We need to pick up groceries and make dinner. We want to care for aging parents. We are required to work over the weekend in order to finish the report for our boss. No matter who we are we must determine how to navigate these types of demands, and the demands don't come neatly in containers. They collide all at the same time. The night that a critical meeting runs late at the office is the same night our daughter performs in *Fiddler on the Roof.* Or just when we get that promotion at work, our son makes the travel team for soccer. Work and life are inextricably linked.

Technology has further blurred the lines between life and work. The line is blurry because things are moving so fast. The line is blurry because it is going away. It is fuzzy and fading. In fact, some would argue the line isn't simply blurred or fuzzy, it is nonexistent. Because work and life are coming together, we must collectively determine how to create the conditions for work to be a positive experience—one in which workers want to bring discretionary time, energy, and passion to the job. After work, we need the energy to bring our best to our personal lives. In the morning, we want to anticipate a day that allows us to bring our best to our work.

In this blurred world, what are the responsibilities of leaders and organizations? What are the ways employers can help meet these needs? What are the ways we can more effectively bring work to life and life to work? This book explores answers to these questions. Work-life supports are the benefits, policies, practices, and organizational cultural norms that help employees navigate demands. They are benefits that offer provision for both maternity and paternity time off for an adoption. They are policies for telecommuting. They are company norms that allow flexibility for employees who must leave early in order to care for a sick relative. They are tuition reimbursement programs for the workers who want to continue education. They are core work hour arrangements.

However, these are the easy part—these are just the mechanisms that allow flexibility and options for workers. More importantly, these work-life supports must be implemented in ways that ensure effectiveness. It won't work for leaders to simply pick a few work-life supports from a menu and scotch tape them into an organization's policy manual. This book describes not only the mechanisms for work-life supports, but also the factors that must be considered in order for work-life supports to be successfully implemented. This book describes the conditions that will make the work-life supports effective in bringing work to life.

WHAT THIS BOOK IS . . . AND ISN'T

This is not a book about how organizations can wrench more from employees. Instead, it describes how employees can be more fulfilled, as well as the relationship of choice and self-determination that promote this fulfillment. Leaders and organizations create the conditions that allow employees to make more of their own choices more often and work in the ways that work for them. Some workers will want to keep work and life more separate. Some will want to combine work and life. Work is part of life and life should be a part of our work. Leaders and organizations should create the conditions for abundance and joy—plenty of options for choice and fulfillment. Leaders and organizations should create situations in which employees can have it all—as they choose it.

Work-life balance is the wrong notion. We are better served by seeking to navigate and integrate work and life. Balance connotes a zero-sum game in which work and life are separate and mutually exclusive. The concept of bringing work to life requires a broader view that provides for integrating work and life demands, and meeting both fully. It requires a comprehensive approach that increases workers' capacity and helps mitigate demands, and in turn provides support for navigating the complexities we face in the realms of both work and life.

Accomplishing this integration and navigation of work and life is not a prescription with one right answer. Instead, there are multiple right answers. The best options are aligned with where a company is going and what its culture is seeking to create. They are aligned with an employee and where he is in his life course, and they provide for flexibility throughout a worker's life and career. Leaders and organizations must find ways to serve the whole person— and in turn help the person contribute his best to the organization's results.

The topic of work-life integration is not only for women or only for moms. It is for both men and women, since work is a reality for both, and since both men and women lead full lives and manage multiple demands. When we include the whole population in the dialogue and the solutions— not just women—we all benefit. In addition, we gain when we broaden the dialogue to those who may not have children or those who are empty nesters. In 2010 20 percent of women did not have children and 49 percent of those were voluntarily without children.[1] Work-life supports must embrace all aspects of life—those associated with raising children and those that go beyond children.

Peter Drucker, known as the father of modern management,[2] believed that organizations have a responsibility to workers and also to society. He asserted that managers could positively affect workers, who in turn would positively affect organizations, which in turn would positively affect society. Work-life supports are mechanisms that make this contribution to workers, to organizations, and, in turn, to society. This book addresses how leaders create conditions in which workers can bring more of themselves to work, more fully express the full spectrum of their talents in the work environment, and in turn foster a contribution to society as a whole.

Organizations need not provide charity for employees, and leaders should insist on results. Providing work-life supports is good business, and it is good for employees and for organizations. This book builds the business case for work-life supports and articulates *why* they are important. It also pragmatically addresses how to implement work-life supports, how to adapt them over time, and how to leverage them in order to serve employees and serve organizations.

The subsequent chapters advise leaders, influencers, and decision makers within organizations on how to create a work experience where employees are supported and organizations get better results. The recommendations help organizations adapt so employees can bring work to life and life to work, and find a new reality where employees are successfully navigating both.

BUT WHY SHOULD YOU CARE?

Why should leaders and organizations care? There is plenty on their plates already. Here's why: leaders and organizations should pay attention to work-life supports because corporations depend on workers' commitment, engagement, and enthusiasm. Organizations are dependent on workers' discretionary time. If workers "quit and stay" (called presenteeism), corporations may be retaining their physical being, but they're not accessing workers' best efforts, their most creative output, or those few extra minutes or hours after the workday to complete a project in the most thorough way. Providing work-life supports is good for organizations. Ellen Galinsky, who leads National Studies for the Changing Workforce, found that when companies provide greater work-life supports:

> ... employees exhibit more positive work outcomes, such as job sat-
> isfaction, commitment to employer, and retention, as well as more
> positive life outcomes such as less interference between job and
> family life, less negative spillover from job to home, greater life sat-
> isfaction, and better mental health.

For employers, having employees who are more engaged and more healthy results in higher retention, higher productivity, and reduced costs for medical expenses. A 2013 article by Gallup says there is a cyclical relationship between engagement and company performance and hiring. In their studies they repeatedly find that when employees are more engaged, company performance improves, and in turn, companies can hire more workers and economies benefit overall.[4] The Gallup study also found that engaged employees had lower absenteeism, were more productive, and were more likely to remain with their current employer.[5]

Work-life supports are important because workers are overburdened and overtaxed. They are deluged with demands, and they feel stressed. Dr. Kathleen Christensen, program director at the Alfred P. Sloan Foundation, says, "The American Family is experiencing a time famine."[6] As workers seek to navigate all their demands, state and federal policies aren't much help. Work has changed and workers have changed but U.S. federal policy has not. The Family Medical Leave Act (FMLA), passed in 1993, is the most comprehensive U.S. policy aimed at addressing work and family issues. However, the FMLA only covers employers that have fifty or more workers and only offers unpaid leave.[7] While FMLA was recently updated by the Department of Labor,[8] our U.S. federal policies still do not offer workers much in the way of support. As for local ordinances, San Francisco is leading the way with the Family Friendly Workplace Ordinance, which became effective January 1, 2014. It allows workers at employers of twenty or more people to apply for flexible or predictable working schedules in order to care for a child under age eighteen, a parent over sixty-five, or an ailing family member.

Notwithstanding FMLA or San Francisco's new ordinance, in the absence of broad federal requirements, corporate benefits, policies, and practices become even more important for helping families and workers successfully integrate demands of work and life. *HR Magazine* reported recently that human resource professionals expect benefits—such as health care/wellness, retirement savings/planning, flexible working benefits, and career development—to become increasingly important in recruiting efforts. In particular, 71 percent of HR professionals expect an increase in the importance of flexible working benefits to recruit the best and the brightest.[9] Leaders and organizations must pay attention to work-life supports because they are important to employees—both the people they already employ and those they hope to employ.

RECOMMENDATIONS BASED ON RESEARCH

The ideas and recommendations presented in the following chapters are based on evidence and research. Throughout my career, I've worked with hundreds of senior leaders in a broad array of industries and locations. I've conducted formal research as well as informal research. This book synthe-sizes all that I have learned and provides evidence for work-life supports in terms of which strategies are most effective.[10] I've changed some names and details in order to protect anonymity, but the views and perspectives will guide readers in making choices for their company's work-life support efforts.

A ROADMAP

In section one, *Leading to Abundance—Setting Context*, I provide new perspec-tives on today's reality and a new way to consider the current challenges of work and life demands. I define current challenges as well as the his-torical foundation for our current realities. I define work life supports and provide examples from companies that are implementing them successfully. In section one, I also show evidence of how work-life supports have positive impacts on key organizational outcomes such as employee engagement, pro-ductivity, and growth.

In section two, *Leading with Alignment—Considerations for Success*, I describe the comprehensive considerations that must be factored in when implementing work-life supports. Based on my extensive research with hun-dreds of executives, I provide the ten considerations to focus readers' efforts.

In section three, *Leading for Adaptation—Implementing Work-Life Sup-ports*, I explain how to make a business case for work-life supports, how to effectively manage change, and how to measure successes.

The considerations I provide may be either obstacles or enablers to the successful implementation of work-life supports. When I work with com-panies, I frequently conduct a "force field analysis." Despite the *Star Wars*-sounding name, the analysis is straightforward and pragmatic. It defines the forces or variables that move an organization forward and those that hold it back. Often these variables are two sides of a coin. For example, a company's *emphasis* on performance outcomes is helpful in making work-life supports work. The *absence* of focus on performance outcomes can derail work-life sup-ports. The considerations for work-life supports are criteria for success. In order to successfully implement work-life supports—in alignment with the organization's unique needs—they are the criteria that must be met. All of these levers help ensure the successful implementation of work-life sup-ports. They help workers navigate the demands they face. They help workers integrate work and life across the chapters of their life course. When they operate effectively, they bring work to life.

Simple steps to the perfect solution for workers and organizations? Easy tips for bringing work to life? Hardly. It would be ignorant, arrogant, or both to suggest that this is a quick, easy process. On the contrary, successfully implementing work-life supports requires dedication and ongoing effort. It is not a program of the month, but rather a way of managing for the long term. Bringing work to life and creating the conditions for growth, exuberance, fulfillment, choice, and self-determination are worth it for workers and for organizations. Let's get started on bringing work to life.

PART I

Leading to Abundance:
Setting Context

CHAPTER 1

Leading from a New Perspective

Pick up any business periodical or read any business-focused blog, and you will find a great deal being written about how we are working, how we should work, how we will work, and how work is changing. Search online for "mobility," "work flexibility," or "changing work" and you'll get millions of hits. These are well-worn topics and there is significant information in the system that creates noise. Here, I offer some new perspectives—new lenses—on these old topics suggesting the importance of integration of life and work over a lifetime, and the importance of creating perceptions of capacity and abundance for employees. Sometimes, looking at the same thing in a new way offers new clues that we wouldn't have seen otherwise. Leaders who align work-life supports with their organizations and adapt them appropriately will realize business benefits.

PERCEIVING REALITY

Dr. Carl Frost was a slight man, but he was a giant to me.[1] He seemed ancient and wise, and his snow-white hair contributed to this effect. I was fortunate enough to have Dr. Frost as a mentor. He used to say, "What day is it? You have to know what day it is." By this he meant that in order to make good decisions, you must have context and a sense of business literacy. You have to know what is going on outside the organization (context) and within the organization (business literacy). Making decisions without this type of knowledge is ineffective at best.

Dr. Frost was right about the need for a clear lens on reality. Work has changed significantly over the years. The challenge is to make sense of it. What is the world of work today? In addition to the world being a different place, workers are also facing a changing reality. Throughout their life course, workers must make things work, work things out, and work through both the demands of their lives and the demands of their work. Our typical conception of the relationship between the world of work and the world of our personal pursuits is balance. We perceive a dissonance or a mismatch between one world and the other, and we typically describe the solution as effectively "balancing." If we can just balance the scales, we will be able to deal with the demands on each side effectively.

INTEGRATION

One of the perspectives I offer is that balance is not the ideal we should be working toward. Our ability to find solutions is rooted in our perceptions of the problem. Unfortunately, the metaphor of balance doesn't serve us in finding a solution to this dissonance between life and work. Balance doesn't work because it implies a zero-sum game. On a scale, one side is up and the other is down. There is always a trade-off regarding how much goes on each side, and a scale requires a delicate touch lest one side become too heavy. A scale implies an "or" between choices, instead of an "and" in which abundance is possible. Another problem is that there are only two sides on a

Figure 1-1   It's NOT About Balance

scale, one up, the other down. Where do we place our investments for *all* the things that matter to us in life?

An alternative view is to consider the extent to which employees must integrate life and work. Integrating means coordinating, blending, and bringing elements of work and life into a unified whole. The worlds of work and family are deeply connected, and they are also fluid. There is a relationship between work and family and an ongoing effort by individuals within families to navigate work and family demands within the flow of their lives. For this reason, I also use the metaphor of navigation. We're navigating and charting a course as we find our way through the competing demands of work and life.

Some readers disagree with the concept of integration. They argue that employees don't want to integrate, they want to compartmentalize. They want to keep work and life separate. It's semantics. What they really mean is that they want to manage a boundary between work and life. This is appropriate. Managing the boundary is what I mean by navigation. Work is part of life. Life should be part of work, in that we should be able to bring our whole selves to work—or *more* of ourselves, at least. We also deserve to make a choice on how much to bring. There may be parts of our lives we want to keep separate from work. That's the navigation part. We should be able to navigate the demands as they come up. If an employee has to work late on the same night he was supposed to meet friends for dinner or pick up his daughter from play practice, he must navigate—find his way through—these competing demands for his time. Through these pages I'll cover how organizations can provide a level of flexibility that helps workers with this type of navigation.

THE LIFE COURSE

Workers require various types of support throughout their life course: in waves of years, months, and even days. Thinking in terms of years, the work an employee performs and the support she needs when she is just starting her career are very different from those she needs when she has a partner, has young children, has older children, needs to support elderly parents, or seeks a retirement off-ramp. Considering the life course over months, workers may need different types of support through different seasons. This is especially true of workers who have children in school and for whom the school calendar produces differing needs for child care, working hours, and school requirements.

Even day to day, workers may need varying supports. These may take the form of different technology, varied working hours, or even flextime as workers navigate their life demands on a daily basis. Supporting the employee over her life course requires adaptation—creating a context within which the employee can adapt to the changing needs and demands of life. Throughout the life course—over days, months, or years—leaders and organizations are in a position to help employees adapt through providing benefits, policies, practices, and organizational cultural norms. Offering these types of supports has been an underutilized approach to creating a positive experience of work.

DEMAND AND CAPACITY

In 2005, Patricia Voydanoff[2] demonstrated that when we perceive that we have the personal capacity to meet the demands we are facing, we will be more satisfied with both our work and our family life and perform better in both realms. A critical element of this theory is the importance of perception. The relationship of demand and capacity is less about the objective demands we face and more about our perception of the demands in relationship to whether or not we believe we can handle what's coming at us. Does a worker feel capable of handling the tasks before him? Does she feel greater than her responsibilities or do her responsibilities seem like they are outstripping her ability to meet them all? This is a fluid question and typically perceptions vary over time, but in general, when workers feel as if they can handle the demands they face, they will feel less stress and more fulfillment.

Leaders and organizations are key to creating work-life supports that can reduce perceptions of demand and also increase perceptions of capacity. When a dad has the option to work at home because his son is sick with strep throat, the demands on his time are reduced. When a woman has the ability to leave work early on Tuesday to visit her ailing mother, her capacity to both work and support her parent is increased. This is the relationship of work-life supports to demand and capacity. It's a peoples' economics model. Leaders and organizations can support employees in navigating their life course and effectively integrating work and life by offering work-life supports that reduce the perceived demands and provide for greater capacity on the parts of workers. Leaders and organizations can—through benefits, policies, practices, and norms—make the demands a little less demanding and make the perception of capacity a little greater.

CREATING ABUNDANCE:
A WHOLE NEW PERSPECTIVE

Abundance is a belief that there is enough to go around, that there is plenty, and that we can find ways to access it. Shifting to a paradigm of abundance–rather than scarcity–provides a whole new perspective on the challenge of work-life. Years ago, I worked with a company that manufactured earth-moving equipment. As part of a vendor orientation, we had the opportunity to sit on bleachers behind glass and see a demonstration of what the equipment could do. There was a giant arena with piles and piles of dirt. Through a narrated experience, we witnessed the capabilities of the machines—to dig, to move, to drop, and to load dirt. It was surprisingly like watching a dance. During the show, a colleague leaned over to me and pointed out that the whole company was founded on the principle that there was a lot of dirt in the world that was in the wrong places. Abundance is like this. There is plenty of time, there is plenty of really good work to do, there is plenty of recognition, there are plenty of rewards. The challenge for leaders and organizations is to ensure these are distributed and accessible. There is an opportunity to create the conditions for abundance in the work environment. Work-life supports are a pragmatic and effective way to do this. Recognizing employees for a job well done, finding ways for employees to make choices concerning the types of projects they work on, and providing new technological options so employees can work at home are all examples of ways to create abundance.

Leaders must make this real day by day and hour by hour in the ways they lead employees. Countless miniscule decisions and attitudes drive the overall experience that an employee has on a team or in an organization. Early in my career, I reported to a leader who was always full of energy and enthusiasm toward her team and her work. She was the leader of our learning and development team. This was in the years before e-mail, and voice mail was our lifeline. We left significant numbers of voice mails for our team members and we listened to many voice mails from each other. In our team's culture, we could sustain long-winded, even deep, conversations through the exchange of voice mail alone. An important part of the culture that Mary created was in praising team members' accomplishments. We would regularly receive messages about this team member or that team member who had finished a big project to rave reviews, solved a snarly problem, or received accolades from a customer. Mary's messages were not just cheerleading, they had substance. She was aware of the real work the team members were doing and she provided recognition that felt meaningful. In addition, Mary gave us control over our work, our time, and our schedules. As long as we accomplished the "what," we were free to make our own choices for the "how."

Mary was creating abundance. There was plenty of positive recognition and rewards to go around. There were plenty of desirable projects, and we felt a sense of equity for the way they were handed out. The team followed Mary's lead, and while we didn't always agree, we always supported and reinforced one another's efforts. We wanted to succeed. We wanted to contribute. We wanted to engage because there was always an upside with the recognition Mary and the rest of the team members bestowed. This is abundance. It is the feeling leaders foster that there are plenty of great opportunities to go around. Work feels less demanding when we can make our own choices regarding where and how we work. Work actually fuels our sense of capacity when it encourages us and provides for us to accomplish great things in concert with others.

BRINGING IT ALL TO WORK

Abundance encourages people to bring all of themselves—their passions, their creativity, and their talents—to work. It creates a context for joy at work. Abundance provides the opportunity for people to express themselves more fully at work. A leader creates abundance when he provides for employees to engage in the work that inspires them. A leader creates abundance when she aligns work with the creativity and the talents an employee most wants to express. A leader creates abundance when he connects the employee's efforts to a broader purpose. As workers, we all want to build cathedrals, not just lay bricks. Abundance is when we can look up from our brick-laying and see the cathedral that will result from our collective efforts.

Don't misunderstand, abundance does not mean that companies are making additional demands of workers, it means that organizations provide for workers so they can bring their best to their jobs. This is very different from pressuring workers to be perfect. A friend was describing the concept of acting like a "pilot" at work. A professional pilot doesn't fly constantly, he works in shifts. In addition, sometimes a pilot uses the autopilot feature of a plane. However, there are crucial moments when a pilot's skills are necessary: upon take-off and landing, during situations such as turbulence, or during unexpected weather events. Having a pilot's viewpoint at work suggests that workers be prepared to bring their best game all the time, but not be pressured to be 100 percent perfect every minute on every project every time. There are times during which it makes sense to do good work on autopilot and conserve energy for crucial situations that require hands-on flying.

MOMENTS MATTER

Many companies today are focused on the total experience of work and the "touch points" for an employee. These may also be "moments of truth" during which the company provides critical support for an employee, or doesn't. A friend told me a story recently about a coworker whose sixth-grade daughter didn't get off the bus after school one day. Her son called and was frantic. Normally, brother and sister met at the bus stop after coming home from their elementary school and middle school buses and stayed together at home until their parents returned home after work. On this ordinary Tuesday, Lucy hadn't gotten off the bus. The mother was frantic. She called the father. She called the school. She called the bus service. She called the neighbors. No one had seen her daughter. In addition, she had a critically important customer visiting and it was her turn to present within the next half hour. She left work then and there. She dropped everything in order to find her daughter. Luckily, her daughter was safe at an unanticipated sports practice. Fortunately, her boss supported her sudden departure and developed a contingency plan to cover her time with the customer. This is an example of how work-life supports operate at a "moment of truth." The company's culture and leadership allowed for this employee to have the flexibility to leave at the most inopportune time. The experience has remained with the mother for a long time. For her, it is evidence of her company being supportive in all aspects of her life. Work-life supports provide the opportunity to touch employees throughout critical times in their navigation of work and life demands, and to create abundance.

SELF-DETERMINATION AND CHOICE

One of the critical components to successful work-life supports is the self-determination and choice that organizations give employees. Providing more choice, more freedom, and more autonomy is a good thing for employees and a good thing for organizations. By giving more choice, organizations create more ways for employees to contribute. Within our American culture, most people feel more positively when they have greater levels of self-determination, authority over their own choices, and the chance to direct their own courses of action. Autonomy is so important that it is a critical concept not only within social psychology, but within government and politics, medical science, and ethics. When companies provide greater autonomy for workers, they are demonstrating respect for employees' capacity to participate in decision making, exercise sound judgment, and accomplish results.

Work-life supports that provide autonomy give workers more control over where they work, when they work, how they accomplish tasks, which projects to complete, and how to adjust and accommodate competing demands during the day. An employee with autonomy can make the choice to take a longer lunch and pick up the dry cleaning on the way back to the office, and then work again later in the evening to put the finishing touches on the report. Self-sufficiency of this kind allows a worker to attend his daughter's track meet and take a conference call in the car between her events. In this type of "adult-to-adult" relationship, the organization is treating the employee with respect and an assumption that he will do good work. This type of "adult-to-adult" model results in employees feeling greater senses of mastery, confidence, and motivation. Fostering more autonomy also provides for healthy development and growth. As workers make more of their own decisions, and can then learn from those and have the freedom to adjust and improve, both the worker and the organization benefit.

Organizations also create abundance when they provide employees with free choice about projects. A friend of mine works at a technology company in Silicon Valley. All employees are invited to spend fully 20 percent of paid time on projects of their own choosing. My friend conceives of what she would love to do and frames the project in a clear and compelling way. These free choice projects must be serious and adequately developed to produce a succinct statement of the effort. This provides scaffolding for the effort. Then, the statement of effort is posted on an internal company site that advertises the opportunity to others within the company. Employees may invest their 20 percent paid discretionary time on projects of their own initiative, or on those of others with whom they share a passionate purpose. This is an example of abundance. Employees tap their passions. They contribute to and excel in projects of their own choosing. They must still meet their goals and job responsibilities, but there is also an institutionalized opportunity to bring additional interests to work and focus on them. However, this is not only for the employees' benefit. The organization also benefits from employees who are enthusiastically engaged and from the output that is generated.

CHANGING THE GAME

Leaders must change the game for employees and make work more fulfilling and less demanding. When work is perceived as just another demand, workers tend to feel overburdened. On the other hand, leaders can create a sense of abundance that establishes work as a place for employees to fully connect, relate, create, and fulfill themselves. Jim Clifton, CEO of Gallup and author of *The Coming Jobs War*, says that workers must believe the best part of their life is ahead of them rather than behind them, an attitude that is a predictor of well-being. He says, "Nothing great happens in an environment of misery. Inspiration really does matter. No one is productive if they're miserable...high wellbeing—that's a marker for everything good. Unbridled, crazy enthusiasm...That kind of inspiration creates all kinds of energy, and that energy creates jobs."[3]

TYING IT TOGETHER

How does this all tie together? Here's an example: a friend of mine is a senior vice president at a consumer goods organization. She views employee development as her primary task. Every quarter, she sets aside time with each employee over lunch to discuss the employee's career. Her rule of thumb is that the lunch conversation cannot include discussion of mundane tasks or be used to catch up on work-related topics. Instead, the lunch conversation covers how the employee is doing as a person and the employee's professional goals. The personal aspect of the lunches helps the employee feel she can bring her entire self to work. This is abundance.

By knowing her employees deeply, this leader is able to assign tasks based on employees' skills and passions and the best fit for where they are and where they want to be. This is also abundance. She points out that there have been times when an employee's personal goals weren't aligned with the department's needs. In these cases, she was able to help the employees find pathways out of the department. One moved into a finance role and the other went back to school to pursue nursing. This too, is abundance. They were wins for the organization and the employees because they helped change situations where alignment between the job and the passions didn't exist. The perspectives I'm suggesting—abundance, alignment, demand and capacity—are not mutually exclusive. They overlap. They are red threads that weave through the process of leading and weave through the work-life supports that companies implement.

Work-life supports—mechanisms such as benefits, policies, and practices—can help employees by reducing perceived demands and increasing perceived capacity. Giving choice, control, and options for the ways employees work creates abundance. Providing for rewards and flexibility also creates abundance. Options for continuing education and freedom to engage in community activities during working hours create space for abundance. Giving employees control over their working hours provides autonomy and reduces perceived demands. Offering the opportunity to work remotely increases the perception of capacity on the part of employees. These are only a few options. There are many more, but any of the alternatives help employees integrate and navigate across the life course and shift their perceptions of demand and capacity. These concepts, ideas, and solutions will be the substance of the coming sections of this book.

It all sounds like a lot to manage, and it is, but it's worth it. When organizations support employees in these ways, they engage more completely, find work more satisfying, maintain a longer commitment to work, and ultimately perform better in support of organizational goals. Ellen Galinsky, a long-time researcher on the topics of work and life, found in her 2010 study that when workplaces offered flexibility, workers had more job engagement, job satisfaction, retention, and health.[4] These are the types of results that organizations are seeking. Offering work-life supports is a way to accomplish them.

IN SUM

The world of work has changed; we are overburdened and challenged to meet all of our demands and maintain our sanity. Unfortunately, the concept of "balance" is the wrong metaphor and it actually inhibits us from solving the problem of work-life fulfillment. It is more useful to begin solving the problem of work-life challenges by considering how workers can *integrate* and *navigate* life and work across the life course—through years, over months, across days. When employees feel they have the capacity to handle all the demands facing them, they perform better. So how do corporations provide for this capacity and demand? Leaders are key. They provide work-life supports and they create a sense of abundance and autonomy for workers. What's the bottom line? Providing work-life supports is good for workers and good for organizations. There are positive outcomes for both in terms of engagement, satisfaction, and performance.

CHAPTER 2

Leading from Past to Present

Our current reality is informed by where we have been historically and the vanguard of theorists who influenced today's perspectives. Who are workers and what are they facing today? What is the historical foundation for today's reality? Is it as dismal as some of the statistics suggest? How do organizations embrace the whole person at work and how do they bring work to life? How do leaders create the context for joy? This chapter describes our current conundrum of work and life with these questions in mind.

WORKERS TODAY

Work is changing and so are workers. Spillover is the norm for all kinds of workers—men and women, parents and those without children. Workers have full lives and identities both inside and outside of work, and understanding these realities is an important starting point.

AN INCLUSIVE VIEW

Employees are experiencing spillover from work to home and from home to work. In one of my own sets of research, I found women face more spillover than men and those at higher income levels tend to face less spillover.

In addition, in 2007, the American Psychological Association found that 43 percent of Americans were sensing interference from family to job and 52 percent were experiencing interference from job to family.[1]

This spillover is occurring for men and women, and for parents and nonparents. Most research efforts, articles, and books focus on mothers. They leave out men and they leave out those who don't have children. However, the need for successful navigation of work and life is relevant to all.

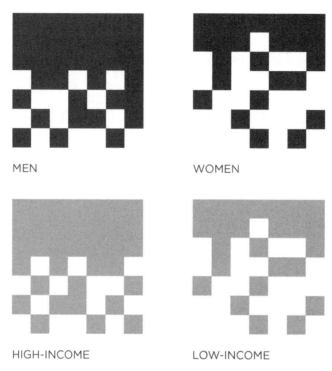

Figure 2-1 Job/Family Spillover Patterns based on gender and income

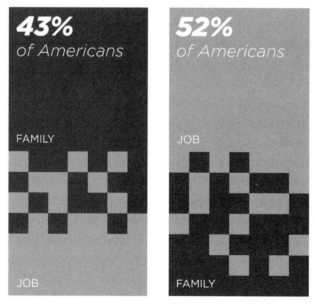

Figure 2-2 Job/Work Spillover Patterns overall

A broader view is necessary. Employees need support for a variety of life responsibilities, not just child care. A full spectrum of life must be attended to, and employees will be most fulfilled when they have time and energy to: spend time with friends, be involved in hobbies, continue education, care for elders, nurture relationships with mates, serve their communities, contribute toward volunteer efforts, and even attend to mundane tasks like housework or fixing the garage door.

EMPLOYEES WITH CHILDREN

Most workers do have children, and in the majority of two-parent families, both parents work outside the home. According to one study, only 20 percent of families fit the traditional breadwinner–caregiver model.[2] The vast majority of women with children under the age of eighteen work outside the home. (The figures are 80 percent to 90 percent depending on which data set you consult.) For employees with children, their experience of work serves as context for their children. Parents' working conditions, wages, and work hours affect children's emotional and mental functioning and well-being. When parents feel better about the work they are doing, they tend to bring this experience home. Whether or not a parent is satisfied with his or her work is more important to the quality of family life than when or how parents work.

For employees with children, school schedules also create a significant constraint. Most schools are still based on an agrarian calendar and do not conform to the typical work hours of parents. Parents encounter problems when schools close for weather or teacher in-service days and, as a result, parents must adjust their schedules to accommodate changes in the school's schedule. Parents want to participate in school activities and this involvement is important to their senses of self. Children's school performance is also positively impacted when parents are involved in school activities. All of this should matter to companies. When companies offer work-life supports, workers perform better, given all the parenting demands they face. Companies should also take a very long-term view of their contribution to the community. The children of today's employees are tomorrow's employees and future adult members of the broader community of which we are all a part. The parent whom an organization supports today through work-life approaches may be raising the daughter who will cure cancer or the son who will be the next brilliant inventor.

FULL LIVES

Employees are multifaceted and companies should treat them as such. They have full lives of which work is only a part. D.J. DePree, the founder of Herman Miller, tells a moving story of the Millwright.[3] It has become a legend in the Herman Miller culture and shapes belief systems and norms within the organization. The Millwright, Herman Rummelt, was a mechanic who kept the factory machines operational. In 1927, around 7 a.m. one day, Herman Rummelt died of a sudden heart attack. D.J. went to visit the Millwright's wife, who showed him handcrafts the Millwright had made and poetry the Millwright had written. This was a defining experience for D.J., who says, "I came to the conclusion that we are all extraordinary." The best leaders recognize this multifaceted nature of people they employ.

PERSPECTIVES FROM THE PAST AND PRESENT

How did we get here? A sense of history grounds these discussions of work and life.

A LOSS OF SELF

Consider the work of Karl Marx. In the 1800s he conceived of a world in which workers were alienated and disconnected from their work because they lost connection to the value of their outputs. Employees were separated from the products of their labor because they did not own them. Deskilling of production meant that work was only a means of subsistence, not fulfillment. In addition, they were estranged from other workers since they were in competition with others for pay, jobs, and ultimately survival. Marx compared workers to animals that were used simply for their physical abilities and not for their minds or their passions. Marx argued there was a "loss of self" because work conditions also destroyed workers' ties to family and friends.[4] This sounds like a dismal reality, but is our current reality any less dismal? Consider these facts:

- 62 percent of mothers and 73 percent of fathers say that work is a significant form of stress[5]
- 68 percent of women and 70 percent of men say that work is a significant form of stress[6]

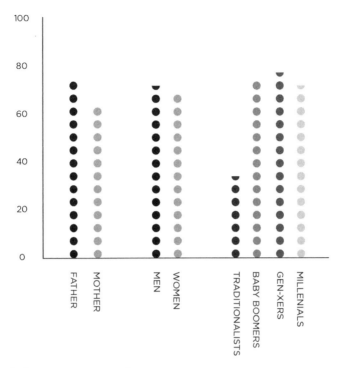

Figure 2-3 Stressed at Work

- 31 percent of the mature generation (sometimes called traditional-ists), 73 percent of baby boomers, 75 percent of gen Xers, and 71 percent of millennials say that work is a significant source of stress[7]
- 51 percent of employees say they have been less productive at work due to stress and 41 percent report they feel stressed or tense during their day at work[8]
- Absenteeism, turnover, reduced productivity, and costs for medical, legal, and insurance coverage due to job stress are estimated at a $300 billion cost annually to U.S. industry[9]
- Worldwide, only 13 percent of employees across 142 countries are engaged (meaning committed and emotionally involved) in their jobs[10]
- Within the American workforce, only 28 percent of workers are "engaged," with 53 percent "not engaged" and 19 percent "actively disengaged"[11]
- U.S. employers lose between $450 and $550 billion per year in pro-ductivity[12] due to absenteeism, lack of motivation, or employees who aren't giving their all

- In interviews with 36,280 employees in eighteen countries, only 3 percent experience high levels of self-governance in their organizations; this was true across countries, industries, economic context, language, and ethnicities[13]

These facts are the result of organizations making demands on employees and the lack of support being provided in turn. There are exceptions, of course, but taken together, the statistics are telling. Rick Wartzman, executive director of the Drucker Institute[14] describes how the social contract has changed:

> The idea of work-life integration, as opposed to work-life balance, is right on. Businesses today need to concentrate on supporting workers in new ways because so many of the things they used to do in this regard have disappeared. The context is really important. Historically, big American companies supported workers through a rich social contract, but today, even the most effectively run companies can't afford to do this anymore. Job security, in the form of lifetime employment; medical benefits with no out-of-pocket expenses for the employee; and guaranteed pensions are almost all gone now. The social contract has eroded tremendously over the past thirty to forty years.[15]

A recent paper by Peter Fleming[16] suggests a new problem of "biocracy" in which the spillover from work to home causes employees to be exploited in ever-increasing ways, even after they leave the workplace for the day. In his view, technology allows organizations and capitalism to tap personal time, interests, and skills. "Biopower" (a term originally coined by theorist Michel Foucault) on the part of organizations allows for all aspects of employees' lives to be tapped—in a way that is intrusive and violates appropriate boundaries between work and life. The positive side of this equation is that those employees who are passionate about their work will contribute discretionary time—the time during which they can choose to do anything—to work. How do organizations tap that discretionary time in a way that is positive and not exploitative of employees? This is the power of effective work-life supports, which I will discuss.

A PERSON-CENTERED VIEW

In the meantime, what are the ways companies should view work and workers? After Marx, a more person-centered, optimistic framework was born. It suggested that leaders must value workers for their contributions and recommended that employees participate in more decision making. In 1933, Emile Durkheim took a stand by saying that workers could contribute value in their work through the unique ways they express themselves. This sounds like an early version of abundance, in which workers are bringing their passions and interests to the workplace and engaging completely. Durkheim also asserted that social relationships drive and solidify economic ties. This is fitting, as most people spend a majority of their waking hours at work and form relationships there.

Consider the effects when companies attend to employees. The "Hawthorne Effect" was conceived based on a study in 1941 in which a researcher named George C. Homans studied employees at the Western Electric Company. Homans was interested in studying productivity so he adjusted light levels at a factory. At first he found that as he turned up the lighting levels slightly, productivity increased. However, as he continued the experiment, a funny thing happened: as he turned *down* the lighting, productivity also improved. Eventually, the factory workers were practically working in the dark, but still their productivity was increasing. Homans and his team scratched their heads and assessed what was happening. They went away to think and stopped adjusting the lighting levels. It was at this point that productivity returned to its prior levels. What was happening? Productivity was increasing not because of the lighting levels—whether they were high or low. Productivity was increasing because of the time and attention being paid to the workers. The very process of being studied contributed to the employees feeling valued, and this was the cause of the increased productivity. This example harkens back to the friend of mine who takes each of her staff members out to lunch once per quarter. They feel valued. They feel attended to, and their work shows it.

In 1943, psychologist Abraham Maslow argued for the importance of work that would help employees reach self-actualization. Douglas McGregor, who studied management and motivation in the late 1950s, also said that people should be viewed as motivated, responsible, mature, competent, and hard working. Treating employees in a way that embraced this positive view was better than treating them as untrustworthy or seeking to be in control of every detail of their work. The reason this history is important is because it demonstrates the lasting nature of these ideas and continuity over time. Through the past, we can better understand our present and our future. By considering how we bring work to life, we are standing on the shoulders of some of the best and brightest management theorists.

One of the tasks of leadership is to create the conditions in which workers can flourish and bring creative potential to their work. A "whole person" mentality, such as D.J. DePree held, views workers as multifaceted. This view acknowledges the talents, personalities, and lives that employees have beyond the work they are expected to perform. Workers must be connected to the broader view and meaning in their work in order to feel fulfilled. They also need the opportunity to be supported holistically in their life, of which work is a part.

IN SUM

Leaders have the opportunity to bring work to life for their employees. During these turbulent, changing times, leaders and organizations must shape a new experience of work for workers. What if companies could create a positive work experience for everyone, men and women, parents and nonparents? What if leaders could help employees find ways to integrate the demands created by spillover, schedule constraints, and the need for fulfilling lives outside of work? What if work were a point of joy and vitality, rather than an additional demand? What if work could be fulfilling and sustaining, rather than burdensome? What if employees had a level of autonomy and self-determination that created a sense of capacity and well-being? This is what it would mean to bring work to life, and providing work-life supports is one way to accomplish this type of new reality for workers.

CHAPTER 3

Leading from Today's Challenges

An understanding of today's trials and realities must inform the way leaders and organizations move forward in responding to employee needs and, in turn, drive organizational results. Here, I suggest ten challenges that companies, leaders, and employees are facing today. In each case they are tensions between the realities: For example, by trying to do too much, companies may not accomplish anything as well as they ought. Or, just when people feel like they lack enough time for connecting, they must ensure they are investing time in relationships. Recognizing these tensions provides a starting point for their resolution.

SAY NO

When my team works with customers, we always start with their end in mind, the goals of their business. After all, *we* are only adding value to the extent that we are helping our customers add value for *their* own customers and shareholders. Before 2008, executives were focused on business drivers such as collaboration and communication, growth and stability, and market leadership. They reported that the most important success factors for their businesses were innovation, corporate image, and culture. They were focusing on attraction and retention of employees, operational efficiency, and customers. They also prioritized the need for safety, sustainability,[1] and community focus. With the economic turmoil of 2008 came a complete shift in priorities. Leaders and organizations were suddenly focused on survival and cost reduction—nothing more, nothing less. Is this ancient history? Far from it, because while leaders have moved back toward a focus on the previous business drivers, they are keeping a firm grip on considerations for survival through continuous cost reduction. This fundamental concern—which never seems to ebb—shapes all their decision making and sense of "what day it is" (as Dr. Frost used to say) for their organizations.

As organizations try to do more with less, they have trouble prioritizing. They seek to meet all their business objectives and cut costs too. They seek to provide fulfilling work at the same time they are asking employees to complete more work. Ellen Galinsky, in 2005, found that one third of U.S. employees were chronically overworked.[2] The total number of hours worked for dual-earning couples increased ten hours per week between 1977 and 2002.[3] Companies have reduced head count, but for the most part they haven't reduced the work, and employees are feeling it.

It is a tension. By attempting to do *everything*, an organization can't do *anything* as well as it should. In order to truly say "yes" and to prioritize certain outcomes, the organization must be able to say "no" to other priorities. Companies are rarely saying "no" to things that are *un*important. Many projects are important, but they must be prioritized. An inability to say "no," and the tendency to add responsibilities to teams and departments continuously, has become an organizational disability. In order to truly say "yes" and accomplish key business drivers, the organization must also learn to say "no" and thereby limit obligations in other areas.

The ability to say "no" and to prioritize is related to work-life supports. Whether making assignments to individuals or to teams, if companies simply continue to add projects and never take a realistic view of what's reasonable for one employee to accomplish, they set employees up for failure. Organizations are adding to the overtaxed, overburdened reality that workers face.

One oil and gas organization with which I consulted has taken a systematic approach to saying yes and saying no. Once a year, management collects a list of all the projects that are occurring throughout the company. They ensure the list is comprehensive and that it includes all of the employees who are working on the projects as well as the necessary funding for the projects. After they have collected all of this data, they sit together in a

Figure 3-1   Say 'No' to Say 'Yes'

day-long session in which they discuss the connections, overlaps, and relationships of the projects to each other. They challenge one another to limit the projects on the list and they review resources so that no one department is overtaxed and so resources (time, people, and money) are allocated to only the most important projects. This annual scrutiny by the executive team is rigorous, but the leaders agree it is the best way to select projects and manage a realistic set of goals and tasks. The process happens once per year because projects tend to proliferate throughout the year and require continual culling. The annual review ensures that the organization is prioritizing and keeping projects in check.

SLOW DOWN

Just when we need more time to reflect, we are under increasing pressure to go faster. "The West cultivates haste," says Jean-Francois Lesage.[4] According to a recent study, we even walk faster than other countries.[5] A children's book by Jamie Lee Curtis and Laura Cornell asks, *Is There Really a Human Race?*[6] This fast pace is created by multiple factors. Work is intensifying. In addition, due to global uncertainty, the context outside the organization can shift at any moment, keeping companies vigilant. Competitive threat has increased globally and as a result, corporations are increasingly under pressure to reduce costs, increase productivity, and innovate at breakneck speed. Getting to market first has always been one of the requirements for success, but the overall speed of innovation has increased. Additionally, many companies are faced with the challenge of having their innovations copied and being able to do little in response. At a recent trade show, the companies that lead the industry in innovative solutions had to stand by impotently while scouts took significant numbers of photos. The scouts were undoubtedly informing companies that would copy the new products within weeks.

From the employees' point of view, cognitive complexity has increased and no one has all the answers he needs. In order to get things done, people must connect and solve problems with others, and this requires time. Additionally, the speed of information is faster than it has ever been before. A few weeks ago, I was at a conference center in the Chicago area. In the restroom, there was a TV screen above every sink. As I washed my hands, I was able to keep up with the latest politics and pop culture. It's this in-your-face, on-all-the-time world that keeps the stream of information flowing like a fire hose. All of this information isn't necessarily bad. IBM CEO Virginia

Rometty says, "Information will be to the twenty-first century what steam, electricity, and fossil fuel were to the prior centuries."[7] Our challenge is to harness this input and make sense of it all. We must slow down. We need time to pause and reflect in order to make sense of an ever-broadening array of options and complexity, but we seem to have lost access to a pause button.

When I was working in an automotive company, there was a motivational poster on the wall extolling the folly of an approach called "ready, fire, aim." At the time it was funny because it *wasn't* the norm. Today, it *has* increasingly become the norm. Compressed time and heightened expectations cause us to run so fast that we are frequently taking action after action without taking time to pause, reflect, and determine whether our actions are even the right ones. The effect is that of a rushed reality, and one in which we may be doing the wrong things, albeit very efficiently. Because of technology, some of us have filled every moment of our days. In the past, we had quiet times—such as time in the car, or time waiting in line at the grocery store—to reflect and ruminate. Now those times are overfilled by phone calls, social networking, and staying in touch via our smart devices. We may think we're gaining efficiency, but we're losing the opportunity to reflect. Reflection makes us smarter because it keeps us sane and because it helps us consider options. In the classic Plan-Do-Check-Act model (also called the Deming Cycle for Dr. W. Edwards Deming), there are formal steps for the important work of planning and checking. When we lose time for reflection, we risk going into spin cycles of decision making and reactive responses.

Again, it is a tension. We increasingly require thorough thinking in order to make good decisions, however we are less likely to take the time to step back and choose wisely among well-considered options.

Leaders who bring work to life find a way to carve out time for employees to reflect and prioritize, identifying the vital few priorities from the

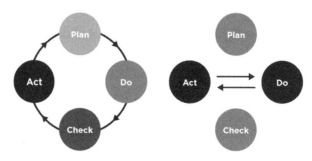

Figure 3-2   Spin Cycle

miniscule many tasks. Providing work-life supports is a way to bring realistic expectations back. When employees can work from home occasionally in order to focus on a significant project, or when the company's culture allows employees to ignore e-mail over a weekend, it provides for employees to slow down, reflect, and be more effective and creative.

SET BOUNDARIES

We have more "time-saving devices" but we have less time. Technology has proliferated and as a result, information is coming at us faster than we can receive it or make sense of it. In 2008 there were three million Apple iPhone mobile devices in the world. At the start of 2014, there are over one billion smartphone users and more than 420 iPhone mobile devices.[8] In 2004 there were one million Facebook users. Today, there are 1.23 billion registered Facebook users. In 2006, the iTunes App Store didn't exist. Today, the iTunes App Store has 900,000 apps. All of these are sources of information that are coming in droves. The challenge isn't so much that the information is coming too fast, but that we can't make sense of it *as* fast. The speed of technology is outstripping our human mechanisms for sense making and this is what tends to overwhelm us. In addition, we struggle with spillover from work to the personal arena and from personal areas to work because we're always "on."

Sometimes this is helpful. I can deal with the issue at work while cheering on my son's baseball game or during intermission at my daughter's concert. On the other hand, this kind of habit puts us into situations where there is never downtime and the present moment is always full. We must develop the skill of boundary management. Technology enhances our ability for boundary-spanning (also known more negatively as spillover), but technology is selfish so the next frontier will be to manage our technology and set boundaries, instead of allowing technology to manage us. Bringing work to life means finding life outside of work and managing the boundary successfully.

Another frontier is the process of making technology invisible. Surely, fish don't think about water. Technology has become ubiquitous and it is infused in the way we work, but still, it can be a point of discord or difficulty. Real change will occur at the point that technology is absent from our conscious awareness—similar to fish and water—something that surrounds us and facilitates our lives without requiring our conscious awareness. This also relates to work-life supports. When organizations provide mechanisms that allow workers to both span and manage boundaries, easily and without a lot of conscious effort, they are bringing work to life by leveraging work-life supports.

TAKE TIME FOR RELATIONSHIPS

The less time we have for social relationships, the more we must take the time for them. Leaders regularly hear from workers that they are so consumed with accomplishing tasks, they don't feel they have time for relationships. Yet, it seems the less time we have for relationships, the more important they are. When we're moving quickly, it's important we have strong relationships on which to fall back. It's also critical that we have the ability to span boundaries in our relationships. A couple of years ago, I had the opportunity to lead an engagement with Yellowstone National Park for an initiative they called the Greening of Yellowstone.[9] The session brought leaders in education, industry, and government together with park leaders in order to share ideas across fields of expertise and set a course for environmental stewardship for the park. The session was instructive in its green mission and also instructive in its boundary-spanning approach. It points to the trend that has already changed lives significantly: the network.

We are getting things done with and through others to a greater extent than ever. In the past, we would hit "send." Now we hit "post" or "share." Some companies view the social network as distracting to productivity. On the contrary, encouraging this connecting and networking is a powerful way to provide work-life supports. When employees solve problems in new ways through the network, or reach out to the network for a break or to refresh themselves, they boost their sense of capacity and abundance. (I'll discuss this in more detail later on.)

Another aspect of our new collective reality is that relationships are collateral. Employees and organizations are forming coalitions. Many of them are being held accountable for solving broader problems and are accountable for wider spans of responsibility. Workers are finding that they cannot deliver results exclusively within their own areas of responsibility because no single function is adequate for the challenges that face the organization as a whole. In response, leaders and teams are forming alliances across departments such as HR, IT, finance, and real estate/facility management. These coalitions are designed to span boundaries, produce results, spread accountability, and foster diversity of thinking. Networks are becoming a support mechanism because they spread risk and they connect people with information to increase effectiveness.

NURTURE CONNECTIONS

Business competition is becoming fragmented. The competitors that were previously medium sized have now come together and are larger-sized, more significant forces. In addition, during the downturn of 2008, many employees who lost their jobs launched their own consulting businesses. The barriers to entry were low and they needed work. Many of them survived and as the economy turns upward, they are benefiting. This proliferation of consultants has contributed to fragmentation of the competitive market.

Fragmentation and confusion are also increasing because of strategic partnerships. Vendors—whether firms or individual consultants—are seeking to get further upstream in the buying process. When they are successful, they are in turn able to dictate which other partners are able to gain access and at what points. In order to compete, organizations that are competitors today must collaborate as partners tomorrow in a state of co-opetition. Customers are looking to their suppliers and partners to play nicely together, but this can be a challenge when competitors are keen to protect intellectual property and differentiators. Leaders must help workers make sense of this new landscape and provide a backstop when there are questions of judgment or discretion. When leaders provide guidance and lead by example in this new reality of murky relationships, workers will feel more supported and therefore be able to take appropriate risks in order to benefit the organization.

SEEK TALENT

Another aspect of our changing context is the bifurcation of the labor market. Low-skill jobs are requiring even fewer skills and less education on the parts of workers as technology automates many tasks that previously required employee judgment or decision making. At the same time, higher-skill jobs are requiring increasing levels of skill and education. The implication is that there is little remaining in the middle.[10] Americans are feeling this reality: In a Gallup poll only 52 percent of respondents—down from 81 percent in 1998—perceive there is enough social mobility for the average American to get ahead.[11] New college graduates are experiencing this effect as well. They struggle to find positions matched to their education level or field of study: 42 percent are in jobs requiring less education than their degree provides and 41 percent are unable to find work in their chosen field.[12] In addition, attraction and retention continue to be buzzwords among leaders. It is difficult to find the right people to fulfill the skill sets companies require. There seem to be plenty of candidates, but not necessarily candidates who are a perfect match—or even a good-enough match—to the jobs that are open. Sometimes, finding the right candidate is like hunting for a needle in a haystack. Because of the previous downward spiral in the economy, that hunt has become even more challenging. The process still entails finding a needle—the right candidate—in a haystack, but now the haystack of other candidates seeking work has become even bigger. This has made the tasks of recruiting and selection increasingly difficult. A key task of leadership is to put the best team in place and ensure that the right people are in the right positions on the team.

HONOR AGE

Companies also face the challenge of shifting demographics. There are more generations of people working today than ever before, and they must learn to work together despite having different backgrounds and worldviews. At my company, we knew this was true when our colleagues' children began appearing as our coworkers. These were the same kids about whom we traded stories when they were losing their teeth, getting their drivers' licenses (and sometimes getting into trouble with their newfound freedom), and choosing colleges. Now they are working side by side with us.

On the flip side, there are colleagues who are still in the workforce who hadn't planned on being around so long. In 2008, a woman at our company was literally one week away from her retirement. The parties were planned and the honorary monogrammed pen had been ordered. When the economy faltered, she cancelled her retirement then and there. She thought she would be delaying retirement by a year, or perhaps two. Today, years later, she is still working and adding value, but this was not her planned course, nor does it create the opening that the less-experienced members of the organization were hoping to grow into.

Lately, executives say that we are allowing the pendulum to swing too much toward worshipping the younger worker. Surely younger employees have a lot to offer, but their talents shouldn't overshadow the talents of all the other workers who are also contributing. Despite the younger cohorts, many of the executives with whom I work report their workforce's average age is fifty-something. Companies must capture the organizational memory that resides in the more senior generation before they retire. At the same time, they must find ways to engage the full spectrum of workers at every age. Work-life supports in the form of mentoring and partnering are good solutions, allowing senior workers to share their knowledge with younger employees who will be present long enough to leverage it within the organization. I'll discuss this topic in more detail later.

CHOOSE WISELY

The proliferation of choice makes choosing more difficult. A recent study explored purchase behavior at the jam/jelly kiosks that spring up during the holidays. It turns out that when too many samples are presented for tasting, potential customers tend not to purchase anything. On the opposite end of the experience, when too few options are presented, people also tend not to purchase. There is a "just enough" quality to choice making. People apparently want enough options to feel satisfied they have chosen the best from an array, but they want few enough that they don't feel overwhelmed.

Jams and jellies relate to business in this way: employees must make sense of the options open to them, create meaning out of the chaos, and synthesize the disparate parts of a whole so they can take the best actions. Leadership involves helping employees make sense, and synthesizing is a significant value-add in a world of increasing complexity. With so much coming at employees all the time, leaders have an opportunity to connect the dots, to explain, and to help distinguish patterns. They must communicate the company's monthly financial results and also bring meaning to the data, helping team members interpret and translate it to their own roles. Leaders can help buffer some of the noise as well. When the organization encounters bumps or makes changes that can be distracting to employees, leaders can act as shock absorbers for these changes.

One well-loved leader, Katrina, has announced nine organizational changes to her team within the past four years. These have included changes in departments, changes in leadership, and changes in members of the team who have taken other roles. She grounds the team with two pieces of advice.

The first is that they should always stay focused on the customer. If they are focused on what the customer needs, they will rarely be wrong or irrelevant. The second is that if they just wait long enough, things will change again. She means this in the most optimistic and appropriate way. She knows it is the reality of her organization and Katrina is helping her team to see it too—and survive it.

Another challenge in choosing wisely is the breakdown of authority. The proliferation and accessibility of information means that it has become more difficult to really know what to trust. It is frequently difficult to discern whether information is from an authoritative, credible source. Information is readily available, but there are no quality controls. The onus is on individuals to determine whom and what to trust. Caveat emptor–let the buyer beware–has a whole new meaning when it is applied to what we're "buying" and choosing to believe from among the information coming at us. Leaders who help make sense of complexity, communicate expectations clearly, and help employees work through change are offering work-life supports.

EXECUTE STRATEGICALLY

The real advantage of strategy is in the execution. Previously, organizations judged people's skills based on whether they were more strategic or more tactical. Today, both are necessary and the ability to flow between these skills is a primary determiner of success. Companies have upped the ante. Organizations and leaders are facing increasing pressure and higher expectations. Work that differentiated them previously is today just a ticket to entry. Leaders are being called on to hit higher marks with their performance. Strategy and execution are both critical, but they are quite different. Effective strategic planning makes choices and places bets on an uncertain future. It requires choosing among options in order to reduce risk for the future. It is fraught with ambiguity. At the same time, organizations report that execution matters more than ever. In a world where everyone has access to virtually the same expertise, companies must differentiate by executing and producing results better than their competitors.

The success of work-life supports lies in both strategy and execution. Work-life supports must be connected with the company's business direction for the future. Tactics must ladder up to strategy, and their execution must be flawless. The tactics companies select—provision of printers at home, core hours for teams, eldercare benefits—are as important as the extent to which they are effectively implemented and managed.

FUTURE PROOF

One trend within organizations is the desire to "future proof" the organization. While many executives point to "future proofing" as an ideal, it is a bit of a misnomer. Companies aren't really looking for ways to hold the future at bay, as much as they're looking for ways to succeed in the future—whatever may come. Leaders want help planning for the unknown and identifying solutions that will work no matter what the future looks like. *Fast Company* recently published five steps for glimpsing the future. Step one: examine what's happening today. Step two: look for anticipated trends ("weak signals"). Step three: apply them to a vision for the future. Step four: create a story of the potential future. Step five: determine what is necessary to reach the potential future.[13]

Regardless of the steps they take to predict the future, companies gain by being future agnostic, finding solutions that work today and are flexible

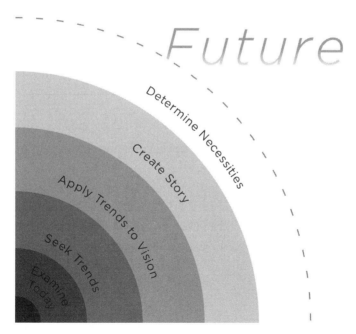

Figure 3-3   5 Steps for Glimpsing the Future

enough to meet the differences that will exist in tomorrow's situation. Work-life supports must be constantly monitored and they must evolve. They should shift as workers' needs and work shift. Part of the responsibility of leaders is to manage this ongoing adaptation and grow along with it.

IN SUM

Our reality calls for new skills, behaviors, and points of view. We must learn to say no, to turn off, and to pay attention selectively. We must maintain relationships and connections at the same time we're selecting the best options and the best talent. In addition, we must think strategically and execute brilliantly. Within this world of challenges, we are facing demands from life and work that are unprecedented. Work-life supports offer a powerful point of leverage with which leaders and organizations create a climate of abundance and fulfillment.

CHAPTER 4

Leading to Work-Life Supports

For organizations to be successful, leaders must create abundance and help employees respond to work-life demands throughout their life course. My research with senior leaders shows that there are a tremendous number of approaches to providing work-life supports. The approaches are as varied and individual as workers and their companies, but this chapter provides some ideas for executives who want to leverage work-life supports in their organizations. These are only the mechanisms available for work-life supports in the form of benefits, policies, and practices; they must be implemented with consideration for the factors I discuss in part 2. These options provide a starting point for the journey and offer examples of companies that are implementing different types of work-life supports.

DEFINING TERMS

I am defining work-life supports as benefits, formal policies, and informal practices that help employees navigate the demands of their work and life. Because there is some overlap between benefits, policies, and practices, examples are useful. *Benefits* are the company-funded options an organization provides to employees. Some are required by law, such as workers' compensation, disability, and unemployment benefits. Other types of benefits are discretionary, and include insurance coverage for family members, life insurance, sick leave, financial assistance for education and training, and retirement benefits. *Policies* are the principles, rules, or guidelines that guide day-to-day operations. They are the documented protocols for the way the business will run. Examples of policies include flextime, caregiving leaves, telecommuting, employee counseling, and legal assistance programs. *Organizational practices* are established patterns for how the organization is managed; they may not be written down, but have become the norm for a group or the organization in total. For example, companies might offer development programs for supervisors or allow employees to leave early now and then in order to meet family obligations.

AN ABUNDANCE OF OPTIONS

Below is a list of some of the work-life supports that exist today. This is only a fraction of the options, as there is a plethora of possibilities. In addition, while they are categorized here, in reality there are areas of gray between each. More important than the way they are organized is that they are selected carefully and implemented effectively within organizations.

Insurance/Benefits

Adoption assistance	Gender reassignment benefits
Health and dental benefits	Rehab benefits
Eldercare benefits	Vision benefits

Leaves

Caregiving leaves	Short-term leave
Parental leaves	Military service leaves
Family leave	Job back guarantees
Long-term maternity leave	Paid sabbaticals*
Long-term leave	

Wellness and Mental Health

Corporate counseling services	Wellness benefits
Corporate medical services	Healthy food education
Employee assistance programs	On-site health/fitness classes

Retirement

Staged retirement	Pension plans and/or defined
Retirement planning assistance/	contribution plans
education	

Care-Related Solutions

Online referral service for child care	Emergency back-up child care
Kindergarten on-site	Near-site or on-site child care*
Summer program for children	Eldercare and/or financial
	assistance for eldercare

Education

Time off to attend classes   Tuition reimbursement

Hours of work

Leave early

Flextime—flex as you wish, anytime, without a formal approach

Core hours

Compressed workweek*

Time tracking

Reduction of hours in the summer or seasonal long-term arrangements

Scheduled working hours same as school days

Overtime requirement limits

Flexibility for alternative hours such as four ten-hour days

Part-time work and/or job sharing*

Option to not work weekends

Leave work early as needed

Extended breaks during the day

Additional Policies

Travel and expense policies

Work location

Work at home option

IT support at home

Financial assistance for equipment at home

Financial assistance for furniture at home

Education regarding how to work at home successfully

Company-provided third or fourth places[1]

Technology

Support/education for new technology skills

Social networking

IT network, storage systems, phone systems, processing systems, collaborative systems, financial systems

IT policies

Choice of device and/or BYOD

800 number for conference calls

Skype

Camera-enabled laptop

Job Content, Job Design, Management

Control over the content of
  one's work

Choice of roles in a rotation
  program

Standards of work for consistency

Independent agent model

Collaboration activities during
  working hours; project stage
  and relationship stage

Choose own projects

Multiple people doing same job

Work aligned with talents,
  creativity, passion

Prioritization of assignments

Mentoring; reverse mentoring

Career development

Recognition

Physical Environment On-Site

Lactation rooms

Food, coffee, lunches

Great places for people to
  meet and connect; coffee
  bar; meeting rooms

Stimulating interiors

Constantly refreshed/updated
  interiors

Light, ambient noise, moderate
  traffic/activity in the space

Wi-Fi, videoconferencing,
  projection, sharing
  technologies

Navigation and way-finding

Lower-height walls, more glass,
  transparency

Private spaces

Phone booths

Protocols for use of the space

Flexibility—user-controlled
  changes

Proximity of leaders

Amenities

Pretax dollars for public
  transportation

Cab service when working late

Takeout dinners

Order-in dinners at the office

Shuttle to/from work

Dry cleaning services

On-site dental services

Car detailing services

Car snow removal services

On-site car detailing

On-site greeting card
  printing/envelopes

Discounts for area entertainment

Parking apps to assist in finding
  nearby parking spots

Community

Community program for area
  children and employee children

Time off to volunteer

Those items marked with an asterisk (*) are offered so commonly among companies in *Fortune* magazine's "Best Companies to Work For" list, they have their own icon in the article.[2] However, a large proportion of companies have not begun offering work-life supports or do not yet offer them to the level they could. For this reason, I'll discuss a number of these approaches, as well as the criteria for their successful implementation, in later chapters.

SOME EXAMPLES

One especially effective form of work-life support is flexible working options. These allow employees to choose when and where they work, as well as the projects on which they focus. As an example, an employee may have latitude in the way she solves a problem, or an engineer may have choices pertaining to which projects he works on during the year. In addition to providing autonomy and control over one's work, flexible work schedules allow employees to meet work demands at the same time they meet the demands of family. A dad may need to drive car pool or pick up his children from school. A woman may need to take a break mid-workday in order to meet the furnace repair technician at her home. Some companies are also increasing flexibility by providing the choice for a compressed workweek. With a compressed workweek, employees work a standard number of hours in a compressed fashion; for example, a worker might work four ten-hour days, taking the fifth day to meet family demands or continue education. Another option is seasonal long-term arrangements. These types of solutions take many forms, including work schedules that shift between summer months and school months. At some organizations, leaders are recommending policies that provide for extended breaks, sabbaticals, or job sharing in roles that would traditionally not have allowed for a job-sharing model. Telecommuting programs and work-at-home programs are familiar options that are gaining attention. Some organizations are experimenting with shortened workdays or workweeks. Other companies are attempting to find ways to limit mandatory overtime or even schedule working hours so they align with school days.

Flexible work schedules go hand in hand with control over one's work because employers must have a degree of trust that employees are working and accomplishing results even when they are not in view of supervisors. A paradigm of trusting employees to do their best work without direct supervision and providing employees with more control over their work is in concert with overall self-determination. In all of these cases, the employee's increased ownership and control over his work is intended to help integrate the demands of work and home. They are typically also aimed at reducing the negative spillover from work to home or vice versa. One notable fact is that the presence of greater proportions of women occupying top-ranking positions at a company is connected with a greater number of family-friendly options as compared with companies that have fewer women in top leadership positions and less family-friendly policies.[3] Is the presence of women driving more family-friendly policies and practices? Or do companies with more family-friendly policies and practices simply attract more women to those top positions? More research is required to answer the question, but the trend remains toward companies increasingly providing options and choices to employees in order to enhance the support of work and life.

TAKING ADVANTAGE—A DISCONNECT

While corporations may have formal work-life support policies and practices, the reality is that many workers do not take advantage of them. This is typically attributed to personal preferences as well as the American cultural ethic valuing work. Economic pressures, downsizing, and reductions in head count on the part of companies are also blamed. As companies eliminate jobs, employees may feel a greater sense of job insecurity or fear, causing them to work harder and longer—and not take advantage of work-life supports, even if they wish they could.

The extent to which employees feel they can take advantage of work-life supports also varies based on norms and unwritten rules within the organizational culture. In some cases, men and women may not take advantage of work-life supports because of a perception that negative career ramifications could result. In later chapters, I discuss ways to increase the likelihood that employees will take advantage of valuable work-life supports.

COMPARING COMPANIES

When I consult with management and human resource departments, they frequently request case studies and benchmark information concerning work-life support policies and implementation. They want to know whether they are keeping up with other companies, or, better yet, staying ahead of the curve. Companies vary widely in their policies and practices. Following are a few examples. While I have changed details in order to retain anonymity, these are real companies provided as examples and thought starters. Whether companies are more conservative or progressive, they can offer a meaningful cocktail of work-life supports which matches their culture and business needs. The Goldilocks Rule is important here. Work-life supports must be right for any given company, and no two companies' solutions will be the same. Companies that are most successful with work-life support implementation avoid having too few or too many work-life supports. Instead, they have a set of approaches and solutions that are *just right*—hence, the Goldilocks Rule. "As much as necessary, as little as possible," is another way to think about establishing the right approach. Keep solutions as comprehensive as necessary for success, but also keep the solution set as straightforward and simple as possible.

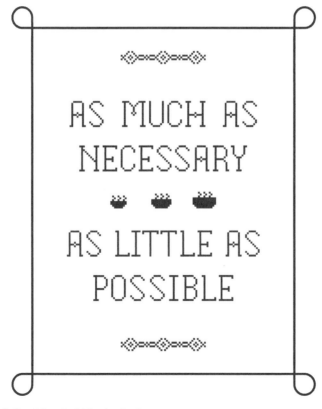

Figure 4-1   The Goldilocks Rule

Example: NalydCo

NalydCo is an oil and gas company that provides an example of a company taking a more conservative approach to work-life supports. It is based in Houston and is one of the largest producers of national gas in the nation. NalydCo is in a constant battle to attract and retain the best talent to accommodate its consistent growth. The company's workforce is quite senior, and NalydCo has little turnover. The company is known for its family-oriented culture and demonstration of care toward employees. NalydCo's culture is decidedly face to face, and employees find it difficult to get things done unless they are in person with co-workers.

NalydCo is stepping into alternative working approaches cautiously. Management believes that work must be accomplished on site, although the company has allowed for a shift in working hours seasonally. During the summer, employees are allowed to come in one hour later, leave one hour earlier, and work from home on Friday afternoons, provided their work in the office is completed. Managers are choosing this path so they maximize the time that employees are face to face in the office and ensure the hours in the office are consistent. NalydCo also has provisions for special circumstances. If an employee has an emergency or an unusual situation or if an employee is working on a short-term project that requires concentration, the employee may coordinate with her manager to plan a work-at-home day. Upon returning to work the next day, the employee is required to demonstrate what she completed while at home. NalydCo is relying on work team leaders to be the primary decision makers since there are no formal policies for flexible working.

NalydCo also offers assistance in the case of catastrophe. Since its region has been affected by multiple hurricanes, the company is second to none at supporting employees through disasters. During the last hurricane, NalydCo purchased generators and loaned them to employees. In addition, the company offered employees and their family members places to shelter—on site as well as in short-term rental housing—in cases where their homes were damaged or destroyed. NalydCo also offered no-interest loans for employees who needed to repair or rebuild homes. For employees who receive such significant support at moments of critical life events, the company's contribution to their survival has resulted in untold levels of loyalty and appreciation, and in turn, employee contribution and retention. While NalydCo is making conservative forays into the provision of work-life supports, the company is an instructive example. NalydCo demonstrates that even when a company only wants to tiptoe into the work-life support arena, there are meaningful ways to do so.

Example: ElsaCo

ElsaCo is a leading manufacturing company that produces heavy equipment worldwide. The company has a bifurcated workforce in which the majority of employees are either quite senior and close to retirement or quite junior and new to the organization. This "barbell effect" is the result of ElsaCo having gone through a period when it wasn't hiring. ElsaCo prides itself on taking care of its employees.

ElsaCo has formalized its work-life support options through a policy manual that provides detail on every specification for each solution. In addition, the company has a comprehensive benefits program including health insurance that focuses on rewards for well-behavior such as participation in health assessments and demonstration of healthy habits, generous maternity leave policies, and eldercare leave. In order to accommodate flexible work, ElsaCo offers a rigorous process for assessment, selection, and application for employees to be part of an alternative working program. ElsaCo allows any employee to develop and propose a flexible work arrangement. Most requests are honored, provided the employee has a good performance record and continues demonstrating positive performance after the alternative working arrangements are implemented.

ElsaCo also requires employees to track their time so leaders can see trends and ensure that employees have reasonable work hours. Some leaders within the organization are skeptical. They say the time tracking sounds like "Big Brother," and sends a negative message regarding employees' trustworthiness, but the company stands firm, insisting the time tracking is intended for the benefit of employees. The program, the company says, flags employees who are working too many hours, allowing management to help prioritize their projects and ensure a reasonable workload. ElsaCo also has rigorous standards for performance and checkpoints in the alternative working process. This organization provides an example of a process-oriented company, offering options for flexibility while also attending to a systematic approach for all the elements of the program.

Example: XelaCo

XelaCo is a well-known global consumer goods organization with consistent growth and shareholder return. As a way to ensure it maintains a focus on employees, the company has formalized an extensive array of policies and practices.

One of the unique perks the company offers is technology support for employees who work at home. With this benefit, XelaCo's IT gurus will go to employees' homes as requested to help set up new equipment if the employees need assistance. XelaCo offers the opportunity for employees to select up to five projects a year of their own choosing as a means for career development. XelaCo also has an extensive offering in terms of benefits, one of which is gender reassignment medical support. Children in the community, as well as employees' children, are supported through community programs for kids during the summer. XelaCo offers on-site day care at most facilities and near-site day care in some of its smaller locations. All the food in the cafeteria is offered at significantly reduced prices and employees who work late may order in or may take home meals from the organization's food service. For the locations within metro areas, XelaCo offers pretax metro cards for which employees may use pretax dollars to pay for mass transit. When the snow flies in its more northern locations, XelaCo offers a service where it will brush, scrape, and warm up employees' cars for a nominal fee.

One of the practices employees are perhaps most appreciative of is the option for sabbatical. After ten years with the company, each employee is eligible for a sabbatical. The length and frequency of the sabbatical increases as seniority increases, and it is available to all employees with good performance records. Several of the senior leaders in the organization actively take advantage of work-life supports themselves, choosing to work from home regularly and taking advantage of sabbaticals. This is significant, as it helps send a message to employees that it is acceptable within the culture to take advantage of the work-life supports the company provides. While this description doesn't include every single option the company provides, it does give a sense of the extensive work-life supports available to employees.

Example: YertCo

In a final example, YertCo, a technology company, is fast growing and has a very young workforce in which the average age is thirty-two. The company is global and works 24-7 in order to be in close contact with its global customers. YertCo has had struggles hiring enough talent fast enough to fuel its growth and views employee attraction as a key priority for its business. In terms of work-life supports, YertCo offers extensive benefits, including medical, dental, and unlimited time off for sickness. In addition, the company offers amenities such as shuttle services to and from parking areas and on-site car detailing.

YertCo also has an alternative working program for which employees enroll online. The online enrollment is not an application for approval, but rather a sign-up for financial assistance to purchase furniture and equipment for a home office. Additionally, at-home ergonomic assessments are available for those who work from home three or more days per week. YertCo also provides a monthly stipend for employees to choose their own technology. Most employees set their own hours and come and go from the office as they wish. There are few formal policies and instead, leaders simply allow employees to work as they wish, emphasizing the results employees achieve rather than whether or not they are present in the office. It is the norm to see dogs in the work environment and the cafeteria even sells Milk-Bones and packaged servings of dog food. Employees at YertCo will tell you that seeing dogs in the work environment now and then is as much a morale boost to them as it is a convenience for the dogs' owners. The company does not believe in formal employee training. Instead, it believes all development happens on the job and it has little use for formalized learning—classroom, online, or otherwise.

IN SUM

A multitude of work-life support options exist and may be applied in a variety of ways. It is most important to connect the work-life supports with an organization's situation for the greatest effectiveness. In the following chapters, I'll share more on how to leverage work-life supports, but in the meantime, the examples above are meant to provide ideas, no matter what an organization's unique context or culture.

CHAPTER 5

Leading to Results

Despite the benefits of work-life supports for employees and companies, not all companies are implementing them. These companies fail to leverage work-life supports to drive their results. In fact, work-life supports produce business benefits such as engagement, productivity, cost savings, and improved attraction and retention of talent.

RESULTS THROUGH WORK-LIFE SUPPORTS

The logic is straightforward. When companies provide work-life supports, they enhance engagement, satisfaction, retention, and employee health.[1] These in turn are correlated with better organizational results. It's a simple logic train in which work-life supports lead to positive business outcomes (better employee engagement, lower costs), which in turn lead to better overall organizational outcomes (profitability, financial performance, customer satisfaction).

This logic train seems straightforward enough, but it becomes nuanced because executives and researchers disagree about which factors produce which results. For example, does improved retention of talent cause other positive outcomes such as improved profitability, or is improved retention an outcome on its own? Is enhanced employee engagement an overall measure of business performance, or a means to achieve an ultimate goal of improved stock price? In addition, which factors lead to which other factors? The relationships among the variables are sticky because for any of them, it is difficult to prove the direction of the relationship—which leads to which—and it is difficult to prove that any factor *causes* another. Instead, the factors are merely correlated, meaning they tend to occur together and appear to have a relationship to each other and to work-life supports.

Regardless, it is enough to conclude that work-life supports have positive impacts. These positive impacts are defined in multiple ways (which I'll describe here), but ultimately, they are positive for business. When organizations serve people, they serve their own business results. There is a healthy tension of give and take. Companies should offer work-life supports for people because it is the right thing to do in order to help them integrate work and life and to navigate through their life course. They should also offer work-life supports for the benefit of the organization, which will reap better outcomes. Greg Parsons,[2] vice president, new landscape of work for Herman Miller, says:

> Most companies focus on what they must *get* in terms of financial results and market performance but the real opportunity is to focus also on what they *give*—the distinctly valuable product, service, or experience that fulfills their purpose for customers. Companies get based on what they give. Companies focusing on what they give probably get more back than those focusing on what they hope to get. They reach their potential more fully–as a company, for their employees, and for the community–by doing both.[3]

I will begin focusing on the business results[4] most frequently identified by executives in this study and most frequently demonstrated in the related research. Overall, executives in this study believe that work-life supports help organizations accomplish goals and reach better organizational performance. Work-life supports result in positive outcomes for employees and for organizations. K.H. Moon, former CEO of personal care goods company Yuhan-Kimberly, has provided multiple work-life supports to his employees and believes they make a difference:[5]

> I strongly believe work-life supports are closely connected to key outcomes such as employee engagement, employee satisfaction, customer satisfaction, company growth, and stock price. We offered maternity leave, employee assistance programs, lifelong learning, and new work systems. The new work systems included flextime and the opportunity to work in a home office. As a result of these programs and systems we saw reduced turnover rates and we built loyalty and a sense of ownership on the part of employees. In addition, innovation grew and employees increased the rate of providing

suggestions to the company. We also accomplished almost zero rates of accidents, waste, defects, and pollution.[6]

Moon's beliefs are well founded. He has won formal awards such as the Most Admired CEO of Korea. In addition, his leadership resulted in Yuhan-Kimberly being named a "Great Place to Work" by the Great Places to Work Institute and one of "Korea's Most Admired Companies."

A gentleman who participated in my research, Kyle (a pseudonym), who is a longtime executive at an oil and gas company, describes a situation in which one of his employees was going through a very difficult time in which her husband was dying of Lou Gehrig's disease. She needed to take a great deal of time away from work, and the company was willing to accommodate this absence. In Kyle's view, this employee's commitment to the company is cemented because she appreciates the support the company provided. "She would walk through fire for us now," he says.

Even in situations that are not as extreme, providing for employees has benefits. Andrew Brondel, director of administration for Diamond Pet Foods,[7] says, "When employees don't have to worry about health care or financial issues, they can focus on success and growing our business. They have the mental clarity . . . to take the initiative and implement new ideas."

Lisa Brummel,[8] chief people officer for Microsoft, agrees that minimizing distractions contributes to employee engagement and contributions. She has this to say regarding Microsoft's work-life supports.

For Microsoft, having an engaged workforce is essential to success. We understand that people who are able to focus on their work with minimal distraction are going to have the highest chance to help the company grow and succeed.[9]

Microsoft offers a variety of work-life supports. Brummel says:

We invest heavily in work/life support outside of traditional health benefits by offering things like back-up day care, on-site health center, fully subsidized athletic club memberships, pickup/drop-off dry cleaning, and many other resources for employees to feel like they are supported at "home" while they are active at "work." We, of course, offer vacation and sabbatical programs along with matching donations for doing volunteer work in the community. In all, we try hard to address those things which our employees feel are important and we work to make sure they feel supported in activities that cross the work/life divide.[10]

Richard T. Clark, previous chairman of the board and CEO for Merck & Co., is featured in a video by the Alfred P. Sloan Foundation. In it, he asserts that workplace flexibility results in better productivity because when you give people flextime, you increase their dedication.[11] In the same Sloan Foundation video, Anne Mulcahy, former chairwoman and CEO of Xerox, says that when workers have personal and professional balance and satisfaction they will perform better than when they are stressed.[12] Rick Wartzman, executive director of the Drucker Institute, agrees and also points out the importance of purpose and self-determination:

> We know that employees who feel supported make a huge contribution. A big part of that is giving them a keen sense of responsibility and accountability, all while providing a deep understanding of the organization's greater purpose in the world. This means ensuring that the individual employee's own objectives and their team's objectives align to the overall mission and purpose of the organization. It's also about letting the individual employee figure out the best way to drive results, rather than this coming from the top down, command-and-control style. Indeed, there's a lot of research that tells us that when employees are treated this way, they consistently deliver superior experiences to delight customers and that, in turn, drives performance and financial returns. This is the greatest support we can give workers: a real sense of responsibility, accountability, and purpose. When you do that, there's no doubt that employees wake up every day excited about what they do. Work and life melt into one.[13]

RECIPROCITY AND OBLIGATIONS

A basic concept related to our human condition is reciprocity. As humans, we tend to want to respond in kind to others around us. When others help us, we want to help them. This is true in the workplace as well. When a leader helps an employee or when an organization provides assistance, the employee feels a desire to reciprocate and to respond in a way that mirrors the benefit he has been provided. It's part of our basic nature. As a result, helping people feel valued enhances their commitment.

Hence, the organization has an opportunity and an obligation to serve employees. Barbara, head of Human Resources from a banking organization, says that because people work so much, the organization is obligated to allow some flexibility. Barbara is turning the reciprocity argument around: she believes that when employees work significant hours, the company should reciprocate by providing more flexibility. In addition, Barbara builds an argument for results. She argues that flexibility leads to better engagement, which in turn leads to better productivity, creating better results for the organization. Michelle, an executive I interviewed, is the chief administration officer for her global manufacturing organization. She links the provision of work-life support to productivity:

> If you increase engagement and retention, you keep costs down because you have employees who are productive. If you give them flexibility, you're meeting them more than halfway to facilitate that productivity.

In her comments, Michelle too demonstrates our deeply felt human desire for reciprocity.

ADVANTAGES OF HAPPINESS

When workers are engaged, committed, passionate, and happy in their work, there are plenty of benefits. In *The Happiness Advantage*, Shawn Achor makes a case for various benefits that arise from happiness. He argues that happiness is the origin (not the outcome) of motivation, efficiency, resilience, creativity, productivity, and performance.[14] Thomas Wright, a professor with the Fordham University Business School, finds that the performance of happy and less happy employees varies between 10 and 15 percent.[15] Gallup's studies of happy salespeople find they sell 37 percent more, and they have less absenteeism, with 23 percent fewer symptoms of fatigue.[16]

Leaders have the opportunity to create the conditions for more employee happiness. At the same time, an adult-to-adult model suggests that we are only responsible for our own behavior and outcomes and not for others'. Leaders can, however, create conditions for others' success. While employees are responsible for their own happiness, employers should do everything

possible to help them achieve it. Creating abundance and fulfillment by providing work-life supports helps create the conditions for more happiness on
the parts of employees. This in turn leads to all the positive outcomes of
happiness. Ross, who participated in my research, is a COO with an oil and
gas company, agrees:

> You win the hearts and minds of your employees, which is about
> ensuring their needs are met as well as the business needs. The
> employee is going to work for you because they want to and because
> of respect and appreciation, as opposed to an employee that is just
> beaten into submission and is just going to punch a time clock.
> You'll get much more innovation, much more out-of-the-box think-
> ing, trying to improve the business as opposed to someone who is
> just doing their job.

The most powerful reciprocity comes not only from an emotional experience, but also from a cognitive experience. When companies provide for
people emotionally—win their hearts, for example by offering caring and
concern—they engender a higher level of commitment. Likewise, when
organizations provide for people in a way that they logically believe is
beneficial—win their minds, for example with policies that allow them to
manage multiple demands in their lives—they also engender employee commitment. What is most compelling is the opportunity to win both hearts
and minds. When companies win both hearts and minds, they achieve a
level of employee engagement that is more powerful than either of the two
separately.

PROOF THROUGH BRAIN CHEMISTRY

New brain research also bears out this connection between hearts and
minds. Neuroscientists Adam Waytz and Malia Mason[17] have identified
multiple neural networks that control aspects of our thought and behavior.
An affect network controls the ways we experience emotion and the ways we
make decisions based on these emotions. A control network affects the ways
we consider, weigh, and evaluate options for the long term. Leaders must
create conditions that positively affect both emotions and thoughts. Leaders
appeal to emotion and appeal to cognition by providing work-life supports
that powerfully reinforce what individuals need. Neuroeconomist Paul Zak,

author of *The Moral Molecule*,[18] has also proven a link between brain chemistry and behavior. He finds that when oxytocin is released in our brains, we tend to demonstrate more cooperative, collaborative, and pro-social behavior. We can facilitate the release of oxytocin in others by demonstrating love, caring, and trust toward them. This creates a reinforcing loop of positive outcomes for individuals and organizations. (See my interview with Paul regarding work-life supports in this chapter.)

The Neuroscience Connection with Work-Life Supports: An Interview with Paul Zak, PhD

Paul Zak, PhD, neuroeconomist and professor at Claremont Graduate University, has written a book called The Moral Molecule. *In it, he highlights the importance of brain chemicals on behaviors. He finds that oxytocin, a neuropeptide, is the basis for all kinds of pro-social behavior. Paul's research provides a perspective on the importance of providing work-life supports as part of a high-trust, high-performance work environment.*

What is the relationship of neuroscience to work-life supports?

PZ: Companies that provide work-life supports are creating the conditions for positive environments. I like to think of the POP model—people, organization, purpose. What I mean by this is that when employees are selected properly and put into an organization where they are empowered to face challenges and take ownership with a sense of purpose, they are more highly motivated and engaged, they feel closer to each other, they are more productive, and more innovative. When work is challenging, they will experience more physiological arousal as well as relaxation. In other words, they will be focused *and* relaxed. They will be in flow. This is the signature of a highly engaged employee.

So arousal and relaxation occur together?

PZ: They can. During a challenging task, the employee is in a state of arousal and then after the task is done, the heart rate quickly returns to normal. This is helpful to our physiology because it allows us to come back to baseline after the task. From a work-life support point of view,

(Continued)

this means that employees don't take any stress home with them. They can quickly decompress. When work is over, it's over.

What are the conditions for that kind of "flow" state?

PZ: It tends to occur when employees are challenged and rewarded and praised and feel a sense of ownership with their task. Building a high-trust organization is the key.

What is the relationship of this "flow" to a work environment?

PZ: A high-trust environment allows personal choice for the employee. It allows the employee to choose how they work and where they work. It is an environment that subscribes to Peter Drucker's principles of management by objectives, using milestones and objectives to manage the work. The best environments make the work engaging and fun. They provide challenges that require hard work but are attainable, not impossible.

What about the relationship of individual work and collaborative work?

PZ: In their work, people need time alone but they also need time together so they can bump into others on purpose. Those random opportunities to connect are valuable. We're working with a company right now and when their employees show up each day, they receive a picture of another employee in the building. During the day they have to find that person and find out his or her birthday. Then, they have to enter it into the system and they get points. It's a game-like way to have people develop new connections with others in the workplace.

Sounds like the beginning of creating friendships.

PZ: Yes. The only way to have a high-trust environment is to be friends with the people you work with. You want a situation where people really look forward to seeing their coworkers.

What about self-determination? Any neurological connection for that?

PZ: Absolutely. When people are more engaged with control over what they're doing, they have better cardiovascular response. When they lack autonomy it can lead to burnout and stress.

I've heard you talk about re-set. What do you mean by re-set?

PZ: Companies violate work-life integration when they don't give employees a chance to re-set. Companies that require employees to work enormously long hours—fourteen- or fifteen-hour days for too long—are abusive. Neurologically it's unhealthy to have neurons constantly firing without a break. We can experience extreme physiological fatigue. We need a refractory period like a weekend. We've seen companies who will have employees show up on a Monday after the accomplishment of a project and be given tickets to a game or an amusement park and told to take the day off, on us. This is a great re-set.

Sounds fun.

PZ: Fun is really important in the work environment so that all challenges don't seem like work. Work is work but we need to give people the opportunity to have fun too. At work, you can give something a "water cooler test." In other words, what will people say at the water cooler? This is just as important as the "tell your spouse test," which is what you tell your spouse when they say, "How was your day, honey?" You want employees to carry home something positive and engaging and fun.[19]

THE POWER OF BEHAVIOR

There is value in demonstrating commitment to employees through behaviors. Simply telling employees they are valued only goes so far. Really acting in concert with this declaration is key. In my first job out of college, I worked with an executive who regularly reminded his staff, "You're behaving so loudly, I can hardly hear what you're saying." Likewise, many years ago, an international brand had a "This We Believe" statement of its values. Over time, the company received feedback that the statement was seen as hypocritical based on the behavior of a few key leaders. The company responded by launching a "This We Behave" complementary statement. It was important for the organization's leaders to go beyond rhetoric and behave in alignment with its values.

How does this relate to work-life supports? Work-life supports send a strong message to employees regarding the extent to which they are valued by their organization. Providing work-life supports within the context of clear organizational principles demonstrates commitment to employees in a way that is tangible and meaningful. The executives in this study refer to this as employee engagement and loyalty. According to Xavier Unkovic,[20] global president of Mars Drinks, Inc.:

> We are unique because of our commitment to our Five Principles, which are: quality, responsibility, mutuality, efficiency, and freedom. We are putting these into action, and for us it's all about the people, planet, and performance. As the third-biggest food manufacturer in the world, we have a great impact on the planet. We want to make a better life at work for people and for the planet. This relates to everything from the way we source our products, run factories, reduce packaging and energy consumption, to our provision of work-life supports. The principles are very visible but we're not just talking about them, we're also acting on what we do. For us it's about how we put our principles into action. People play a central role here and it's all about the people.[21]

This engagement is also related to the amount of time employees spend working and the extent to which work is a prominent part of employees' lives. They must have a sense of purpose. Xavier goes on to say:

> Work-life demands are a challenge. We spend more time at work than we spend sleeping or we spend with family and friends. If people aren't happy or satisfied it will impact their work and beyond, then they aren't at their best. They need to know *why* they are working and have the opportunity to express themselves as individuals. People need a sense of purpose and need to know they are unique and a part of a project in a community. We do everything possible to ensure our actions are aligned with our values. When people enjoy working and come to work with a smile, we all benefit. Mars helps you to grow and gives you the opportunity to bring ideas to the table. In every role in the company, people know they are important and respected.[22]

According to Michelle, chief administration officer at a global manufacturing firm, providing work-life supports sends a message to employees that the company cares about them as individuals. It affects their engagement because workers feel better about a company that provides work-life supports, even if they do not personally take advantage of every program or policy. Diane, a participant in my research who is an executive vice president in charge of administration, from a media company, believes that work-life support programs build enthusiasm and bonding as well as the feeling that the company cares about the individual. She believes that people will always "go the extra mile" when they believe the company has a stake in employees' well-being. Like Michelle, she believes this is true whether an employee personally takes advantage of all the work-life supports available or not. The point to note is that there is benefit to be realized simply by making work-life supports available, even if not all employees utilize them.

Organizations that fail to provide work-life supports run the risk of alienating workers and losing their mindshare. An executive related a story: within her company, there was a new mom who was ready to return from her three-month maternity leave. The Sunday before she was to return to work, her baby contracted a very serious respiratory virus that required him to be hospitalized. Her boss didn't handle it well. She insisted that this employee work from her son's bedside. The employee quit. Her boss's insistence that she work despite the critical health situation her infant faced was too much for the employee to bear. This is just one example. There are more, but the message is this: when work-life supports are not in place, employee engagement can be damaged.

SAVING MONEY

Leaders also believe that providing work-life support saves money. Frank participated in my research and is in charge of engineering, real estate, facilities, and quality for his manufacturing company. He calculates that, by giving an employee work flexibility and allowing the employee to work from home, he saves $100,000 per employee in facility costs because he avoids the expenses of maintaining an office for that person on-site. Isaiah and Lee, executives I interviewed, also lead real estate and facilities departments at the technology companies for which they work. While they have not quantified the savings, they both agree. Leaders in this study also believe they save money because they ultimately reduce absenteeism. When employees have little flexibility, they are forced to take full days off or call in sick in order to accommodate personal needs such as doctor visits or caring for children on a snow day when school is closed. On the other hand, when they have the ability to adjust their work hours—to come in late and work late in turn—they are able to perform their daily tasks in an adjusted way. Likewise, if employees have the ability to work from home, supported by the necessary technology, they are able to be productive from home even when children may be home sick. This type of flexibility results in cost savings, these leaders argue, because the organization isn't losing money through absenteeism. Instead, it is gaining the benefit of an employee's continued working time despite personal commitments that must be met throughout the day.

ATTRACTING AND RETAINING TALENT

Organizations must manage the experience people have as employees, but they must also consider how they entice people to join the company in the first place. The economy has a strong bearing on supply and demand and the balance of power between employees and employers. Before 2008, companies were offering work-life supports as a way to attract employees in a tight labor market. With the economic downturn in 2008, businesses were cutting head count and eliminating employees, and the power shifted to companies. Employees were afraid of losing their jobs and they were working harder than ever to stay employed, as they watched friends and colleagues flow to the unemployment lines. More recently, as the economy begins its tentative return to economic wholeness, employees have more power again. They are choosing to work in multiple careers over their lifetimes and in multiple organizations over their careers. Work-life supports can be the differentiating factor in an employee choosing an employer.

In 2013, Mars, Inc. was one of *Fortune* magazine's "100 Best Companies to Work For,"[23] so as global president for Mars Drinks, Xavier Unkovic's perspectives are telling. He says:

> Anytime you look at your market share you always compare yourself with industry competitors. When it comes to attracting talent, you compete with every company in the world from GM to Boeing and more. The biggest challenge we have is in finding people. In order to have a great company, you have to have great people who want to work for your company and who have alignment with your values. This is about creating better lives and work. Our legacy is that people are happier when they feel they have an impact on other people. Life is too short and if we only have one life,

it is important to enjoy it. A company should make you want to stay and you should have fun and be able to smile. It's not about perks, it's about at the end of the week or the month whether employees can say they're enjoying the company they work for and whether they feel their personal values are aligned with the culture.[24]

Ross, a COO with an oil and gas company, agrees:

Work-life supports are especially critical now. You're not going to get the top talent that you require to deliver results unless you've got an atmosphere and culture in your company that gives you a good balance between the two. Work-life supports are a benefit that separates one organization from another. Employees are becoming more astute and demanding. In order to attract (and retain) the best and the brightest, work-life supports and work flexibility will be critical. There are exceptions to be sure, but in general, leaders in organizations are recognizing that employees worth hiring have raised the bar in terms of their expectations of the organization. Regardless of their generation or job, they want more from a company in terms of benefits, policies, and practices that support a fuller range of options for their navigation of work-life demands.

Retention has positive financial impacts. In general, turnover costs three times an employee's salary. This is the cost for replacing the employee in terms of lost productivity (when the position is vacant), recruiting, training, and orienting the new employee. This impact is significant and it does not include the lost knowledge from the departing employee, or the potential negative impact on motivation among remaining employees. Adding to the complexity is the fact that those employees most likely to leave are typically the most talented, as they are in demand and have the most to gain from shifting to a different company. Work-life supports provide a solution by contributing positively to retention. In a 2013 study of workplaces, the American Psychological Association found that turnover was only 6 percent for companies that promote well-being and performance through work-life support measures. This was compared with a national average turnover rate of 38 percent.[25] Creating an environment of abundance, where people are drawn in and want to stay, is worth it to the bottom line.

PURCHASING FLEXIBILITY

We had a saying at a company where I worked in the past: "We're so fortunate here, you can work your eighty hours whenever you want." We weren't kidding. The culture in the organization was to work intensive hours, but in addition to our wages, we were paid in flexibility. The culture of the organization allowed us to come and go as we pleased—for dentist appointments, for little league games, to attend violin recitals, to drive for Meals on Wheels—as long as we delivered results. Delivering results usually meant working long hours to get it all done. We knew we'd made a deal with the devil, and we discussed it openly. The trade-off was worth it to many of us. Our sweat bought us the opportunity to be the moms, dads, mates, and community members we wanted to be. We may not have been serving ourselves—our sleep suffered—but we were serving our families and communities. While I'm not necessarily advocating for this level of intensity and intrusion into nonworking hours, work-life supports can be a powerful draw for employees who are seeking to integrate life and work and navigate across their life course.

Isaiah, an executive with a technology company, says that his organization is in an extremely competitive market for talent, and work-life supports are a critical component of attracting people. Recent research corroborates that flexibility in the workplace is attractive: specifically, one study found that when workplaces offer flexible options, they are more attractive to 90 percent of workers.[26]

HIRING "10S"

In an article in *Inc.* magazine,[27] Martin Jacknis explains key hiring dynamics: in order to *have* the very best talent, you must *hire* the very best talent. Jacknis argues that 10s hire 10s because they are smart enough, and secure enough, to know that they should surround themselves with others who are as smart as possible. Leaders who are below a 10 tend to hire just under their own capability level so they look better. That is, 9s hire 8s, 8s hire 7s, and so on. So the real advantage only comes when you have 10s in an organization, and they in turn hire the best. The effective strategy is to hire so you're always surrounded by people who are as smart, or smarter than you are.[28] Otherwise, you'll always have good—but not great—talent.

Regardless of whom you're hiring, attracting new talent is fundamentally a matter of power dictated by supply and demand. Lorraine, an executive in charge of administration, philanthropy, and corporate communication with a media company, points out that the availability of work-life supports can vary based on how challenging it is for a company to recruit talent. She has seen that as the market for talent becomes more competitive, her company offers more work-life supports. When the market shifts and it is easier to attract talent to the organization, the work-life supports are reduced. She describes a hierarchy of needs in which, when the economy is poor, employees are just happy to be working and demand less in terms of work-life supports.

While there will always be some pendulum swing between good economic times and bad, leaders in this study believe that there is an all-out war for talent today. Baby boomers are retiring now or will very soon. In addition, these leaders believe our education system is not birthing as much talent as it once did and, moving forward, it will be very difficult to find the right talent. Work-life supports will be a differentiator, and companies that don't offer these supports will pay the price in terms of the talent they are—and are not—able to attract.

SELF-DETERMINATION AND SELF-GOVERNANCE

Earlier, I discussed the need for self-determination and the importance of work-life supports that provide for choice making and autonomy. This control also results in positive organizational outcomes. Organizations that have a high level of employee control and self-governance perform significantly better than other organizations. They are more innovative, have greater employee loyalty, and higher customer satisfaction. In addition, they see less misconduct on the parts of employees and better financial performance.[29]

POINTS OF RESISTANCE

If work-life supports are so positive and beneficial to employees and the companies for which they work, why don't all companies offer them? Rick Wartzman, executive director of the Drucker Institute, believes that it is related to the costs that are out of companies' control:

The social contract has eroded over the past thirty to forty years primarily because of cost. In the two or three decades immediately following World War II, major American corporations could afford to be generous; there was hardly any competition from the rest of the world. With the rise of the global economy, companies have needed to cut costs in order to remain competitive. As a result, what I call the "hard side" of the social contract that employers have with their employees—job security, pay, benefits—has been shredded. At the same time, there are lots of ways that companies can support employees on the "soft side" of the social contract—that is, in terms of the ways that employees are treated, the ways they are engaged with their work, and the ways they are given a sense of purpose. These are all well within the control of a company, even in an age of brutal economic competition.[30]

Some executives resist providing work-life supports because they believe it's not the role of the organization to do so. Their push back is "it's not my problem" or "it *shouldn't* be my problem." This sounds like a classic Democrat/Republican debate. Regardless of your politics though, this resistance— that it's not an organization's problem—doesn't hold. In reality, men and women are under increasing pressure to integrate the demands of work and family. Lacking comprehensive federal support for this work-life integration, the support offered by corporations is imperative. When companies serve their employees they win in the end because the employees in turn work harder and that's good for organizational performance.[31] As a result, it *is* relevant and necessary for organizations to pay attention to work-life supports.

Some leaders argue that it is difficult to measure the impact of work-life supports. They are right. Work-life supports are always part of a larger system and a broader experience of work. It is nearly impossible to isolate the variable of the work-life support options provided to employees from all the other variables in an organization. Elements such as the overall economy, reward systems, measurement systems, training systems, and employee personal life issues (to name just a few of multiple variables) will always have a bearing on an organization's results. In addition, costs are often easier to measure than benefits. Lisa Brummel, chief people officer for Microsoft, says:

> Leaders often get caught up in the cost of an activity because it is a more tangible metric than trying to measure the benefit of an activity. I would encourage all leaders to put a "benefit" list side by side with a "cost" list and take a hard look at where they can really create

high satisfaction for their employees. There is immeasurable return in a happy and engaged employee, and leaders must not lose sight of that.[32]

It is possible that the argument of difficulty in measuring the impact of work-life supports is simply a smoke screen for a leader who doesn't believe in providing them. Despite the difficulty measuring, it is still important to provide work-life supports and there are significant amounts of data that support this as a worthy endeavor. In part 3, I'll provide detail regarding how to measure effectively.

PERSONAL EXPERIENCE

In general, executives who embrace the idea of providing more work-life supports are typically those who have benefited from them personally, or whose family members have benefited. We all form opinions through our personal experiences, and it is impossible to totally separate ourselves from that personal experience. Senior executives are no different, and those who tell stories of being helped by work-life supports—for their father's illness, for their partner's job loss, for their own knee surgery—tend to be those most likely to advocate for work-life supports. It's helpful to think of senior executive viewpoints on a continuum from anti-sponsor to detractor to supporter to advocate.

Personal experience tends to move an executive left or right on the continuum. In fact, a senior leader's personal experience may even be on behalf of an employee. My research shows that even if a senior executive has had to tap into work-life supports for her team member, she tends to be more of an advocate for them.

It is important to note that the leader's enhanced support for work-life mechanisms was true only if the employee was a strong performer, and

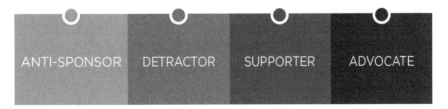

Figure 5-1 Sponsorship Continuum

the leader believed the need was legitimate. Senior leaders are actually less likely to advocate for work-life supports if they believe they have been taken advantage of by an employee in the past. This is the Slacker's Rule. When leaders have high-performing employees who are served by work-life supports, the leaders' own advocacy for work-life supports tends to increase. On the other hand, when a leader believes that an employee has played the system or benefited unjustly from a work-life support system, the leader will be less likely to be an advocate for work-life supports generally. Such experiences can even result in the leader becoming a detractor or anti-sponsor of the work-life supports, and standing in the way of implementing them. The solution? Accountability. Leaders who hold individuals on the team accountable tend to get the best results from the whole team. The way employees are treated and the extent to which leaders hold them accountable sends a message to the whole team, and the message has powerful repercussions for overall performance.

IN SUM

When companies fail to pay attention to work-life support, they run the risk of *not* attracting good people, of *not* tapping the best energies of their employees, of *not* retaining employees. The bottom line? Work-life supports are good for the bottom line. They are the right thing to do for people who are seeking to integrate all the parts of their work and life. They are also the right thing to do for the organization because the company will reap rewards from enhanced commitment, effort, and performance.

PART II

Leading with Alignment: Considerations for Success

CHAPTER 6

Aligning with the Nature of the Work

When implementing work-life supports, a key factor that must be considered is the nature of the work employees are performing. Work-life supports such as medical benefits or amenities can be easy to apply more equally across workers no matter what their job. However, flexibility of hours or locations for work can be more challenging to provide. This chapter describes some of the situations in which it may be more difficult to provide flexibility as well as creative ways to implement work-life supports despite the limitations.

In my research, I find that work-life supports are significantly more available when work meets certain conditions. I also find that the question of whether work is conducive to more flexible working options can be a matter of perception. It is important here to define terms. Many work-life supports can be available to anyone and everyone on a policy basis. These are policy-related supports such as parental leave or education reimbursement. However, things become more nuanced in the application of the policy. For example, it is straightforward to provide a certain level of educational reimbursement as a work-life support to everyone. It is more of a judgment call—often made by work team leaders—as to whether certain employees or those in certain jobs should be afforded time off to take classes. The real issue in these cases is work flexibility.

LEGITIMATE CHALLENGES

There are some jobs for which it is challenging to provide flexibility. Work that requires an employee to be connected with machines, equipment, or lab supplies that are only available in the building is less conducive to flexible working options. Manufacturing, production inventory control scheduling, engineering, receptionist/concierge, and IT support are examples of positions that may be less conducive to flexibility. Another example is work that requires employees to have regular face-to-face interaction with other employees or with customers in order to get things done.

In general, there is a relationship between work and flexibility that can be described by a parabola curve. Employees with the most flexibility afforded to them through their work tend to be those who have medium levels of pay and are at medium-to-high professional levels within their organizations. Those with the lowest pay/professional status and those with the highest pay/professional status tend to have the least flexibility. Why? Because often the jobs at the lower ranks are more tied to desks (such as customer service team members), machines (skilled trades), or customers (repair technicians). At the other end of the continuum are senior managers and executives who must be in the office more frequently in order to lead people in the moment and be available for spontaneous decisions with colleagues. Their face time is usually a part of their work on a day-to-day basis. For every example there are exceptions, but in general, research suggests

Figure 6-1   Work-Flexibility Curve

this relationship between pay/professional level and degree of flexibility available.

Barbara, a senior leader at a financial organization, says that traders are required to be at their desks and it feels "nearly impossible" to provide them with flexibility of their hours or the location for their work. Lorraine runs the administrative function for her media organization. Her company has a large contingent of call center employees who are tied to their desks, and to sitting in close proximity to work teams in which problems are solved moment to moment. No matter how strong the will to provide flexibility in working hours, for some jobs it is more challenging than in others.

A major sticking point for one organization—in this case a media company—is the challenge of the "lowest common denominator." Lorraine's company is seeking to standardize the employee experience across all jobs and locations for the organization, with equal access to benefits, policies, and practices for all employees. The problem is that a large percentage of employees are technicians and call center employees for whom it is more difficult to provide flexible working options. Unfortunately, this emphasis on equality misses the point. It is certainly possible to offer options that provide equity. Just because every job doesn't have the exact same access to flexible work options doesn't mean that equitable solutions can't be found. If no one can progress until everyone can progress, there is no platform for trying new things and learning. Lorraine is advocating for a shift in mind-set toward equity (not equality) in order to catalyze creative solutions.

CREATIVE SOLUTIONS

Even in situations where jobs are seemingly less suited for flexible working approaches, companies are finding creative solutions that allow for worker flexibility, while ensuring the employees in those jobs are still able to accomplish their work successfully.

TRAVEL

Jobs requiring significant travel present situations in which it is more difficult to provide flexibility. A colleague of mine, Kelly, worked for a multinational legal firm and traveled extensively. Unfortunately, her boss would not allow any flexibility in her schedule when she traveled. Kelly would regularly travel from the West Coast to the East Coast on red-eye flights so she would spend fewer nights away from her children and husband. However, her boss still expected her to show up at the office from 8 a.m. to 5 p.m. Sometimes this meant she would have to go straight from the airport to the office at 7 a.m., after having spent a short four-hour night on a plane.

Kelly would freshen up in airport bathrooms and do her best with clients the next day, but it didn't last. Despite being a successful rising star in the firm, she left and found another firm. Her departure prompted a shift in the firm's approach to work-life supports. The firm began affording more flexibility of work hours. When staff was traveling, the firm provided one day off per month to compensate for extensive travel. Additionally, the firm provided employees with camera-equipped laptops so they could communicate visually with their families from the road. Unfortunately, it was too late for Kelly to benefit from any of the policy changes at the firm. The lesson here? Creative solutions are usually possible, even in jobs with challenges such as travel. Importantly, leaders must be aware of the constraints of the work they're requiring of employees or risk losing them.

REGULATIONS AND SAFETY

Another example of work that may be more difficult to accommodate with flexible working choices is that which is controlled by regulations and security measures. One executive with whom I spoke described how certain employees weren't able to work at home or work on laptops because of the sensitive nature of the data they were handling.

Interestingly, each of these employees was also mandated to take an annual vacation of at least two weeks with no connection to the office. This mechanism was designed to protect against financial fraud. The company believed that any questionable activity in which an employee might be involved would be unsustainable if he was away from the office and completely out of touch for two weeks at a time. The forced vacations had the consequence of giving employees time away.

For employees who must be in the office, and not able to use a laptop for their work, the company is exploring on-site child care so employees can check on their children during the day. The company is also experimenting with creating a partnership with area restaurants, arranging for these establishments to deliver dinners when employees have to work late in the office.

An oil and gas executive with whom I spoke also cited regulations and security concerns as a reason for less job flexibility. He reported that some work was constrained by the unwillingness to load laptops with too much information that could potentially put the organization's infrastructure at risk. His company began providing each employee with a tablet device on which to perform portions of their work away from the office. By decoupling the work from the device, the company maintained security for the portions of the tasks that were sensitive while creating flexible options for those that were not.

A GENIUS SOLUTION

Recently I worked with a company that set up a new coffee bar within one of its facilities. One of the features designed to support people was a "Genius Bar," which was a part of the coffee bar. This solution was simply an IT expert who sat at the end of the coffee bar with a brightly colored name tag and a table tent identifying her as the on-duty genius. The concept worked so well during the move in process that they've kept it going, and now there is an IT expert at the coffee bar every Monday through Friday from 10 a.m. to 3 p.m. This is a perfect example of a role that is tied to a certain location (the genius/coffee bar) and tied to a certain degree of contact with others. However, while the role has these limitations, it is still possible to provide work-life flexibility to those who perform the role. The way the job is designed—with a trio of employees serving in the role of "Genius on Duty," instead of one person—there is plenty of flexibility for the people who are part of the genius squad.

CYCLES OF WORK

When companies seek creative ways to accomplish flexible work, the cycles of that work are also important to consider. I worked with a marketing team within a large consumer goods organization. A key part of the work in what was known as the "creation center" was designing, developing, and producing graphics and packages for the organization's customers. In this case, there was a need for the team to be together at certain times to brainstorm the unique ideas that would drive the package. In addition, there were times when team members needed access to the specialized production equipment and times when the team needed to be present to assemble materials. The work team leader was able to offer plenty of flexibility to each team member by discerning the moments when face-to-face work or on-site work was necessary. When it was, the team was there contributing. For the times when work on site wasn't necessary, the team had plenty of flexibility to come and go, as long as the work was accomplished effectively.

CYCLES OF COLLABORATIVE AND INDIVIDUAL WORK

When companies are designing and provisioning for work-life supports, they also benefit by assessing the dynamics and cycles of teams, because work sometimes changes at various points in the team's cycle. Consider two dimensions: relationship and task. At the outset of a project, there is frequently a need for face-to-face, in-office collaboration in order to establish task-oriented starting points such as ground rules, protocols, direction for the team, assignments, working agreements, and key milestones. Once these foundational elements are in place, it is possible to proceed more effectively. In the example of the marketing team above, there was a need for face-to-face collaboration at the outset of each mini-project to establish unique ideas that would drive the remainder of the project.

There are also key moments that require more face-to-face communication and collaboration that are driven by the team's need to manage relationships. In general, when team members do not yet know each other well, more face-to-face collaboration is useful. There is a degree of trust that is built through face-to-face connections that helps the efficiency and effectiveness of a project as it moves forward. Trust may also be established through virtual means for team members who aren't in contact with one another in the same location. There may be moments when the team receives new members or members change. There may also be a point where a new leader takes over, or a point where conflict has occurred and must be resolved. These key relationship points require greater face-to-face communication in order to reinforce interaction norms, work through challenges, pick up non-verbal signals, and deal with disagreements in a constructive way. It's not that these processes can't occur without face-to-face communication, it's just that face-to-face processing makes it more effective.

CUSTOMER-FACING WORK

Customer-facing work is another example with requirements that affect a company's ability to offer flexible working hours. When team members must meet with customers at certain times—either on the phone, on site, or at customer offices—flexibility is clearly more challenging. However, with proactive planning, when work team leaders can identify portions of a day or portions of a week during which this customer work is necessary, flexibility can be available for the portions of the day or week that are not customer facing. Some leaders are also experimenting with providing rewards and recognition for employees who are tied to customer schedules. In one example, a company provides a yearly retreat to a nearby water park for employees and their families.

PROJECT-BASED WORK

One of the trends on the horizon is the "Hollywood Model." As it relates to the way people work, this means that much of our work—both inside and outside of organizations—will be project based. The "Hollywood Model" derives its name from a comparison with the way movies are produced. A group of individuals gets together for a time-limited duration to produce a movie. When the movie is complete they disband, and each moves on separately to a new movie.

This is distinguished from a typical corporate model, in which people take jobs within departments and work as members of a team for the long term. Work in the corporate model is more continuous and not based on the episodic nature of projects. In the newer Hollywood Model, projects may be for the long term or for the short term, but they are the organizing feature of work. Work is organized to a lesser degree by functions or departments. A worker may still bring a core competence in accounting, but her work is focused on XYZ project. When XYZ project concludes, she is assigned to a different project or must find the next project herself. The implications for this type of approach are far reaching.

In this project-based reality, workers' identities will be based on the projects they are part of more than the department to which they belong. Workers will potentially have less job security in the traditional sense. At the conclusion of a project, a worker may have to find another assignment based on his merits and reputation. This denotes more of an "independent agent" (find your own work) type of world, even when the worker is still a regular full-time employee of that organization.

This type of model also has implications for the work itself. The leader will either need to contract with the agents on the project to stay until the end of the effort or create a fulfilling enough experience that workers want to stay on the project and see it through to the end. If companies are managing work effectively, they are making work its own magnet, so this model drives to that type of management.

For particularly progressive companies, the Hollywood Model may already be reality. In other cases, the Hollywood Model is taking hold within the ranks of external contract labor. In this case, contractors may trade off the training, development, and insurance benefits a corporation provides in exchange for greater autonomy, freedom, and creative license for their work. In a world where there is heavy competition for talent, companies must either find a way to compel loyalty or create situations where it isn't necessary. The Hollywood Model suggests a way to leverage loyalty for the short term of a project. This benefits the organization. Career coaches recommend that each worker think of her career as a portfolio of contributions through which she creates value and generates new knowledge for herself and her organization. This knowledge is portable to all future projects and roles, whether the worker is an employee of the organization or a free agent.

LEADERSHIP LESSONS FROM PROJECT-BASED WORK

What are the leadership lessons from the Hollywood Model as they relate to work-life supports? First, leaders must ensure that employees have a strong sense of identity associated with the work they do. Whether people are working in a more traditional team with a more traditional schedule or working in a less traditional way with a less traditional schedule, a strong sense of purpose and identity with their work will be helpful in creating a sense of fulfillment.

Another lesson from the Hollywood Model pertains to passion. In this model, workers have some degree of choice regarding the content of their work and how it aligns with their passions. Finally, there is a strong aspect of accountability in the Hollywood Model. Workers are held accountable by the team leader and by the other project team members. Employees' currency is the value they bring to their work, and success on a project helps drive the worker to the next project aligned with his passions. Leaders who are able to provide identity and purpose in the work, align people and their passions, and ensure accountability are able to increase an employee's sense of capacity to fulfill demands and reduce the perception of demands as well. Each of these contribute to work-life support overall.

DEMAND AND CAPACITY

Previously, I described the importance of employees' perceptions of capacity in relationship to demand. When a worker faces daunting demands, his perception of his own capacity has an impact on his ability to meet those demands. When the load feels too heavy to carry, he won't pick it up. Work-life supports, implemented successfully based on the considerations in this model, work on both sides of the equation. They reduce the demands that workers face.

Successful implementation also works on the capacity side of the model. Providing work-life supports increases workers' capacity to face challenges. Through these solutions, companies can accomplish better results in ways that allow flexible options for employees. Embedded in many of these solutions are self-determination and autonomy through which employees are making choices regarding how they work, when they work, and where they work, within the context of delivering results and meeting the requirements of their jobs.

PERCEPTIONS AND MIND-SETS

Often, the question of which jobs are more or less conducive to work flexibility is based on personal perception. Such a perception is easy to hear in these comments, from a senior executive in an oil and gas company: "Few of our employees can work from home because our work is in the building." His statement makes a generalization affecting the jobs of literally thousands of workers within his organization and demonstrates a more traditional attitude toward work. In shifting perceptions and in taking steps to provide workers with flexibility, it is useful to think of a continuum. While there may be jobs and situations that are, by definition, less flexible, there are plenty of jobs in which some flexibility is possible. Providing flexibility should not be a yes or no decision, but rather a decision of degree.

Organizations can and should adopt a mind-set of openness toward work flexibility. These overall beliefs can then guide the ways in which organizations experiment with flexible working approaches. Here are some starters: *Our organization sets out to provide as much flexibility as is possible and reasonable. Our organization aligns flexible options with the nature of the work.* While every job can't have total flexibility, most jobs can have some flexibility. These types of mind-sets point the way toward creative solutions. Despite all of the situations in which providing work-life supports and flexibility are challenging, leaders *can* find ways to provide work flexibility. Creative solutions provide flexibility within limits and boundaries of many jobs. Organizations must expand work-life solutions beyond simply considering work hours and location. As we've seen, work-life supports come in many forms from benefits to education, and from recognition to project selection and amenities.

IN SUM

Some work is more difficult to accommodate with work-life supports, but it is important to consider the limitations leaders may be imposing based on personal opinions. Whether the work situation is limited by travel, by collaborative needs of teams, or by some other parameter, creative options for work flexibility are usually possible to find.

CHAPTER 7

Aligning with Global Work

Many organizations and employees are finding that work is increasingly global in nature. This chapter provides recommendations for how to make global work effective, and how to provide work-life supports for more global types of work. It also addresses social networking as a tool for connecting employees and thus bringing work to life.

GLOBAL WORK, NEW DEMANDS

In my study of work-life supports, I find that when companies have a greater proportion of work that is global, they tend to be more amenable to providing work-life supports. There are a few reasons for this. When employees are working with individuals from other countries and time zones, companies—even those that consider themselves to be more traditional and less supportive of flexible work schedules—are forced to provide for a variety of working hours. The U.S. employee who is on a call with another region of the world at 9 p.m., or on a videoconference with another at 5 a.m., is no longer required to be in the office from 8 a.m. to 5 p.m.

Global work also tends to support and catalyze the provision of more work-life supports because leaders learn about the work-life supports and integration available in other countries. In general, the United States has some of the most paltry federal supports for everything from parental leave to vacation benefits. Executives in my study report that as global work increases, the exposure to differences in countries' policies does too. Sometimes this inspires leaders to make increasingly convincing business cases for enhanced leave or improved vacation allotments using the ammunition of other countries' policies and the results they achieve. Brent is a senior leader with a manufacturing company. He says, "We are experiencing a shift where we have almost as many workers in Asia as we do in the United States, and the workforce in Asia is a stronger proponent of work-life support than we are in the U.S. and they're going to help the rest of the company acclimate to that environment."

Effective global work requires new skill sets and approaches, and developing these can be demanding. For some, global working may be perceived as a significant set of demands without enough rewards in the "plus" column of the personal balance sheet. Given that one of the ways to provide support for work and life is to reduce the perception of demands, providing effective leadership and systems can be an effective way to offer work-life supports. Some companies are offering training on culture sensitivity. They are providing online and classroom-based learning on the nuances between cultures in order to make working between cultures easier. Other companies are offering foreign language training.

WORK-LIFE SUPPORTS FOR GLOBAL WORK

One company with which I consulted was implementing a new process that required teammates in the United States and Mexico to regularly interact and travel between countries. In order to facilitate what would be a multi-year process, the company ordered language training DVDs for employees so the English-speakers could learn Spanish and the Spanish-speakers could learn English. Even if employees did not become fluent in the teammates' language, they had an increased understanding of the vocabulary. When the Mexico team was hiring new employees for the project, language skills were paramount, and the U.S. team participated in the interviewing process in order to help evaluate the candidate's proficiency.

When teammates had to travel between the U.S. and Mexico, the company paid for one additional day of travel for each of the team members. U.S. employees enjoyed tours of Mexico's historic and government districts and extensive art museums. Employees from Mexico visiting the U.S. attended a hockey game. They also visited one of the more northern U.S. sites in January and were able to experience snow for the first time. There were also a few teammates who also set up informal lunchtime phone conversations in which they attempted to speak exclusively in either English or Spanish and learn through this immersion. They discussed aspects of their personal lives as a means of enhancing their vocabulary and language skills. The company also instituted weekly conference calls to ensure that the team stayed connected. The calls were successful in keeping the lines of communication open, so there were fewer misunderstandings in translation. All of these tactics were in service to a strategic goal of supporting employees through the work and contributing to a capacity to work across borders. A situation that could have yielded tremendous stress instead became the context for new and fulfilling experiences and relationships among team members.

Work-life supports for employees who work with global clients or teammates may also be provided in the form of flexible working hours or technology that enables employees to work from home. Employees should be able to call in to conference lines using a local 800 number or using a phone with global capabilities. Employees who must use videoconferencing should be able to do so from a laptop computer equipped with a camera to enable a quality videoconference.

MANAGEMENT APPROACHES TO WORK-LIFE SUPPORTS

Another way to provide work-life supports is through leadership and management approaches that make working globally more effective. A couple of years ago, I worked with a global company that supplied well-known consumer goods. Its growth strategy was to acquire and also build capability outside the United States. In particular, it had established a branch of its organization in India. Despite the fact that the employees in India were regular full time employees of the organization, many in the U.S. did not think of them as members of the same organization. Instead, they tended to think of them as members of a totally different organization at odds with the parent organization.

Realizing this was a problem, we took some specific steps to unite the entire organization. These were strategies to provide work-life supports, making global work not only more manageable but more fulfilling in terms of the relationships that were fostered:

• First, we clarified direction, expectations, and business literacy. The company's leadership clearly identified locations outside the U.S. as full members in the business and set expectations for a global team. Leaders regularly reported on all the global locations. They kept these locations visible to all employees at monthly all-employee business meetings.

- We established a U.S. leadership sponsor for each of the India counterpart departments (finance, design, engineering, customer service). This leader's role was to ensure success for that portion of the India contingent and hold those in the U.S. accountable for success.

- Next, we addressed concerns of job security. We were clear with U.S. employees, educating them on the international growth strategy and clarifying how a strong global organization would translate to a strong organization in the U.S.—one in which jobs were more secure, not less secure. There was one department in the U.S. that was under consideration to be shifted off shore, and we worked with that department directly and honestly, helping them understand which jobs would be affected, which wouldn't be affected, and what options were available to those whose jobs would likely be affected.

- We also ensured that all portions of the organization shared a common purpose and goals. We asked both the U.S. and the India teams to participate in articulating and shaping these. We did this through joint development sessions in which we facilitated dialogue via videoconference.

- Additionally, we did some problem solving with the team. We discovered that certain functions were working well across borders—specifically, engineering and some design functions. For the functions that were working less well—in particular, one of the financial functions—we pointed out the differences and reminded them of the accountability the entire team had for success.

- We created standards for the work that needed to be accomplished. One of the more troubling points of resistance to the India team's success on the part of the U.S. team was a belief that their work wasn't up to the quality levels of the U.S. team. Because of this, we increased the training available to the India team and created standards so that both teams were using the same playbook.

- We established specific lines of communication between the U.S. team and the India team. We established an every-other-week phone meeting in which we discussed what was working, what wasn't working, and what we could continuously improve and work on together. We kept the meeting to thirty minutes and worked efficiently so that it wasn't perceived as a burden, and was instead seen as a quick, effective way to communicate and accomplish work together. We also emphasized the use of e-mail communication between teammates so that accents wouldn't be a hindrance to understanding. For communication that had to be verbal, we established an 800 number. We didn't want anyone to say, "I didn't know how to call

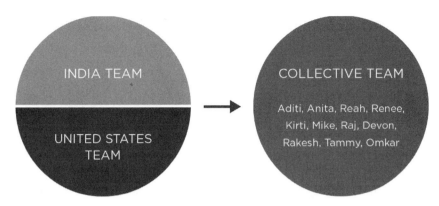

Figure 7-1 Global Team

them." Instead, we wanted coworkers to pick up the phone and speak with one another in order to achieve common objectives.

• Additionally, and this was perhaps most important, we called people by their names. We reinforced that all the team members were people with identities. Instead of a team on the other side of the world that was a monolith made up of foreigners, we ensured that every employee knew the names of those with whom she was working across borders. Instead of the "India team" or the "United States team," teammates became Aditi, Anita, Reah, Renee, Kirti, Mike, Raj, Devon, Rakesh, Tammy, and Omkar.

• Finally, we held people accountable. We added teamwork to the expectations we set as performance goals and identified constructive work as a point of accountability. After all, "what gets rewarded gets done" and this was no exception. We recognized the team and celebrated their accomplishments.

Has it worked? Absolutely. Teams are working well together and productivity among the teams is at an all-time high. Positive feedback from customers is also at record levels. The teams have challenges, of course, but they now have communication channels and mechanisms to work through the challenges. One of the measures of success is satisfaction scores. Those working on these teams feel more satisfied and report less stress than they did a year before the changes, and this has made a big difference in reducing the overall demands they perceived. The provision of work-life supports reduces the perception of demand and increases the perception of capacity, and these tactics were effective in bringing work to life in the context of global efforts.

THE CONNECTION TO SOCIAL NETWORKING

Global work is also related to social networking. Specifically, social networking via Facebook, Pinterest, LinkedIn, or other platforms can serve the purposes of helping employees connect and develop relationships, find others with common interests or competencies to collaborate on tasks, or even take a break from work in order to refresh and regroup. The reason social networking emerges especially in global companies is that their employees are often working with one another more virtually and less face to face. As a result, they must find ways to connect personally that are not dependent on running into each other at the coffee machine in the morning. Global working generally drives leaders to manage employees for the results they create, instead of their presence in the office from 8 a.m. to 5 p.m., Monday through Friday.

Global companies tend to be more open to employees' use of social networking sites to collaborate virtually. Social networking has also become a way in which many workers stay in touch with other elements of their lives during the workday. Sometimes it is the primary vehicle for connecting with another mom to RSVP for her son's birthday party—through Facebook's message feature—or checking in on a teenage daughter's evening plans via her Twitter feed. A LinkedIn discussion group may be a vehicle for solving a problem or obtaining information. One study of investment traders found that those who learned from the input of the network achieved the highest returns on their investments.[1] The network can have real benefits in getting work done effectively.

Social networking may also provide a brain break from an intensive project. Sometimes it offers a gateway to supportive family or friends on a hard day. Whether employees are using social networking to connect with one another and accomplish tasks, or are checking personal social networking sites during working hours, access to social networks is essentially helping to reduce the perception of demands and increase perceptions of capacity by providing support for getting these types of activities done. Kevin Knebl, social networking guru and coauthor of *The Social Media Sales Revolution,* believes that social networking is integral to the way we work and the way we relate to others (see my interview with Kevin Knebl).

Work-Life Supports and Social Networking: An Interview with Kevin Knebl

Kevin Knebl is coauthor of The Social Media Sales Revolution: The New Rules for Finding Customers, Building Relationships, and Closing More Sales Through Online Networking *(McGraw-Hill), as well as a contributing author of* Learn Marketing with Social Media in Seven Days *(Wiley). He is the most recommended business speaker in the world and he speaks, trains, and coaches internationally on social selling, relationship marketing, networking, LinkedIn, and personal development.*

What is the relationship between social networking and work-life supports?

KK: The world is more interconnected and hyper-caffeinated than it ever has been. If you think back to the '80s and '90s, work life and personal life were more separate. With the world of Facebook, Twitter, and other platforms, the line isn't blurred anymore, it doesn't even exist. The question is, "Does an individual have enough common sense in their professional life to be sure they're not overstepping the boundaries?" Generation Y and Z and whatever is next are so used to being connected that the skill is to set a line in the sand. It is hard to separate work from life. In our 24–7, 365 society with electronics and cell and Skype, it isn't work-life balance, it's the balance of overall life, and work is just a part of it. It's easy to teach people about the bells and whistles of social media, but I remind people to enjoy their life. Using social media, they can add value to others in so many ways. At work, we don't turn off the person.

How does social networking add value to people's lives?

KK: We're wired to connect from the moment we are born. No one is wired to be Tom Hanks on an island with a volleyball named Wilson. Through social media we now have the ability to connect with anyone on earth. Every human with a cell phone is a media company. We can add value to others through these channels in many ways, financially, spiritually... like mosquitoes in a nudist colony of opportunity. Social media

(Continued)

shows us that we're so much more alike than different. For example, we may work at different companies and live in different states but we all love and appreciate our families, and this is what we post on Facebook. Social media breaks down the barriers between people. It shows us that we're more alike than different. It opens lines of communications between people. Social media enables us to connect more and it facilitates relationships.

What are our responsibilities as they relate to social media?

KK: In some ways, it's the same as what we learned from our parents and grandparents years ago. For example, "If you can't say something nice, don't say anything at all." The way we were raised at home has a ripple effect in the way we function in the world. The values we were raised with affect us. You can't outrun your character. If you're a jerk, you'll leave a wake of jerkiness behind you. With social media, a jerk is still a jerk, it's just that more people know it now. With social media, we all live in glass houses. You can't legislate morality or etiquette, so a good rule is to leave the world better than you found it. We all have an impact on everyone else whether we realize it or not, and we need to treat that with a level of responsibility. The Dalai Lama says, "My religion is kindness." I agree with this. It would be great if we could all just be a little nicer. The challenge with social media is, there is no context. Because of this, we need to err on the side of being kind, because posts can be taken the wrong way. We are responsible for what we say and do, both online and offline.

What is the role of social media in the work environment?

KK: It can add value to the end customer and internal employees. Think of birthdays. If we're friends on Facebook and I know it's your birthday, now I can wish you a happy birthday. Or I can wish you a happy work anniversary based on LinkedIn. I can pay it forward and add value in so many ways. It can help employee morale and retention. Externally, it can help with customer service. It can also help a company monitor the competition and see new opportunities. Both internally and externally, it can help increase the effectiveness of teams and strategic partnerships and alliances.

What are the trends regarding companies' adoption rates for social media?

KK: I'm seeing increased adoption of LinkedIn and Facebook and Twitter by organizations. Even the more traditional companies are figuring out that these tools can be helpful to them. In addition, the way they respond and whether they allow employees to use the tools sends a message about whether they respect and want to empower employees. If a company doesn't allow employees to use social media, it quickly sends a message that they don't trust employees to communicate to the world, and this can lead to a disengaged employee. My experience in business is that the tone is set from the top—from senior management and chief executives. They don't have to be experts with social media. They can accept the tools and empower the organization or they can pretend the tools don't exist. The little things CEOs do have a ripple effect. This happens through their attitudes and how they interact and what is tolerated or not and how they treat people. We need to have empowering environments in this interconnected world. We have a tremendous opportunity to create great relationships.

Are there particular guidelines you recommend?

KK: Companies just have to be cognizant of the communication tools and provide guidelines for using social media. The guidelines create the environment for employees to build strong relationships. The right guidelines all depend on your company's size, industry, and other factors. It doesn't have to be a fifty-page edict, but things like "never respond negatively to customers," "never criticize each other publically," "never air dirty laundry," "always be polite and positive," "always take the high road," are good examples.

Any final words on social media?

KK: Social media at its core is about relationships. The more enlightened organizations will use it to empower and strengthen their employees and their relationships.

MAKING RULES

Companies that do not already allow employees to spend time on social networking during working hours are sometimes concerned with employees taking advantage of the system. Unfortunately, there will be some who will. Most won't, however. One of my first jobs was chairperson of one of the company's "equity committees." The equity committees were our answer to dealing with issues of fairness and policy. The committees provided a vehicle for employees to voice concerns in a representative system through which the committee members could process policies and issues. There was a committee for each part of the business with an overall committee for the company as a whole. Each committee met monthly and was made up of representatives from all functional groups within that part of the business.

Nick was a long-term employee who had been with the company for more than forty years. He had a vast network across the organization. Beyond Nick's tenure and job, he was vastly networked because he was a good listener, easy to talk to, and patient. When he offered his response to a problem, he usually approached it from an angle that was new or unconsidered, so chatting with Nick always helped us think differently. One day, in an equity committee meeting, we were debating whether we should adopt a new policy that would impose greater controls on employees. Nick listened through the debate. Then he spoke up and asked us whether we were creating policies for 95 percent or 5 percent of employees. His argument was that 95 percent of the people would do the right thing because it was the right thing to do. Only 5 percent of the people wouldn't do the right thing.

Companies should create policies for the majority of the people who want to do the right thing. Expect the best and create rules, policies, and guidelines that are liberating and provide the broad outlines of expectation, rather than creating policies that seek to control every detail of an employee's work. For some leaders, a point of resistance to work-life supports is that people will take advantage. They're worried about the minority of people who cannot be trusted. To think as Nick did, it is best to create approaches that serve the majority. Some employees may take advantage of social networking options or work flexibility, but in general, you'll win because 95 percent of your employees will set the bar by performing well and by doing the right thing.

IN SUM

Global work has shifted realities for many workers by requiring new hours, new types of communication, and new problem-solving skills. When organizations provide work-life supports in the form of many different solutions—flexibility of working hours, language development, travel time, social networking—they provide for an employee experience that is positive. With this positive experience, employees contribute to the organization and the outcomes they are expected to accomplish. Companies are also wise to create solutions that serve the majority of people who want to do a good job and make a positive contribution.

CHAPTER 8

Aligning with Technology

In this chapter, I discuss technology and its relationship to work-life supports. Technology is the proverbial double-edged sword as it relates to navigating work and life demands. While it provides tools that allow greater flexibility for where and when people work, it can also tether employees to their work constantly. This chapter describes why employers should offer technology provisions for employees, and how they can best do it. It suggests new skills and behaviors that will be necessary as work and workers respond to shifts in technology, and it recommends some ways workers can use technology to navigate work and life.

In my research, I find that companies that provide more technology for employees tend to also have greater work-life support options for employees. For companies at the forward edge of technology provisioning, this chapter will feel like well-known terrain, but there are many companies with their entire workforces still tethered to desktop computers. This is true even for companies with brands that are known for being forward thinking and innovative. The future will arrive, just not everywhere at the same time.[1] Technology is correlated with greater work-life supports. Technology itself is a work-life support, but it also creates new demands that *diminish* successful work-life navigation. Technology is complicated.

THE PROS AND CONS OF TECHNOLOGY

Within the last few years, there was a popular commercial for a wireless network. It features a beautiful mom with a cell phone and three beautiful daughters. The girls are getting ready for the day and want to play and go to the beach instead of spending the day with a babysitter who watches TV all day. Unfortunately, the mom can't go to the beach because she has an important meeting with a client. One of her little girls says, "Mommy, when can I be a client?" This changes everything. The mom responds by leaving the babysitter home alone watching TV, taking her girls to the beach, and taking her client meeting on a conference call from there. This is all thanks to her superior cell phone and wireless network. Cindy Lauper's song "Girls Just Wanna Have Fun" provides a triumphant chorus.[2] The ad is testimony to the complexity of technology. It liberates us from the physical office while it also chains us to schedules and work in a way that can be limiting.

Linda, a general manager for the software division of a global technology company and who was part of my study, provides a starting point for exploration: "Technology is accelerating the breakdown of the barriers of a traditional work schedule and a traditional office environment. Companies have two choices. They can either resist it or embrace it and actually use it to their advantage." Livia, an executive with a media company says, "It's great to have a flexible work schedule but you're given a smartphone and the objective is that you're going to respond immediately. That is unhealthy. It creeps into your whole life. It is important to take time off and be away from the device."

Experts agree that staying connected and working 24–7 is damaging to health. An article in *Inc.* magazine[3] reported on research that found:

- Working eleven hours per day rather than eight hours resulted in a 67 percent increased risk of developing heart disease.
- Working more than fifty hours per week led to three times greater risk of developing a problem with alcohol abuse.
- Twenty hours without sleep was the equivalent of a .1 blood alcohol level (five or six drinks for people 160 to 180 pounds), resulting in problems with judgment.

67%
increased risk of developing heart disease with an 11 hour work day

3x
greater risk of alcohol abuse when working 50+ hours per week

.1%
blood alcohol level is equivalent to 20 hours without sleep

Figure 8-1   Health Impacts

Recently, I spoke with a senior executive who had progressed quickly in her career and found herself in her late thirties with two small children, a great house-husband, and a job as a high-level vice president. The problem was that she was frantic and she never turned off. This senior executive was not well liked by her peers, and this caused her significant difficulty in accomplishing her work and feeling satisfied with her relationships with colleagues. She confided that she slept with her smartphone under her pillow. She was so afraid of the CEO to whom she reported and so afraid for her job security that she felt the need to respond immediately to whatever messages she received. Her solution was to sleep with her phone. While this example is extreme, it is a true story. It demonstrates the disadvantages of technology when people don't have the skills or feel empowered enough to manage the boundary issues it can potentially create.

RESISTANCE

It is perhaps these negative effects on health and well-being that create resistance to the provisioning of technology for work-life supports. Livia, Diane, and Lorraine are all employed with media companies. All three women say that, for their companies, cost is a significant obstacle in providing technological support to workers. Lorraine betrays a deep-seated resistance to employees working at home when she cites the added costs of filling the shoes of employees who aren't in the office. She believes that if you give employees technology that allows them to work away from the office, they will get less work done and the company will be required to hire more people to "fill the holes left by a worker who is flexing her hours." Technology must be considered in relation to both its cost and its payback. For leaders who increasingly want to provide technology options to employees, they must make a business case to justify investing in the technology.

In which situations do leaders and companies experience less resistance? Interestingly, there is a relationship between technology provisioning and other work-life supports. Again, technology is a mechanism to support work-life and it also creates the conditions for more work-life supports such as flexible working and more choice making by employees. From my research it is clear that companies that have provided more technology for longer periods of time—in the form of devices such as smartphones, laptops, and tablets—tend to have greater work-life supports in other forms as well. They have climbed the curve before other companies because their access to technology has allowed them to experiment with how employees can work from other locations and still be productive, connect with others, and remain engaged with the organization.

One company is testing remote working by providing a handful of employees with enhanced technology. The catch? They must trade off their assigned workstations. Those employees who choose to receive the goodies (a smartphone, a printer at home, access to applications such as Skype that aren't available to all employees) must in turn choose to relinquish their traditional offices. Companies are willing to pilot a new approach that involves workers coming to the office less, but they require the benefit of providing less office space and thus spending less per square foot than they traditionally allocate.

SYSTEMS

Technological supports are more than just the devices that companies provide to employees. They are the broader systems of the network, the storage systems, and the IT policies that allow employees easy access and connectivity. Isaiah, a senior executive with a technology company, describes the types of systems that must be part of a technology support system. He says, "If a company doesn't have the technical systems that allow employees to work remotely—phone systems, order processing systems, financial systems, collaborative systems, or others—it will have a hard time keeping employees engaged and productive." When companies make it easy to work from anywhere, with comprehensive consideration for these types of systems, they provide employees with a greater level of support. Sometimes it means employees working from home early in the morning or late at night. Sometimes the support means working from an airport or a hotel. Sometimes it means working from a daughter's lacrosse game between halves.

A related system is travel and expense policies. At first blush, they may not seem related to technology-oriented work-life supports, but they are. In one company with which I consulted, there was a finance department that was known for applying extremely stringent policies to travel and expense activities. One of the policies it implemented removed all financial support for wireless connection in hotels or on airplanes. This was a cost-savings measure—the company was looking for any and all opportunities to reduce costs—that made sense on paper. Unfortunately, the policy had negative consequences for employees and their families, especially those employees who traveled most frequently. Employees were expected to pay for each of these connectivity points, which amounted to between $10 and $25 per connection.

The manager in charge of travel argued that the company didn't expect people to work on airplanes or in hotel rooms, and that employees should have downtime. However, people wanted to choose when and how they had time away from work. Employees argued that they wanted the ability to work in multiple settings, such as airplanes or hotels, without undue personal cost. In this way, employees felt they could enjoy more time with their families and friends when they were home, instead of having to spend personal time catching up on what they weren't able to accomplish on the road. The moral of this story? Offer choice. When employees are able to choose their own approach and allocate time as they wish, they benefit. Self-determination is significantly satisfying. The company also benefits because employees are effective in producing results through multiple settings and situations.

TRENDS

A current trend is BYOD—bring your own device. In this approach, employees supply (and pay for) the devices they prefer, and are expected to use them in order to accomplish their work. In addition, employees must obtain support for their devices on their own. Increasingly, IT help desks are directing employees to cell/data carriers or device manufacturers, leaving employees to seek assistance elsewhere. This trend has significant implications for employee well-being and work-life supports. With all the demands that employees are facing, this practice potentially places additional demands on already overloaded employees. Companies that choose to take this approach should consider the ramifications for employee levels of stress and their perception of challenge with their work and life.

Many companies are also reducing the amount of technology training they offer. This reduction places additional burdens on employees as well. As employees are seeking to integrate and navigate demands, some will see this as a boon: they can learn on their own as they choose. Other employees will experience additional stress because of the requirement to learn the new technology independently, placing additional demands on their discretionary time.

Talk to any IT professional and she will tell you about another trend organizations are facing: an "internet of things,"[4] in which technology links tangible objects (such as cars, traffic lights, desks, homes, toys, or shoes) with one another and with humans. In *Harvard Business Review*'s September 2013 issue, H. James Wilson cites Pew Research in which 21 percent of workers were found to use self-tracking technology such as apps to support journaling or apps to support health habits and biometrics.

The Economist asserts that technology will soon offer predictive value. For example, when we arrive at a hotel on a business trip to a foreign country, our phone may suggest directions to our customer meeting.[5] Or as we approach our front door, the phone will sense our presence, thanks to an iBeacon, and unlock the door and tune the television to our favorite show.[6] In these cases, the implications for work are fascinating. We could have offices that recognize us as we walk in, changing over all devices and amenities to our preferences. Work-life support would be enabled by an office that responds to the worker by removing the necessity to even consider the physical space—no matter where a worker chooses to work that day.

Another trend is algorithm-assisted decision making, in which we leverage technology to collect, filter, and analyze massive amounts of data for better, quicker decisions. An example is a worker who commutes to work and whose GPS suggests an alternate route because of a traffic jam ahead.

WHAT PEOPLE DO AUTOMATICALLY

To consider how technology is changing the way people work, think about how our automatic ways of getting things done are changing. On one hand, people may use technology to do the same tasks in different ways. For example, Brittany could send a letter with a stamp through the U.S. mail, she could send a memo through the internal mail system, or she could send an e-mail. Brittany is performing the same task—communicating with a colleague through the written word—she's simply accomplishing it in different ways, enabled by different technology.

On the other hand, think of finding an unfamiliar location. In the past, Brittany might have obtained a map or a TripTik to plan her trip ahead of time. If she were lost or needed coaching along the way, she would potentially stop at a gas station to ask directions or drive around until she found her destination. Today, reliance on technology has changed the way people accomplish tasks. Now, Brittany is not planning with a map or AAA

TripTik. Instead, she is plugging the address into her car's navigation system or her smartphone's GPS while pulling out of her driveway. Her automatic response if she's lost is less likely to include stopping for directions or simply driving around. Instead, her automatic response is to consult technology. When automatic responses change, skills also change. For example, the skills of navigating are becoming less acute as people, like Brittany in this example, simply follow the auto-voice on their smartphones.[7]

In another example, when my children need to make a list, they automatically reach for their smartphones in order to type the list on a notepad app, instead of using paper and a pencil. In this case, where people are typing rather than *hand*writing, there is an effect on handwriting skills. Some schools no longer teach handwriting skills—they teach printing skills, but the act of writing now happens by pressing keys on a keyboard more often than by holding a pen and forming script on a page. Spelling skills are reportedly on the decline as spell-check becomes the norm and text messages are rife with abbreviations and autocorrect. Why does this matter to work-life supports? Because as companies provide support for the demands that people face in their work, it is helpful to consider technology that will help them accomplish tasks more easily. If tasks have changed, then the way companies support people with technology also needs to change. Quentin Hardy, deputy technology editor for the *New York Times,* believes technology is changing civilization at all levels (for more, see the featured interview). The challenge will be to manage technology for our own purposes.

Work-Life Supports and Technology Today: An Interview with Quentin Hardy, Deputy Technology Editor, *New York Times*

Quentin Hardy is the deputy technology editor for the New York Times. *In this, his "best-ever career," he "gets paid to find out about the world and tell people what he finds." Quentin's specialties are telecom, history, wine, international relations, international finance/economics, and geography.*

(Continued)

In what ways will technology change the way we work?

QH: So what's going on now with technology? It's the Internet with powerful offshoots of cloud computing. It is dominated by software, and software is used to recapitulate processes. Increasingly, software is a kind of potential object which is continually revised. Data is shared in a network model. With that as a framework, think of what that's likely to do with an organization of labor and the organization of life. Just as data is less and less regulated to a specific domain, so are labor and life. For example, data may be part of an airline schedule but that's part of a pricing model or a calendar system. Data takes on different functions. It's hard to say where one part of labor begins and another ends. It's hard to say where work begins and ends, or where home begins and ends. Specific domains are collapsing into each other and that's temporarily stressful for people because domains are changing and identities are changing with them. In the agrarian model, work and home were totally blended. That blending isn't handled well today, but that's a question that's working itself out. If I take a call during dinner, that's not good or if I discuss the softball schedule at a meeting that's not good. We need new systems for blending these together.

How are companies responding?

QH: Companies are getting used to it quickly. BYOD (bring your own device) is an example. You come with the product you're most comfortable with and the company is responsible for security. This makes sense because it gets to the heart of what companies want from a worker, which is productivity. In the industrial model, it was pretty straightforward. You could judge output by goods produced. But in a knowledge economy, it's harder to measure. I may want to measure how well a worker is writing software but this isn't judged by number of lines of code, it's about creating delightful experiences, which is difficult to measure. We've gone through a curve of flexibility where it used to be hard wall offices with doors and then it was cubicles and now it's long tables where people can gather and work in groups. Information flows as we work with each other and specific to the task. We can informally overhear others and readjust when there are changes in the work. Headphones are the new cubicle. When we want to be alone, we just put on our headphones. They are not just a design feature, but a functional feature expressed into design. This is moving into the physical world in other ways as well. A food truck is a restaurant that pulls up temporarily and then goes away again.

What are the responsibilities of organizations in this new technological terrain?

QH: [Peter] Drucker wrote that the goal of a manager in a knowledge economy is to maximize a person's sense of actualization and to give him a sense that what he is doing here today is exactly why God put him on the earth. It is the idea that whatever is best in me is expressed through this task. It's preposterous to think that I will be rewarded with this every moment, but within the larger goal is this paramount good. Top managers especially have a clear need to articulate the function of the organization in a way that provides meaning to the employee and the world in the most profound sense.

How will technology change the way we do this?

QH: With technology, there are more points of measurement, with sensors everywhere. Metrics are helping to ensure that at all times I am maximizing the well-being of associates because this is connected to productivity.

With all that you know and see in this new world of technology, is there anything that's surprising you about the way technology is changing our society?

QH: It is transforming it. It is creating an entirely new civilization. This is broad and deep and there is no aspect of life that is untouched at this point.[8]

NEW BEHAVIORS AND SKILLS

Technology is changing social norms and requiring new behaviors and skills. Patterns of behavior relating to selective attention and novelty are shifting. In addition, workers must learn to set boundaries and be present with others in new ways.

SELECTIVE ATTENTION

Another consideration for the provision of work-life supports is the additional skill of selective attention that people require in order to survive in a world of technological complexity. From a perception standpoint, anything new in an environment tends to gain attention. This continues until the feature in the environment is no longer perceived as new and is filtered out by the subconscious. This process of novelty and selective attention is largely outside awareness.

Consider a person who moves into an apartment in the heart of a city that is situated near train tracks. At first, he'll hear the train go by every time. It will wake him up, interrupt his thoughts, and generally be noticeable in his day-to-day experience. However, he'll eventually grow accustomed to the sound and won't register it anymore. This is the skill of selective attention. Human consciousness tends to identify and filter out stimuli that are constantly present until they are no longer experienced as stimuli. In the example of the city apartment dweller, if the train schedule changes, or if he is home on a weekday and therefore experiencing the weekday train schedule, which is different from the weekend schedule he's accustomed to, he will again hear the train more keenly. Technology is similar to this.

People are learning new social norms for attending to or ignoring technology, and selective attention is a collective skill as much as it is an individual skill. When a smartphone buzzes in a meeting, sometimes the meeting participants will interrupt their conversation and wait for the recipient of the call or message to attend to it or turn it off. As group members become more familiar with one another and with their technology, they are more likely to simply ignore the interruption with no discussion, no lost time, and no nonverbal signaling regarding the interruption. The group is selectively attending to the content of the face-to-face activity without allowing the technology to intrude.

NOVELTY

People must also adjust for things that are novel. As technology evolves, people reshape their thinking. When something is new, people tend to think of it as "technology." As they become accustomed to it, they stop thinking of it as "technology" and instead simply take it for granted. At one time, a refrigerator was the best new technology around. It changed life immeasurably. More senior generations remember how their first refrigerator changed the need to haul ice. It reduced the requirement to shop as frequently. It changed the type of food they ate. It altered how food was prepared (less spices and salt because it could now be kept cold in the refrigerator). It changed how and where food was stored. At first, a refrigerator was considered technology, but today it is simply a fixture in homes that people take for granted and can barely live without. Why do I mention this here? Because we're on the cusp of a new generation of technology, which will soon become invisible and taken for granted. When technology becomes a seamless, invisible, inevitable part of providing work-life supports, employees and companies will benefit.

BOUNDARY MANAGEMENT

Another skill related to technology is boundary management. Both organizations and individuals must improve their skills in setting expectations and managing boundaries as they relate to technology. Recently, our family was dining out. Nearby, there was a table of eight teenagers. As they sat together, each one was on his handheld device. I was struck by the sociological changes we're witnessing. Every one of them was sharing time with someone who wasn't at the table, either virtually, by looking at Facebook or Twitter or Tumblr posts, or literally, by exchanging text messages. In some cases, there were two kids leaning together over one small screen, but in general, they were gathered together enjoying the company of *other* people, not the people they were physically with.

Technology is fundamentally changing the way people share time and relate to one another. People are less present when they are on their devices instead of being in conversation with others. They are less engaged with the real life of being in the same place, at the same time, sharing the same activities, undistracted by a device. The more technology allows people to work anywhere and communicate in multiple ways, the more they must treasure their time together. This is true at dinner. It is also true at the office.

Boundary management is also playing out at the office through a new movement called "Be Here Now." I first saw "Be Here Now" on a poster at a very large health insurance company. The following week I was at a law firm and saw the same sign on bulletin boards there. The week after that I was at a broadcasting company, and saw again the same saying. This time it was taped on doors of collaborative spaces. The idea is gaining traction. It means that it is necessary to be present in a meeting with colleagues and to be "lids down," so distractions are minimized and employees can bring their full attention to the discussion within the group. These companies believe that when employees are more present for meetings they will get more done and, more importantly, they will be more effective in maintaining strong relationships with colleagues.

In another example of work-life supports that encompass boundary management, one of my colleagues believes that as a leader, she has the responsibility to create and manage boundaries for her team. In order to do this, she never sends e-mails over weekends unless it is an emergency. She regularly works over the weekends herself, but she post-dates her e-mails so they are not delivered to her team members until Monday. She expects them to turn off their devices over the weekend and manages their workloads so they do not have to work undue numbers of evenings during the week.

PRESENT BY PROXY

As technology changes, people must learn to make connections in new ways. A classic sociological concept is the idea that "proximity is the number one determinant of relationships." In other words, those people who physically see and interact with one another most often will tend to have the closest relationships emotionally. There are exceptions, but in general, proximity breeds familiarity and closer relationships. For example, when Lily and Edith see each other regularly, they have a greater basis for casual conversation and connection. Lily notices that Edith was absent and asks about her time off. Edith says she was at a college visit for her son. This provides Lily more information about Edith and fodder for future conversations ("How's the college selection going?"). Lily and Edith have the basis for a reinforcing loop in which they're building knowledge of each other. This type of proximity demands presence. When people are present, they benefit from the relationship-building effects of being in close proximity.

Technology can be a proxy for physical presence. When employees are working with remote teams in multiple locations across the globe, across town, or across the building, technology is a powerful way for them to connect and feel close. In digitally mediated relationships, people get to know each other through their e-mail or IM persona or through social networking. A leader within my team, Bailey, is expert at being present when she is not present. Despite being across the country from all her team members, she has found a way to be accessible and personal from a distance. She does this by answering her phone when people call, by responding to e-mails quickly, by including personal notes in e-mails, and by using tools such as Skype, e-mail, IM, and Lync. Her commitment, dedication, and leadership come through.

Contrast this with another teammate, Zach, who is remote but never accessible. When he "never" answers the phone and when he takes days to respond to easy e-mails or urgent requests, the team begins to wonder whether he's spending too many hours improving his golf game. Consistency is key. Bailey is predictable. She sets appropriate boundaries and people know when to expect her to be available. Zach is consistent as well—in his lack of availability. Work-life support is evident when leaders and teammates are consistently accessible to one another. Technology facilitates this accessibility.

In another example, technology helped a struggling team make important connections. The team was just forming. The members of the team had been together only months and had been reorganized multiple times during their collective tenure with the organization. This constant shuffling had worn the team members thin and they questioned their value to the organization. "They don't know what to do with us" and "We're stepchildren who don't have a place" were refrains from team members. To make matters even trickier, none of the team members worked in the same location. They didn't know each other well and didn't understand one another's roles on projects.

The organization took action to support the team, improve the way it was working, and thus support work-life integration. The leader established common goals in order to link the team members' work. In addition, he set up mentoring relationships between team members so they could learn from one another and create personal and professional connections. The leader also established "communities of practice" for group sharing and learning on key topics. He also increased lines of communication by initiating more frequent e-mails and conference calls among team members.

The team also initiated a daily "water cooler time." At first, team members sent calendar invitations for certain times each day so they could log onto the IM system at the same time and connect casually. Eventually, this planning became unnecessary and team members would simply log on and invite others to chat during a virtual coffee or lunch break. This helped build strong relationships, and team members would increasingly phone one another to check in during an average day. Far from intruding on productivity, the check-ins actually enhanced engagement and effectiveness because team members were learning from one another and felt reinvigorated after a brief human connection with others on their team. This is an example of how technology can be a proxy for presence.

Being present by proxy also applies to the *life* side of work-life. I've coined the term *text parenting,* in which parents reach out, connect, coach, guide, and support their children via text. This, too, represents a work-life support strategy for employees who are free to text during the workday. Moms and dads can check in with their children during school or work—about after-school logistics, Lego Robotics sign-up, or encouragement before an exam. Leveraging technology to be present in their children's lives allows employees to be in two places at once, effectively contributing at work while finding additional points of connection with their children. Of course, this text parenting can also apply to other relationships, too (*text relating*). It is

Figure 8-2   Text Parenting

therefore an effective proxy for nonparents in reaching out to friends or other family members. Leveraging technology allows life into work.

IN SUM

Our technology has developed to the point that people need new skills and capabilities in order to use it to the greatest advantage. People are developing new social norms and habits, and learning to set new boundaries. Technology can be a proxy for presence, but a ringing cell phone or the ping of an incoming text is rarely as important as the person in front of us now.

CHAPTER 9

Aligning with the Physical Work Environment

When leaders and organizations implement work-life supports, they are well served to consider the physical work environment, which has a significant impact on the extent to which workers feel supported. Attention to the physical environment is also one of the vehicles through which organizations can help employees meet demands. This chapter offers suggestions for creating a work environment that embraces work-life supports, including strategies to make certain the environment serves employee needs. It also includes approaches to achieve optimal density, make the workplace a magnet, and align functional groups to provide a work environment that is able to serve workers more holistically.

PLACE MATTERS

One of my first jobs out of college was as a manager of training and development. I worked in an older two-story building. The upper story was for management and professional staff and the lower story was for manufacturing. It featured a bare-bones "cafeteria" with vending machines. The chair at my workstation wobbled, and the office had mice. One day, I came into work and my entire desk was flooded. The ceiling had leaked and many of us lost everything on and in our desks. It took weeks for the company to replace our equipment. We had ripped carpeting, pest problems, inferior technology, and leaks, and I asked how we could get some of these problems fixed. My manager explained that we wouldn't. She explained that our customers—the big three automobile manufacturers—regularly toured our building, and if we were sitting in office space that was perceived as too plush, they would believe that the prices for our company's products were too high. As a result, providing basic accoutrements for employees wasn't a priority. Work-life supports would have to take a backseat to the organization's concern for customer perceptions.

Contrast that example with this one. A few years later, I was doing some consulting with one of the top ten liberal arts colleges in the nation. I was leading a team-building engagement with the real estate and facilities team. The team was a seasoned, skeptical crowd, but we made headway in enhancing trust and improving their working relationships. Among the factors that kept them motivated to stay at the college was the value the institution placed on its physical environment. The college knew that the buildings, the interiors, and the grounds were all critical to parents' and students' assessments of the college. When parents and students came to visit, they would judge the college by many factors, and one of the primary factors was their experience of the physical place. The college invested in the place and the hosting experience, and these became differentiators that secured tuition income as well as donor dollars. The manufacturing organization and the college were two very different experiences of spaces used strategically to accomplish certain business outcomes. In both cases, the physical place was a leverage point. It is for every business.

SPACES AND THEIR STORIES

Spaces tell a story about an organization. This is true no matter what the story is, and organizations must manage the story their space is telling. How many areas does the space have for connecting and collaborating? To what extent does the space have amenities for employees? In what ways does the space support individual, quiet work? How old is the equipment or the furnishings? Does the space feature explicit connections with nature or the community? All of these features send cues to people regarding the values of the organization. As humans, we regularly judge books by their covers, and the physical workplace is the cover for an organization's book.

I once consulted with an insurance company that had redesigned its space. The new space was well received. It featured the best of optimal density, with enough people that it felt energized, but not so many that it felt over-crowded. It was beautiful, functional, and offered choice. People were productive and satisfied in the space. The space worked so well that the organization used it as a recruiting mechanism. This is not so unusual. Space will either attract new employees ("Wow, I can't wait to work there!") or it will put them off ("Really, I have to work *there?*"). This insurance firm was national and it was struggling to attract and retain the best talent at a time when the industry couldn't hire enough good people fast enough. So when the company decided to leverage the new space to recruit employees, it would fly prospective employees to this, its newest facility, and provide a tour. Predictably, the candidates would be impressed with the space. The problem was, the position offered usually wouldn't be based in that facility, as it was one of the smaller offices. Instead, the new employee would be assigned to another office. The company was attempting to use the physical space as an attractor. It worked, until employees realized they wouldn't be working in the new space, and they would be working in older space that wasn't up to the conditions of the new.

Xavier Unkovic, global president of Mars Drinks, Inc., has a perspective on physical spaces at his organization:

> We are a storytelling culture and we continuously communicate about our Five Principles through storytelling. Each office has the Five Principles on the wall, along with our vision and mission. Everyone is aware of the Five Principles and can speak to them. The stories we tell demonstrate how we are putting the principles into action and how they are impacting our personal lives. It's a habit to share. We also have similar architecture for our offices, whether you go to Tokyo, Shanghai, Dublin, or Philadelphia. There will be similar feelings and experience of our culture. The architecture aligns with our culture. We don't have enclosed offices and not even our CEO and president have their own parking spots. We are growing fast, so one of our challenges is to make sure we keep embedding our Five Principles to our new associates. We measure our line managers on this, so we're sure we have consistency across all locations and areas and maintain our strong culture.[1]

Space will tell a story regarding what the organization values and how the organization supports employees. Organizations must ensure that the physical space is effectively supporting its employees. This in turn tells an authentic story that will both attract and retain employees.

MAKING SPACE A DESTINATION

Space is important. Paradoxically, due to technology, the less people need to go to the office in order to accomplish work, the more the workplace matters. In other words, the more technology allows us to do our jobs from anywhere, the more important it is to come to work in order to connect with others face-to-face and accomplish collaborative tasks more effectively. The workplace must be a place that offers a value equation to the worker. It is in competition with a multitude of other locations so it must offer the very best solution to a worker getting her needs met.[2] It is important for organizations to design spaces that are compelling magnets for employees.[3] How do spaces attract employees and cause them to want to be on the premises? What are the factors that keep people engaged with the physical space?

Having worked in the industry for many years, I'm often asked for my recommendations on creating a supportive work environment. One consideration is food and drink. Great places typically offer great coffee, great lunches, great smoothies, and the like. (Sometimes these are even made available for free.) Frank LaRusso,[4] vice president at Mars Drinks, Inc., says:

> When we want to connect with others, we usually don't say, "Let's have a conversation." Instead, we say, "Let's have a cup of coffee." It's also related to behavior and surprisingly, to better listening. Leaders need to be better listeners, and when we're drinking, we have a closed mouth and an opportunity to listen well. Drinks are creating these moments of connection and listening. Connecting over coffee or other beverages gives us a chance to bring better life at work. We can have informative discussions with others and know about their kids or how they did in their hockey game.

Research demonstrates the benefits of warm drinks and caffeine. A study by Lawrence E. Williams and John A. Bargh found that when participants held a cup of warm coffee in their hands briefly, they were more generous and caring, as judged by others, than those who held cups of iced coffee.[5] Sleep-deprived rats become more alert when they smell coffee, and humans demonstrate improved cognitive performance, attention, and better mental performance, creativity, and relaxation after consuming caffeine or drinking tea.[6]

Beyond food and drink, companies can provide work-life supports through the physical work environment in the following ways.

- Offer great places for people to meet and connect. Make beverages available at a coffee bar, provide stimulating meeting rooms, and create inviting spaces for people to bump into one another unexpectedly and stop for a discussion. Recently, a senior executive made a request of his facility designers. He asked that they find a way to "drop him in the middle of the information highway." A coffee bar was the solution. It provided the executive with the opportunity to connect and learn from employees in a casual setting.
- Create space for creativity. Everyone wants some degree of stimulation in his or her work. Granted, this will vary by the person and the job, but in general, offer environments that are interesting and spark creativity, both because of how they are outfitted and because of who they attract to the space. Offer views, natural light, and access to the outdoors as additional ways to enhance stimulation in the space.
- Keep the place fresh and changing. In *Allegiant* by Veronica Roth,[7] one of the main characters, Tris, says, "It's strange how time can make a place shrink, make its strangeness ordinary." This is similar to the novelty effect I described earlier in relation to technology. From a perception standpoint, people become accustomed to elements of their surroundings, and the environment is no longer as interesting or stimulating as it once was. An element of regular change is necessary to keep environments continually stimulating.
- Create buzz in the environment by offering plenty of light, ambient noise, and people in the space. Beware of creating space that is deathly quiet. Most people are attracted to space that has some life and energy and commotion—just the right amount.[8]
- Offer a place with plenty of power outlets as well as superior technology, including Wi-Fi, videoconferencing, projection capability, and sharing technologies.
- Make the physical place easy to navigate, so when people arrive they are able to find what and who they need in order to do their best work.
- Make the workplace transparent, with lower-height walls and panels and more glass. This allows workers to see others, find others, and connect in order to make decisions, accomplish tasks, and relate as humans. When

we ask people what they need for success in their work, the number-one thing they say is "privacy." The second thing they need: "opportunities for collaboration." Give people choices so that each of these tasks—and everything in between—can be accomplished effectively in the space.

• Expand people's ideas about how to use the space. Remind employees that "their space" isn't just their individual workstation, but the whole floor or the whole building. Liberate people to work in the portion of the space that best meets their need for the task at hand instead of expecting every task to be best served with time at the individual's desk.

• Ensure that the workplace is authentic. If it is true that "design begins when the people move in," then let people be free to create, re-create, and continually adjust their spaces so they are constantly reworking to fit the project, the people, and the process of the work.

• Create places where people can rub shoulders. One of the factors people say they desire from work spaces is the opportunity to see and interact with leaders. They want a space in which to see and be seen so that they can build relationships and network with leaders casually and naturally. Space that creates a destination—with food or coffee[9] or people—and that provides casual space to sit or lean or have an impromptu conversation—provides this "rubbing elbows" effect.

SOCIAL NORMS

Perhaps one of the most important elements of the physical work environment isn't physical at all. It is the protocols and social norms that are established in the space. Frequently, leaders are being asked to catalyze culture by leveraging the physical space. Sometimes they are being asked to foster the existing culture. Either way, the space is designed to support, spark, or maintain certain behaviors. One of my architect–designer friends says, "We aren't designing new spaces and asking that people continue their old working habits in the new spaces, we're designing new spaces so that new habits of work will be created. We're not asking that you work the old way in the new space. We're asking that you work in a new way in the new space."

For many organizations, flexible working will be new to employees, to teams, and to the organization. This will require leaders to set new protocols for when and how people work and for how the space is used. Explaining these expectations clearly is critical to building a process that works. This is true for the use of the physical space as well as for ways the teams work together.

ACCOUNTABLE SPACES

Employees will vote with their feet regarding how well the workplace is serving them. Sometimes this means they stay away from a workplace that isn't working. Sometimes it means they spend little time in their workstations because their needs are better served in collaborative or community zones.[10] Sometimes it means they gravitate to certain parts of the work environment because they provide a better experience than other areas of the work environment. Our human nature is to want to make our own choices. This means not only having the power to choose, but also having good options from which to choose in the first place.[11]

The workplace must be accountable to the organization and it must be accountable to people. By this I mean that work environments must accommodate the needs of the organization and the people who work for it. Work environments are a significant investment for organizations and they should provide a return by attracting employees and stimulating productive work. Organizations should measure and determine which elements of the work environment employees are using more or less.[12] This quantifiable data can help optimize the space.[13]

A friend who is a leader of real estate and facility management for her company likes to say that there is plenty of office space in the United States, it's just not properly distributed (sounds rather like the earth-moving equipment company I discussed earlier, where the value equation of the earth-moving company is the premise that a lot of dirt in the world is in the wrong places). However, the ideal is not to assign as many people as possible to a space. The ideal is to find the right ratio of people to space. This optimal density supports work-life integration efforts by supporting stimulating work and fostering connections between colleagues.

OPTIMAL DENSITY

There are some famous sociological studies that explored density. In one, a volunteer went to a busy city sidewalk and dropped a pen, then recorded whether anyone stopped to pick up the pen and give it back to him. There were various scenarios, as you can imagine. There were people who didn't even notice the pen and continued down the sidewalk. There were people who noticed and ignored the pen and the volunteer. There were people who noticed the pen and picked it up and kept it for themselves. There

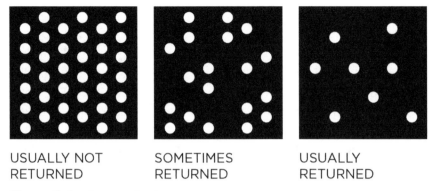

USUALLY NOT   SOMETIMES   USUALLY
RETURNED   RETURNED   RETURNED

Figure 9-1   Density Study

were people who noticed the pen, picked it up, and returned it to the volunteer. The experiment was repeated on city sidewalks with differing amounts of busyness (density), and the results were remarkable. The cities with the greatest population density were those least likely to return the pen.

In another set of experiments, the likelihood of returning the pen was correlated with socioeconomic levels. In cities where the per capita income was highest, the likelihood of returning the pen was lowest. This data on density can be stretched to apply to the workplace. Granted, it is an extrapolation—taking conclusions from one set of circumstances and applying them to another—but there does seem to be some validity on the face of it.[14] In a workplace an optimal level of density can be achieved. We've all been in places that were so empty that we wondered where everyone else was, or if we'd shown up in the wrong place at the wrong time. This type of space lacks energy or magnetism. Likewise, we've all been in places where there is so much commotion that it is disorienting and distracting—like the city street on which we can't get our pen returned.

Another sociologist, Edward A. Ross, studied dangerous mob behavior in the 1800s. He found that when people lacked enough personal space they lost selfhood. He argued that positive behaviors and positive social conditions would result from physical surroundings that were inspiring, stimulating, and not too dense.[15] When companies manage the workplace well, they accomplish optimal levels of density. There are enough people in the space for it to feel interesting, relevant, and vital. At the same time, there are still enough seats to go around, you can hear yourself think, and you can settle in to get some work done. This is the concept of optimal density. It also points to the concept of workplaces that serve employee and organizational requirements. When a workplace serves organizational needs effectively, it is designed in a way that is optimal in terms of cost, efficiency, and its effects on productivity. When a workplace serves employee needs effectively, it is designed in a way that is optimal for employee use. It serves employees and offers the best possible options for them to accomplish their work and connect with others effectively.

BERLIN WALLS

Workplaces that serve employee and organizational needs also point to another consideration: the extent to which the organization sets up a Berlin Wall. The year that my daughter's class studied the Berlin Wall, many of the children were surprised to learn that it wasn't built in order to keep enemies out and protect citizens, it was built in order to keep citizens *in* and regulate their movement. Specifically, it was built to control citizens, limit their choices, and ensure they stayed where the government wanted them to stay—within the walls of the community. The best workplaces are not built to the specifications of the Berlin Wall. The best workplaces—the workplaces that contribute to quality of work-life—are those that compel people to come and stay because they want to, not because they aren't allowed to leave.

Many companies still restrict employees' choices and movements. Employees must be at work for certain hours of the day and in certain locations (mostly at their desks or in the building), but the more progressive workplaces are providing plenty of freedom and choices for employees to get their work done however they would like. Those organizations provide great work spaces, which are one choice among many for employees. Those organizations trust that employees will get their work done in the most expeditious way and in the most effective work environment. One leader with whom I spoke says that every employee goes home at night. The workplace needs to be a place they want to come back to the next day.

ALIGNMENT AMONG SOLUTIONS

When creating space for work-life supports and work flexibility, companies must ensure alignment between HR, IT, and real estate/facility management groups.[16] What is this alignment? It is consistency and synchronization between the departments. This means they are aligned in terms of policies, practices, and leadership approaches. For example, if there is an HR policy that allows working from home but an employee doesn't have the necessary technology to support working from home, the effect will be that working from home is impossible. It's analogous to the game of rock, paper, scissors, where one factor can trump another.

The workplace may offer unassigned spaces for employees to drop in and work for a short period of time, but if HR hasn't supported leadership development in a way that leaders allow employees to work in places other than their assigned stations, the new unassigned spaces will get little use. Likewise, a company may have a stated workplace strategy for workers to move around the building freely and choose where they get different elements of their work accomplished during the day. The company may even have work team leaders who are amenable to this approach, but if the building doesn't have reliable Wi-Fi across the campus, this strategy won't take hold. All the necessary factors—across HR, IT, and real estate/facility management—must be in place for alignment to occur and for the space to effectively support work-life integration.

IN SUM

The physical work environment offers the opportunity to provide work-life supports in multiple ways. Food and drink, places that are alive and buzzing, spaces in which to connect and create, and work environments that tell stories about organizations are all powerful elements of an abundant, fulfilling experience that brings work to life.

CHAPTER 10

Aligning with Generations

It is a rare conversation about work, working, or workers in which the topic of generations doesn't emerge. It's a vogue topic, and the popular press reminds us regularly that there are now four generations in the work environment. Millennials and late-career employees in particular, have unique needs which are driving changes and providing a catalyst for work-life supports.

MILLENNIALS

Millennials (generally considered to have been born between 1981 and 2000) are widely reported to be changing the face of the work environment. They, in addition to gen Zs (born between 2001 and the present), are distinct from any generation that came before them. While the rest of the generations are "digital immigrants"—having arrived in a land where digital technology is new and they're learning—millennial and gen Z generations are made up of "digital natives." They've grown up in a digital culture. I observed a young toddler recently who was looking at a book. It was a bound version with paper pages. She clearly hadn't had much experience with real books, and she kept swiping the bottom of the page to cause it to turn. She was experiencing the book through the lens of her digital upbringing. She is a true digital native. Millennials and gen Zs have the unique experience of being the experts on digital technology in their homes. Their experience is dissimilar from other generations who, for the most part, were still learning what their parents already knew (even when they thought they knew it all). Members of younger generations have a level of power, authority, and influence in the home based on this technological expertise, and it shapes their upbringing. So how do work-life supports relate to younger generations?

There are a significant number of stories in the press about younger generations and what they're demanding. Some of these tales may very well be real. Some may be born of unwarranted preconceptions. Rather than generalizing about whole groups, it is most valuable to understand people at a singular level, as the differences between individuals are more meaningful than the differences between groups. However, biases regarding generations are everywhere, and whether or not we agree with them, when people generalize about millennials, they typically say the following: millennials are demanding more technology than their predecessors. They are also requesting more face time with leaders in order to grow their careers. They are demanding more flexibility with their work. Millennials are less willing to invest long hours for a company or to allow work to invade their personal lives. They are more likely to turn off their work at 5 p.m. and to set personal boundaries. They use technology as they breathe—naturally and without thinking consciously—connecting through technology in ways no previous generation has. They are likely to be free agents or have multiple careers over the course of their lives. They require significant attention and recognition, however they have valuable skills in connecting, learning, and collaborating in teams. Understanding what people are saying about millennials, how do companies make sense of these characterizations?

CATALYZING CHANGE

One of the implications of the biases people hold about millennials is that *whether or not they are true*, the assumptions are driving changes in the world of work. As a result, we don't need to spend a lot of time disagreeing or seeking consensus on whether generational differences exist or what they are. We can move quickly to a conversation pertaining to what changes the perceived generational differences are catalyzing in the workplace. The executives in my research set believe that work-life supports are being enhanced and expanded because of the presence of greater numbers of these younger generations in the work environment. In particular, they believe that younger generations are creating more demand for better technology and more flexibility in where they work. Isaiah, an executive who participated in my study and who is a global leader for finance, information technology, real estate, and facilities, says, "Millennials don't view the workplace as a place anymore, they view it as the technology they have at their disposal. They'll figure out where they need to work, but they must know what technology they'll have that allows them to get their work done." Lisa Brummel, chief people officer for Microsoft, agrees that millennials are changing the terrain of work:

> I think we are encountering a new generation in the workforce that expects work-life support to just be a part of the deal of going to work. Very different than our parents and the parents before them, there is an expectation that those in business understand that work-life is one unified thing and not two separate things. I often hear people talking about the work ethic of the millennials. I think it is really that they are so much more integrated between their work and their life that they don't understand why one should get more attention than the other. As we move forward with a diverse workforce I think the idea of work/life supports will be even more critical.[1]

Linda, who is the general manager of the software division within her global technology company, believes the millennial cohort is better equipped than other cohorts to deal with the changing conditions of the work environment because of their comfort and facility with fast-changing technology.

While the millennials may be driving the visibility of technology and flexibility, the employees who are embracing multiple ways of working are not limited to the millennial generation. Based on perceptions of millennials' demands, though, companies may be able to make an increasingly compelling business case for better technology, more flexible working models, and more options for where and when employees work. In addition, the mix of generations helps ensure a more fulfilled experience through work because of the opportunity to connect with and relate to people who bring multiple points of view. One way to provide that fulfillment is through relationships and learning. To this end, a growing practice among companies is reverse mentoring or reciprocal mentoring. In this approach, a more senior employee is matched with a younger employee with the intention that they will learn from each other. Instead of a more traditional model in which the senior employee is expected to teach and the junior employee to learn, the expectation is that the teaching and the learning will be reciprocal.

LATE-CAREER EMPLOYEES

Another group that is changing the way companies conceive of work-life supports is the group of more senior employees. Most members of this group are baby boomers, sometimes referred to as late-career employees. Since the economic crisis of 2008, many are still working to rebuild their nest eggs for retirement, and for financial reasons, they're not ready to exit the workforce. In addition, they are still healthy, which keeps them feeling younger than their parents did at the same age. As a result, many of them are not going anywhere. This means that the opportunities for advancement for the following generations can be limited in some companies. There are a lot of baby boomers already occupying the best positions and there is tremendous competition for those roles.

ORGANIZATIONAL MEMORY

It is critical for companies to capture the knowledge and experience of more senior employees before they retire. Organizational memory is a factor that separates effective organizations from less effective ones. It is the institutional memory that represents the sum of a company's experience, including its experiences, knowledge, stories, and insight that help guide actions and decisions. Organizational memory is useful only if companies codify the knowledge. That is, if they capture it and document it within the organization. The power of organizational memory is in the company's ability to learn from and build on history, rather than to reinvent it.

One of the ways to capture an organization's memory is through storytelling. In fact, years ago when I was redesigning our organization's New Employee Experience, I went to senior employees and gathered stories about the company. I put images on a large board, and at key times during the new employee training, I would ask a participant to choose an image. Each image corresponded to a video of a senior employee telling a story about the company, its culture, or its legacy. Organizational memory is a critical connector between more senior generations and younger generations within the company. With the graying of our workforce and the increasingly competitive nature of business, it becomes a critical competitive advantage to capture knowledge and ensure healthy organizational memory.

The requirement to capture organizational memory presents the opportunity for mentoring. The primary way that people learn is through watching others—learning experts call this "modeling" or "social proof." People will be more likely to do things when they see others also doing them. This is especially true if they perceive these people to be similar to them in some way.[2] If people learn through watching and interacting with others, then it is critical that organizations provide vehicles for this modeling/teaching and learning to occur. The benefit to the organization is that experience is not lost and valuable expertise is retained for the organization's benefit. Herein lies an opportunity for leveraging work-life supports. Mechanisms such as staged retirement and part-time work are methods to meet the needs and desires of more senior employees who want to keep working and who are fulfilled by sharing their knowledge, but who also want to slow down a bit and reduce their working hours. Instead of simply needing to choose between working and not working, progressive companies are finding ways for more senior employees to ease out.

OFF RAMPS

My friend Agnes has learned to navigate her company's unique culture better than almost anyone. A few years ago, Agnes went to her work team leader and explained her desire to slow down but not stop working. Her advocacy has resulted in the opportunity for her to test some new approaches for work and work hours. Her off ramp will take a few years.

During her first year of this process, Agnes reduced her working days to just four per week. For the following two years, she worked only three days per week. Next year, her last, Agnes will work just two days per week. After she retires, her company will still be able to access Agnes' talent on an hourly consulting basis as needed. As her hours recede, the projects she leads are being reassigned to other people on her team who are ready to receive them after having learned from her over time. The model rewards Agnes' long-term experience and it provides a field of learning for those who must build their skills in order to begin to fill Agnes' sizeable shoes. Soon, Agnes can update her LinkedIn profile to read "gainfully retired."

Work-life supports such as this approach provide options for Agnes and learning opportunities for her younger counterparts. Creating options helps create abundance. This approach emphasizes supporting employees throughout their life course—early, mid, and late career. Whether generalizations are positive or negative, it is preferable to avoid ageism or sweeping statements about any group. Usually, focusing on individual people is most constructive when designing effective work-life supports. Companies need structural and policy frameworks that allow for individual solutions and the flexibility to customize for individual needs.

Agnes' case is a good example of a policy tailored to individual desires, but which addresses a need that is likely to arise repeatedly as other employees advance in their careers. The company had a policy that allowed for her staged retirement to be explored and addressed. The work team leader was open and sufficiently aware of the overall culture to work with Agnes on her request. The technology at Agnes' disposal allowed her to work adjusted part-time hours in locations away from the office. These are examples of the alignment of HR, IT, and real estate/facility management. They are also examples of successfully aligning overall policies and corporate approaches with the unique needs of an individual, bringing work to life.

IN SUM

The unique perspectives and needs of millennials and late-career employees are affecting collective expectations of work-life supports. The work-life supports organizations implement to meet their expectations will contribute positively to work-life supports for all workers. Creating programs for capturing knowledge and mentoring, offering flexible work or staged off-ramps, and providing technology that makes work more connected and more mobile are meaningful improvements for all workers. Herein lies the value of focusing on these two generations. When companies serve them, they serve the broader set of employees who require work-life supports in order to contribute fully to their organizations.

CHAPTER 11

Aligning with Gender and Diversity

In addition to considering factors such as the generations of workers and their needs throughout their life course, as discussed in the previous chapter, organizations are well served to consider diversity and gender in their approach to work-life supports. This chapter explores these connections and recommends ways that work-life supports can be implemented with diversity and gender concerns in mind.

THE BENEFITS OF DIVERSITY

Organizations that focus on diversity in hiring, in training, or in other programs for inclusiveness are generally seeking to tap the talents of *all* their employees and to ensure their business benefits from these multiple contributions. Diversity is a core value in many organizations. A recent McKinsey Global study found that 60 percent of respondents reported that diversity was a core value for their organization.[1] These diversity programs typically embrace all types of differences, including those regarding ethnicity, race, gender, sexual orientation, age cohort, and more.

Linda, an executive in my study who is the general manager of a software division for a global technology company, describes her organization's diversity program: "By definition, a more diverse community making decisions leads to a better outcome. When you have diversity of thought in that collaboration, it yields better results. If you want a diverse workforce, you have to be able to accommodate diverse lifestyles." In addition to their employee base, some companies also focus on diversity because of their customer base. Rita, who participated in my study, and is the chief diversity officer with a global consumer brand, says that $17 billion of her company's $20 billion in sales are from purchases made by women. However, 78 percent of the people who make the decisions in her company are men. Her company is seeking to shift that proportion to a greater percentage of women.

Gender diversity has positive business impacts, according to Gallup. Its recent study found gender-diverse business units had 14 percent higher revenue and 19 percent higher net profit when compared with units that had less gender diversity.[2] In addition, the organizations with the greatest representation of women in executive committees achieve 47 percent greater return on equity and 55 percent better earnings.[3] Rita's organization is also seeking to introduce more general heterogeneity—beyond gender diversity—with a diversity program that is "...built around causing more dissonance, interrupting the status quo constantly, being more market facing and a better representation of and to our customers." Diversity efforts tend to provide education, training, networking events, and affinity groups for employees, partners, families, and the community.

DIVERSITY PROGRAMS

One of the surprises I discovered during my research was the connection between formal diversity programs and the presence and success of work-life supports. When companies had formal diversity programs that were part of the fabric of an organization, work-life supports also tended to be more far reaching and more successful. In most diversity programs, companies have established a formal statement of the importance of diversity, in alignment with the company's overall values. The typical approach to diversity also includes some statement of the company's goals and objectives relative to diversity. For example, companies often state that they expect to recruit, hire, and promote diverse slates of candidates. They also frequently state the importance of treating one another with dignity and respect within the organization.

The connection between diversity programs and work-life supports is striking. If a company wants to implement work-life supports, it does so in order to accommodate diverse lifestyles. In addition, connecting work-life supports to a diversity program that is already part of the organization and for which a strong business case exists is especially efficient and effective. Work-life supports in the form of benefits, policies, or practices that are connected to diversity programs gain advantage from the funding and focus those programs receive in an organization. It can be strategic to integrate work-life supports with diversity programs. In a recent article on diversity, leaders of global organizations cited supporting flexible work arrangements as one of eight practices[4] critical to creating an organization that benefits from diversity.[5]

Many of the more comprehensive diversity programs actually started as gender-related programs—they were originally designed to support women and then grew to support all types of employee differences. A few of the executives I interviewed were seeking to emphasize gender in their diversity programs and some were seeking to do exactly the opposite, to essentially *de*-gender the issue of diversity. As with all implementation of work-life supports, the right answer is specific to a particular organization, but seeing each perspective is useful.

Michelle participated in my research and is the chief administration officer with a global manufacturing organization. She believes that de-gendering the company's diversity program is the right thing to do for two reasons. One, she wants to remove the stigma that can accompany work-life support programs, essentially removing the "mommy track" thinking or the idea that women—even those without children—somehow need more support than their male counterparts. Two, she recognizes that men face similar issues as women do, desiring to "see their kids grow up," attend family events, care for elderly parents, or spend time in their community. Michelle goes on to say, "We do panels on work-life flexibility and I make sure I have dads on the panel and plenty of people addressing the issues from multiple vantage points."

GENDER EMERGES

In the interviews that formed the essential starting point for this book, I did *not* ask specifically about gender, because work-life supports are necessary for all employees, regardless of their gender, age, or other defining characteristics. Despite my *not* asking, every single woman with whom I spoke raised the issue and not one man raised the issue. Why? Because for women, a focus on gender was a key part of their personal experience. Why didn't the topic arise for men? I believe it is because men are not as aware of gender-based biases and therefore the topic of gender did not emerge as a priority in the conversation. A recent McKinsey study also found this difference. Their research of 1,421 men and women found that men were much less likely to see the challenges women face in the workplace.[6]

For women, work-life support is personal. Each of the women in my study reflected on her earlier years as a mom (except Lorraine, who is single with no kids). Diane, an executive vice president of administration with a global media company, says, "I was stretched and I was bananas. I was crazed trying to do it all, but I didn't want to put a spotlight on me because no one else was dealing with this. I was on a trajectory and I didn't want it to take away my opportunities."

A recent McKinsey Global study agrees with this attitude of sacrifice. It found that 81 percent of women were willing to sacrifice parts of their personal lives to achieve a top-ranking position.[7] Livia, an executive in charge of real estate and HR for her media company, has four children who are teenagers today, but she says that when her children were small, she never took a day off or worked from home. "There was a stigma," she says. She believed her boss would lose faith in her ability to perform if she was not on site at all times. This is a theme that many women expressed. They were trying to do it all: career, home, marriage/partnership, kids, and community. Not only was life difficult to juggle, but the enormous effort it required was also something they wanted to keep hidden. Each of them believed it was important to her career that others not see how fast she was paddling—like a duck—under the surface, while seeming to glide effortlessly across the water.

MOTHERHOOD AND ORCHESTRATION

The popular press has argued for years about whether it's good or bad for women to work while they are raising children. The press does not ask this same question pertaining to men. A study by work-family researcher Ellen Galinsky, described in her 1999 book, *Ask the Children,*[8] determined that the ideal situation for women, children, and families is when women's choices are in alignment with their preferences for working. It is ideal when women who want to work part time, do. It is ideal when women who want to work full time, do. It is ideal when women who want to stay home full time, do. It is when women are working, or not, in a manner they *don't* prefer, that families have less satisfaction and fulfillment. One of the problems is guilt. A woman in my study says:

> I heard a long time ago that children spell "love," T-I-M-E. So I must be there for my children a lot. The only way to have quality time is to have enough quantity that you're there when they need

you. You can't turn them on and off. You have to be there enough to experience the pick up after a stressful school day or the tough call from the girlfriend who just dumped him.

Another woman believes that her children are resilient and will forgive a lot of her mistakes and her time working because they know she loves them. That, in her opinion, speaks loudest. Finally, there is this: women who take care of themselves and their own needs and passions are also positive role models for their children. They send a strong message about selfhood, self-confidence, and the need all humans have to care for themselves.

Another theme the women raised was the responsibility they felt to orchestrate all the family logistics. Whether or not they had children, they were orchestrating multiple parts of their lives such as volunteering, extended family gatherings, or social events. This was true for women with children, even if they had husbands or partners who participated at home. The husbands and partners were only "helping," instead of owning the challenges and logistics. One woman said that for her, a husband who "babysits" is the epitome of this type of dynamic. When she is with the children, it is inherent to the relationship and bears no special description such as "babysitting." But when her husband is with their children, people consider him to be "babysitting," as if they're not his to begin with.

MANAGING MULTIPLE DEMANDS

Some argue that women are better able to handle multiple tasks due to female brain chemistry. A recent study by Ragini Verma and her colleagues at the University of Pennsylvania studied the way men's and women's brains are wired. They found men's dominant brain connections occurred *within* hemispheres, while women's occurred *between* hemispheres. They hypothesize that these wiring differences help women remember better and multitask better, while they help men in the area of coordination and motor abilities.[9] The conclusions are yet to be proven.

In the meantime however, demands at home, demands at work, and the need for multitasking are greater for women than for men. Linda, who participated in my study and who is the general manager for the software division of her global technology company, even has company annual survey data to prove it. While there are certainly exceptions, women in Linda's data set reported that, on average, they had more tasks to juggle at home.

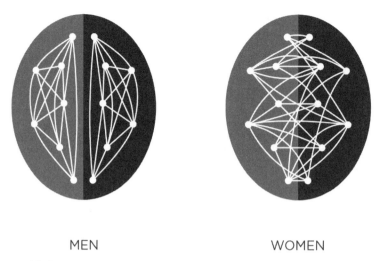

MEN   WOMEN

Figure 11-1   Dominant Brain Connections

Arlie Hochschild, a sociologist, refers to this as a "second shift,"[10] in which women work all day and then must go home to work for their families in the evenings. One woman, a VP of human resources, who is married with children, tells this story: she once received poor marks on her performance review because her team didn't believe she had enough balance in her work and life. She believes that she would not have gotten this type of feedback if she'd been a man.

In general, women tend to compare themselves with other women and not so much with men. In an interesting twist on the traditional "keeping-up-with-the-Joneses" scenario, women tend to look at other women with children and compare how much they're doing. They are less likely to compare themselves with men or even their own husbands or partners. If they did, they would see that they generally are doing more than their partners in terms of pulling the weight at home. Family counseling experts would say that it is beneficial to foster partnerships that allow for open dialogue in which the partners can ask each other for help and more equal levels of contribution.

ADVANCEMENT

Women in my study also discussed advancement and its relationship to long hours and caregiving—for children or other family members. Many of them believe that women are underrepresented at senior levels of their organizations. Barbara, who participated in my study, is the global head of HR for her financial organization. She cites statistics for her company, saying that: at lower or mid-grade job levels, 49 percent of employees are women. At senior roles, that percentage drops to 23 percent. In *Harvard Business Review's* April 2013 issue, Morten T. Hansen, Herminia Ibarra, and Urs Peyer, authors of "The Best-Performing CEOs in the World," report that only 1.5 percent of the CEOs of large public companies are women. Many of the interviewees in my study believe that getting to the top and staying there requires long hours. At some organizations, it also requires travel—sometimes internationally and sometimes for weeks at a time. Barbara says, "It all comes down to child-care resources. Many women do not have the resources to accomplish that kind of time away from home."

Almost all the women in this study at the most senior levels are in one of three situations: they have a stay-at-home husband, they do not have children, or they arrived in their senior level position after their children were grown and therefore did not face the same challenges with child care. One woman said that she believes every family actually needs two and two thirds parents in order to be successful if both parents work. Her point was that it frequently feels nearly impossible to manage all the demands of work and home and life with children with (only) two full-time working partners. Women also discuss how important it is to have two incomes. There are few families who can survive on one income, so both parents must work, and this is a demanding effort for families. Dr. Kathleen Christensen, program director at the Alfred P. Sloan Foundation, calls this need for two incomes a social and economic seismic shift for both the country and for families.[11]

The popular press has lately been reporting on the "likability index," which notes that as men climb in their organizations, they tend to be perceived as more likable. For women, it is the opposite. Achieving a higher rank in the organization is usually accompanied by the perception of less likability for women. The ideal leader is perceived similarly to the ideal man, with traits such as determination, assertiveness, and independence. At the same time, women are expected to be nice, caretaking, and unselfish. This puts women in a double bind, according to Herminia Ibarra, Robin Ely, and Deborah Kolb.[12]

Women in my study also assert their belief that there is a significant amount of unconscious bias they face in the work environment. Diane, who participated in my study and who is an executive vice president in charge of administration, points to a friend who is a senior leader of a well-known consulting practice. "He is a big proponent of women [sic], but he thinks twice before he hires them because in the past he has put time and effort into training women and then they leave the company when they have children." Sheryl Sandberg, author of *Lean In* says, "...there are differences between men and women both in their behavior and in the way their behavior is perceived by others."[13] These biases and perceptions can lead to real consequences. For example, there is an absence of women in senior roles. Only 15 percent of C-suite jobs are held by women and only 17 percent of board seats are held by women.[14] Women who are leading significant, visible projects receive smaller budgets than men by two to three times. Also, they are less likely to have financial P&L (profit and loss) responsibility for their companies.[15]

Lorraine, a participant in my study, is an executive in charge of administration including philanthropy and corporate communication for her global media company. She says that despite media coverage on women who opt out of the workforce because they want to, she believes they are actually opting out as a result of inadequate work-life supports. This is a "mafia offer." It's similar to an ultimatum, or to being caught between the proverbial rock and hard place. When someone makes a "choice" among poor options, it's questionable whether it's really a choice at all. A choice to leave the workforce can have long-lasting negative ramifications in terms of career advancement and earnings. For a woman who takes a hiatus from her career track in order to raise children or attend to other obligations, the financial impact of lost salary and promotions is estimated at $1 million.[16]

WHAT ABOUT MEN?

There are few studies on men and work-life integration, but Kathleen Gerson's work offers one perspective. In Gerson's book *No Man's Land*,[17] she demonstrates that in the aggregate, men statistically have better wages, better positions, and faster career advancement. However, individual men generally do not experience this feeling. Instead, they are experiencing stagnating wages and fewer opportunities. Men are redefining their identities. "A range of social shifts has spawned confusion, ambivalence, and disagreement over the guidelines, models, and definitions of manhood,"[18] says Gerson.

Nicholas W. Townsend, a researcher on the topic of men, work, and family, finds that men increasingly value their lives based on a "package deal," in which emotional closeness, provision, protection, and endowment are four elements that become a composite for men's lives and cannot be viewed in isolation.[19] Men lead full lives of which work is one component, and work-life supports are important so that all aspects of their lives may be fulfilled. Thus, men are important recipients of work-life supports. When organizations support women, they must also consider supporting men who have needs for connection to families and communities outside of work in order to be completely fulfilled.

IN SUM

What are the implications of a gender-based lens on work-life supports? Organizations must make work-life supports an issue for both men and women. Effective work-life supports—those that create the conditions for abundance—help both women and men integrate work and life demands over their life course. Leaders and organizations must take responsibility for creating these conditions. It is not enough to insist that women or men must simply work harder or longer in order to do it all. Leaders and organizations have a responsibility to understand the unique needs of all workers and provide supports that allow them to bring their best to work and maintain wholeness. Programs must adjust in order to meet the needs of women and men as they change over time and over the life course. There will be multiple right answers for women, men, families, and organizations. These work-life supports must provide more options, choices, and personal control, which will in turn provide returns because employees are able to engage more completely when they are at work.

CHAPTER 12

Aligning with Performance

Companies that are most successful in implementing work-life supports ensure they are creating environments where success is measured based on outcomes and performance, rather than simply on employees' physical presence in the office. Before technology allowed employees to work anywhere, traditional management often focused on the number of hours spent in the office. Did the employee come to work each day? Was he on time? Did she focus on her work while she was there? As companies seek to implement work-life supports, flexible working options are often where they begin.

While work-life supports include significantly more than flexible working, alternative working arrangements are most germane to the challenge of managing performance. Why? Because flexible working places pressure on leaders to lead and manage differently, as the metric for performance must go beyond an employee's physical presence. This chapter addresses the need for leaders to focus on outcomes. It also addresses factors that contribute to performance in the first place—such as matching jobs with the right people, and developing and rewarding positive performance.

MANAGING FOR OUTCOMES

"Whites of the eyes" management is when leaders expect employees to be in the office regardless of the nature of their work, or when an organization uses the number of on-site hours as a barometer for employees' success, rather than evaluating the results they achieve. A company with which I consulted had a "whites of the eyes" culture that gave rise to plenty of legends. One of the stories was that its senior executive team tracked what time people left the office at the end of the day. Before the company had a badge tracking system installed, the executive assistants, whose desks were situated close to windows overlooking the main exit, would monitor people leaving. Toward the end of the day, they would take careful note of which employees were leaving early, which left at 5 p.m., and which headed home later than 5 p.m. Those who left later were viewed as superior performers with more commitment to the organization.

In addition to leaving later in the evening, employees could also gain favor by regularly working on Saturdays. Another story has arisen, now that the company has its badge tracking system installed. People say that employees show up on Saturdays to earn positive regard. However, an enterprising employee has discovered one remaining door that was not connected to the badge tracking system. He and a handful of other employees have devised a system where they enter every Saturday morning through the main door and leave immediately through the unconnected door. Voilà! Freedom. Employees have invested time and energy into playing the system. Imagine what they might have been able to accomplish if that same time and energy had been devoted to the substance of their jobs.

While this style of eyeball management is prevalent in some organizations, the majority of the executives in my study see the need for focus to be placed on productivity. Linda, who participated in my research and who is the general manager of her global technology company's software division says, "The bar needs to be on productivity and innovation, not time. This is hard to measure, but you don't want to work more hours, you want to work better, smarter. That requires breakout thinking to set the bar differently." Rita is chief diversity officer from a global consumer brand. She says, "I don't care if people are working upside down in the bathtub at home as long as they're exceeding their objectives." Diane, an EVP in charge of administration for her global media company, expresses this sentiment regarding the need to produce results: "It's a two-way street. The employee has to be doing his share and more and then we're really supportive of flexible working arrangements." One of the gentlemen in my study had this to say about the trust related to flexible working, "If you trust your employee, you shouldn't have to ask where he is. If you don't trust your employee, he shouldn't be working for you."

What is striking in all of these comments, in addition to their emphasis on results, is that they position work-life supports and flexible working as *privileges*. Work-life supports are provided as a result of employees who *exceed* expectations. The assumptions all of these executives make is that it is appropriate to provide work-life supports in exchange for superior performance. There is a principle of exchange—the employee will receive the privilege of working alternatively in exchange for performance—and not just average performance, but superior performance. Again, this is an example of employees *purchasing* flexibility with many hours of work and superior performance.

Any employee for whom working outside the office is a consideration should already be a strong performer. If an employee is new or not yet proven, or worse, if an employee has a performance problem, it is not wise to provide him with the option of working away from the office. Flexible working is most effective when it is available to employees who are already performing well and have the skill sets to manage their work successfully. If an employee doesn't have those skill sets or that maturity, it is wise to build the skills first, ensure good performance, and then layer on the option for flexible work.

MATURITY MATCH

Many employees demonstrate superior performance within the framework of flexible working options. In fact, a recent Gallup report[1] found that remote workers logged more hours and were more engaged than workers in the office. In addition, a recent study by Nicholas Bloom found that call center employees who worked at home completed 13.5 percent more calls than those in the office, were less likely to quit, and were more satisfied.[2] Unfortunately, not all employees are performing this well. Employees must be mature enough, disciplined enough, and have enough integrity to be effective with flexible work.

I once consulted with a department that was seeking to build a new capability within the organization. Its team was distributed globally and many of its members were remote, working from home full time. The leader of the team had a significant number of people reporting directly to him, and there was very little structure. He believed in meritocracy and having the best person win with little role clarity or boundaries between jobs. This created a negative, overly competitive culture. The leader wanted to connect with the team regularly, so every other Friday he would hold a conference call with the approximately one hundred team members who were on the extended team. One of the team members would sometimes fall asleep and snore during the call. Another of the team members would brag that he regularly took long, relaxing baths during the calls. This type of behavior was unacceptable and demonstrated a lack of personal maturity and disregard for the team. These were not ideal candidates for flexible work.

One of the interviewees in my research also shared the story of an operator in a call center who has since lost her job. At the time, the company was running a pilot to explore whether call center operators might be able to work at home. This particular call center operator was caught by her supervisor doing laundry during calls with customers. The employee believed she was successfully multitasking, but the supervisor, who would regularly listen in on calls in order to check quality levels, discovered that her laundry activities were audible to the customer on the other end of the phone. The pilot was terminated and call center operators were not permitted to work from home. This one team member prevented the rest of the team from benefiting from alternative work solutions. Barbara, head of human resources for her global banking organization, discusses the importance of considering whether specific employees have the appropriate skill set to work outside the office: "Not every person is wired to work at home. Not every person is mature enough."

The lesson here? Ensure that there is an appropriate personal maturity level and discipline on the part of any employee who is approaching a flexible working program or an option for working at home. Pilot a process to see if it works. Find ways to hold people accountable for flexible working in the same way people are held accountable for their work in the building. These examples are extreme cases, but they are indicative of the need for selection and accountability for those who have the options for flexible working models.

SITUATIONAL MATCH

Another factor in an employee's performance is the extent to which his situation—not only in terms of maturity, but also in terms of his home office or child care—makes it possible for him to work productively when he is not in the office. I consulted with a company that was going to be closing field offices. The company was experiencing a decline in orders and needed to reduce costs. One of its cost reduction strategies was to close smaller offices. The company sent people home, but many workers did not react positively. Some employees didn't want to work from home because they didn't have space for a home office or because they had children at home during the day. Other employees strongly preferred the companionship and camaraderie that the office provided. Finally, there were employees who just didn't trust themselves to be home and remain focused on work.

Unfortunately, there were no other choices at the time. For employees who faced issues with space or child care, the company outfitted their home offices with furniture and educated them on how to set boundaries with their families. The organization also created opportunities for colleagues to come together in third places such as local coffee shops so they could regularly connect and collaborate in person. The company also provided training in the areas of organization and time management. Perhaps most importantly, the company coached leaders, teams, and individuals on how to manage daily, weekly, and quarterly goals so that physical presence was less critical to success.

KEEPING THE DOOR OPEN

When employees do work away from the office, it is valuable to keep doors open—going both ways. Sometimes employees are working in the office and want the option to work from non-office locations. In other cases, employees have attempted to work in third or fourth places and have determined it wasn't effective for them, and have wanted to return to the office. Sometimes employees begin an education program and determine that working away from the office is too much to handle. In these cases it is helpful for leaders to have an open door for discussions and adjustments.

JOB MATCH

Another factor in performance is the employee's fit with the job she is in. Previously, I covered the requirement to match the nature of the work with the work-life support that is offered. Now, in thinking of how organizations foster solid performance, consider how they match the content of work to the employee. It is useful to do so because when work is well-matched to employee skills and preferences, performance tends to improve and managing performance becomes easier.

In the 1990s, my company was having a hiring blitz in production. We could not hire people fast enough, so we took an "all hands on deck" approach and recruited everyone with HR skills to interview and select candidates for the open positions. I was a member of the cadre interviewing literally hundreds of candidates during a period of a few weeks. During this

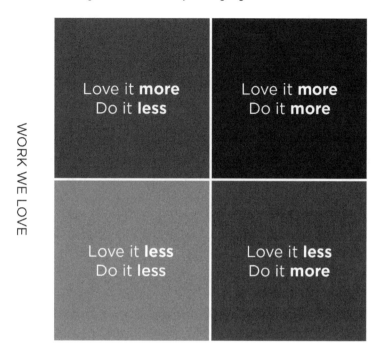

WORK WE DO

Figure 12-1   Love-Work Patterns

time, one of the principles we applied in the selection process was "work we love/work we do." For each of us, there is work we love to do and work we don't especially enjoy. Likewise, any job has a mix of work that must be done. We can think of this in a two by two matrix.

The ideal scenario is when we're in a job for which the required tasks are a match to the activities we love. There will always be tasks we're less excited to perform, but in the ideal situation, these will be tasks that are less demanded and less frequent in any job we occupy.

Having a good match between the job and the person is one way to create abundance. Leaders are in a position to select candidates based on fit and to help employees find alternative projects or roles when there is not an appropriate fit between the employee and the job responsibilities. Leaders can enhance fit by shifting projects within a job or allowing employees to develop their education. Sometimes, the way an employee is allowed to work—in terms of hours and location—can also improve fit between job and employee. Hence, this is another way leaders can provide for work-life supports. People naturally perform better when they feel a fit with their work,[3] and this benefits both the employees and the organization.

SKILL DEVELOPMENT

Another element of positive performance is skill development. Naturally, job performance is better when employees have the skills they need. Learning and skill development can be powerful vehicles to support workers as they face multiple demands across work and life. As work changes continually, so do the skills necessary for success in a job. An employee also needs certain skills to work successfully away from the office. At the top of the list are the ability to communicate, the ability to collaborate both physically and virtually, the ability to manage time and multiple deadlines, the ability to organize work and follow through to completion, and the ability to build trusting relationships with others. Development approaches must fit into a framework of clear goals and objectives.

Companies vary widely in the extent to which they offer formal learning opportunities for employees. Some companies hold orientation at the start of employment and rarely thereafter. Other organizations conduct training for all employees on a frequent basis. In any case, it is rare that companies conduct learning opportunities specifically on the topic of work-life supports. Rick Wartzman, executive director of the Drucker Institute, weighs in on training and learning:

> Much of the business world now centers around the activities of "knowledge workers"—a term Peter Drucker coined in the late 1950s. Knowledge workers have the fortune of not being tied to a clock or an assembly line. For them, work and life automatically bleed together, and should bleed together, as never before. One aspect of this is the need for lifelong learning. Over the past thirty or forty years, corporations have added a host of training programs and provided incentives for people to further their education. In fact, in many ways, companies have become the major providers of continuing education in this country; their investment has risen markedly, even in inflation-adjusted dollars. Lifelong learning

is a huge piece of what Drucker would prescribe, particularly for support of knowledge workers and particularly in this day and age when knowledge becomes obsolete very quickly.[4]

K.H. Moon has been globally recognized for his commitment to lifelong learning when he was at the helm of Yuhan-Kimberly in Korea. Moon offered learning during working hours, for up to 360 hours of professional and technical skills learning per year. In contrast with other organizations which offered compulsory training and required testing, Moon's company offered voluntary training. These classes covered topics such as internet skills, parenting skills, and English and Chinese language skills.[5] Moon provided learning through multiple forms, offering more than simply classroom options:

> We also offered company-borne study groups. Necessities like books and professors were paid for by the company. The learning was available through a "learning cafeteria concept" in which employees could choose their own menu of learning. We also asked employees to identify three to five topics they were interested in and wanted to speak about in front of others. Through this process, employees became facilitators of classes for others and we had hundreds of mini-classes we offered. Because I didn't want to lay off workers during the financial crisis, I implemented a system where they would work for three days and then have three days off. During their three days off, employees could take advantage of these learning opportunities.

Under Moon's leadership, Yuhan-Kimberly saw tremendous results:

> Employees became multiskilled, cross-functional, cross-boundary, and cross-border. They were able to cope with ever-changing work, technology, and processes. This allowed the company to accelerate the speed to market. While our competitors had scale—for example, P&G was ten times our size—we were able to win with speed. Our competitors would typically take three years to bring a product to market. Our average was nine months. Ultimately, we forced P&G out of the market entirely. This was because of our speed and

agility, fueled by employee learning. Employees also became better overall. They were able to contribute more fully to their families and their communities.[6]

DEVELOPMENT PLANNING

Learning and development are most effective when they are targeted for employees' specific goals and unique needs. A development plan is a critical framework for an employee to pursue the most appropriate learning, aligned with the needs of the job and the company. Xavier Unkovic, global president of Mars Drinks, Inc., addresses the importance of training and managing based on desired performance outcomes:

> First, we communicate the vision for the company and ensure clarity
> of vision and goals and allow people to express themselves. In this way,
> they know what this company is doing and how they can contribute.
> An organization also needs the right programs and tools in order to
> develop people successfully. We have HR support and also strong
> management, which are key for us to own associate development.
> Development is important for any position or role in the company.
> We need to celebrate all roles. With the associates, our managers have
> clear responsibility for their team and engagement. We are making
> 100 percent of our associates have a documented development plan. It
> is a seventy-twenty-ten development plan: 70 percent learn by doing,
> 20 percent learn by coaches, 10 percent learn by education.[7]

The connection between development programs and performance planning is a must. At Mars, associates around the globe are involved with a Mars University program which teaches critical skills. The company also utilizes a seven-part development plan which clearly defines goals for development. The company's belief is that this formality helps ensure effectiveness for employees and for the organization. Has Mars seen results from its commitments to performance planning and development? Xavier says "yes":

> Performance will come if you develop your people. This is also
> related to retention. People will be more likely to stay with the com-
> pany when they have the opportunity to develop and contribute.

Even with all the positive results from development planning and learning, one caveat to remember is that training by itself won't change behavior. It is important to determine whether there is a gap in an employee's knowledge or skills before offering training. Frequently, training is implemented as the solution to a problem for which the root cause is lack of motivation, not lack of skill. Training is the appropriate solution when the participant truly needs or desires more knowledge or skills; otherwise, the development efforts will not be effective. Development is most effective when the employee has accountability and takes responsibility for accomplishing his goals. This ownership provides a level of self-determination in how the employee learns, on what timetable over his life course, and on what topics. Self-determination and control are critical elements of work-life supports and of bringing work to life.

MENTORING

In concert with formal learning, either in the classroom or on e-platforms, mentoring can be a valuable tool for knowledge and skill development and behavior change. Progressive companies are carefully selecting mentorship relationships and building mentorship processes into their organizations. Companies are identifying the "organizational heroes" who most embody the desired culture and matching them with high potential employees. The expectation is that both will benefit from a personal relationship as well as coaching and feedback.

MISTAKES AND REWARDS

When offering formal training, development, and mentorship, learning-oriented organizations also embrace mistakes. Curt Pullen,[8] president of Herman Miller North America, offers this perspective on learning-oriented organizations and their approach to mistakes:

> In the room where my team meets regularly, I have a saying framed and hanging on the wall. It says, "Let's make better mistakes tomorrow." This attitude toward mistakes is about learning. Generally, we learn more from our mistakes than from our successes. We can take our successes for granted, but when something doesn't work out, it causes us to study what went wrong. We go back and examine how

we could have done things better. For this reason, mistakes provide a tremendous learning opportunity. When we take a learning approach, it sends a signal to the organization that also relates to decision making. People need to make choices and decisions. If the leader makes all the decisions, there is less opportunity for learning. If people make the decisions, they will own them and the outcome will be something we can all learn from. As leaders we need to back people when they make decisions. In addition, when people own their decisions, and can describe what decisions they've made and why they've made them, it provides the opportunity to increase our collective knowledge. If people are in fear, they won't feel free to make decisions. Decisions need to be made in a context of learning and of leaders who support the decision making of people around them.[9]

Learning and development for leaders and all employees is most effective when it is iterative. Mistakes allow for this iteration. Try, learn, and try again.

ACCOUNTABILITY AND RECOGNITION

When employees perform well, rewards, awards, and recognition are an important type of work-life support. Recognition goes hand in hand with accountability. It is impossible to provide substantive recognition without holding employees accountable. Why? Truly meaningful recognition is specific to a result. It goes beyond a leader saying "great job." Recognition is most powerful when it demonstrates that the leader is knowledgeable about the employee's specific performance and accomplishments. Recognition by peers is also motivating and fulfilling for employees. Mars has an awards program that provides the opportunity for peers to appreciate and recognize one another. Xavier Unkovic, global president of Mars Drinks, Inc., says:

We have a recognition program called "Make a Difference," in which associates nominate each other for awards. We had over 26,000 associates nominated last year. This means that one-third of our entire population was recognized by their peers. We have 16,000 associates who donate over 40,000 hours to their communities through our Mars Volunteer Program (called MVP).[10]

What motivates people to make the effort? Xavier says it's intrinsic.

> There is no financial reward. It's not about the prizes. It's about how
> you as an individual have put a principle into action, and the intrin-
> sic reward that comes from that. The awards are related to people,
> performance, and planet, and it's about how you were able to affect
> these. When people have the freedom to act they can find ways to
> make a better company and they generate fantastic ideas.

Another company, Etsy, an online marketplace for handmade and vin-
tage goods, provides a different example of a formal process for recognition.
There, each employee has the opportunity to recognize another by e-mailing
the Ministry of Unusual Business, which delivers small gifts or cards to
the employee being recognized.[11] Rewards and recognition are elements of
work-life support that motivate and create the conditions for abundance.
This is especially true when they are provided by peers in addition to being
provided by the organization.

IN SUM

Work-life supports are most successfully implemented when organizations
and leaders focus on performance, not simply on whether employees are
physically present in the office. Sometimes this means dealing with performance issues and ensuring that employees demonstrate a level of maturity
and self-discipline. Performance itself improves when employees experience
a match between their jobs, their preferences, and their personal situations.
Skill development, mentoring, ongoing learning, and recognition also contribute to creating conditions under which employees can thrive and are
supported in work and life.

CHAPTER 13

Aligning with Leaders

Of all the considerations for work-life supports I've explored in my research and in this book, work team leaders are the most important and most pivotal. This chapter considers the significant impact of leadership on whether work-life supports will be successful. Peter Drucker's principles of management are instructive regarding the influence leaders have through their decisions and their own actions. When it comes to the way leaders manage, every action they take matters. Organizations must ensure they are developing leaders and setting clear expectations for their behaviors so work-life supports are successful. Effective leadership itself is an important support for employees who are integrating work and life.

MAKE OR BREAK

Leaders will make or break work-life support processes.[1] The key point is that an employee's leader—the person to whom she reports—has the most significant bearing on the extent to which work-life supports are afforded her. There are several reasons that leaders have such significant influence. Generally, companies give leaders significant discretion in assigning or allowing work-life supports for their team members. While company policy sets the overall framework, even the most policy-driven companies require supervisor discretion in the application of various supports. Supervisor discretion is driven by the individual's own beliefs regarding whether work-life supports should be provided to employees.

Work team leaders usually have the power to determine whether a job is a fit for flexible working, whether the individual is a fit, whether a team can accommodate flexible work, whether an employee's education should be paid for, whether the employee may leave work early to attend classes, whether team members have access to technology, and more. Everything comes together with a work team leader's interpretation of situations and how company policies apply. HR also has a role to play in interpreting policy, but the work team leader is on the front line and every decision the team leader makes affects individuals, teams, and organizations because the work team leader is the agent of the company. She has been provided with authority to set direction, make decisions, and take action within the systems that make up the organization.

DRUCKER LEADERSHIP PRINCIPLES

A discussion of leadership specifically related to work-life supports must begin with a more general topic of leadership, and no chapter on leadership is complete without reference to Peter Drucker. Drucker was the father of modern management, and worked extensively with leaders beginning in the 1950s. Effective management is complex, and making sense of it involves a significant number of variables. Drucker helped to clarify. He believed there were five things necessary for success. Managers must set priorities, organize the work, communicate and motivate, measure results, and develop people. Curt Pullen, president of Herman Miller North America and chairman of the board for the Drucker Institute, shares his perspective on how those five responsibilities and Drucker's overall approach are connected to work-life supports:

> Drucker's principles have always been about the full person perspective, since Drucker believed that any company's most valuable asset was its people. Drucker's interest was always in making society better, and he saw companies and their approach to people as a way to accomplish that. In his view, it took good leaders making good choices and decisions to create the conditions for people to perform to their highest potential. This in turn contributed to the organization's success and then in turn to making society a better place. It came down to the job of a manager. Part of Drucker's genius was in crafting insights through his dialogues with leaders. His insights shape how we work today and the decisions we make.[2]

Indeed, the decisions and choices that leaders make about everything, including work-life supports, create the conditions for employees to bring work to life.

Drucker also advocated for transparency, advising that managers be open with their intentions and build trust among employees. In addition, Drucker taught that managers must establish vision and a sense of purpose. K.H. Moon is a former CEO of Yuhan-Kimberly and a former colleague of Peter Drucker. When I spoke with Moon about work-life supports, he had this to say concerning overall management as the context for these supports:

> The first task of management is to be transparent. A manager should establish trust and two-way communication and two-way innovation. Managers need to trust and respect employees and family and community...During my time at Yuhan-Kimberly, we implemented a vision and value sharing system. Through this system we shared our vision and values across the whole supply chain and we emphasized a trust-based supply chain.[3]

The tasks of management also require attention to innovation, performance, and contribution to the community. Moon goes on to say:

> We focused on innovation through collaboration and open connections. We also used management by exception and management by objectives and instituted profit-sharing programs. During this time we maintained our social-cause campaign called Keep Korea Green.[4]

Drucker's approaches, which were implemented by Moon yielded results. Moon says, "Because of this management, we were identified as one of the *Most Admired Companies* and one of the *Best Employers* for ten years. We also achieved 10 percent income return-on-sales." It is difficult to argue with the success of Drucker's management philosophies.

THE LEADERSHIP PARADOX

Managers and leaders are central to employees' experience of work and their experience within the organization. Leaders are always part of a broader organizational culture and the overall culture will outlast any individual leader's efforts. Over time, leaders will shape the culture, but this takes years and affecting this type of change is more similar to steering a tanker—slow and deliberate.

On the other hand, it is also true that leaders create their own subcultures within a company. For example, an organization may be generally very command and control in its operation, requiring adherence to rules and hierarchy for decision making. Within that culture, a leader may behave in a way that is very participative, asking team members for input and making decisions that are more greatly influenced by employees. The subculture of the team can exist within the broader framework.

As another example of the leadership paradox, a broader organization may tout plenty of employee choice making, personal discretion, and freedom but within that culture, a leader may manage team members closely, checking work, checking quality, and checking work process. Leaders create their own cultures, and the cultures leaders create are often mirrors of their own personalities. People join a company because of the nature of the job and the work. People leave a company because of the leader. One's direct supervisor is one of the most essential factors in personal experience of an organization, job, or of work-life supports.

LEADERSHIP DISCRETION

Leaders' decisions are key to the successful application of work-life supports. For companies that have few policies governing work-life supports, as well as those with many formal policies or practices, work team leaders are expected to make decisions for their teams on how the company's policies are applied. Kyle, vice president of real estate and facilities, with an oil and gas company, says that leaders are in the best position to understand an individual employee's situation in relationship to the team and the work the employee must accomplish. At Kyle's organization, before an employee may work from home she must ask permission, explain what she will accomplish at home, and then, when she is back, show evidence of having accomplished the work.

Leader discretion is an important component in day-to-day decisions about working from home as well as episodic or extreme conditions. "The other part of leadership is understanding and getting to know people when they are in stress—when they are at the point when you have to tell them to leave to take care of a personal situation," says Kyle. Leader discretion allows the flexibility in which leaders can tune in to their employees and make decisions that are the most appropriate and supportive.

Allen, director of finance and administration from a banking and finance organization, mentions that his organization's large size makes leader discretion important: "The leader is responsible for interpreting how he wants to address things and the decision-making process is distributed...We lack a consistent [policy-driven] approach." Diane, an executive vice president in charge of administration, from a global media company, says that most arrangements for job sharing, compressed workweeks, or other types of arrangements require employees to "work out a deal" with their managers. Unfortunately, in this situation, the likelihood of an employee having the opportunity to work in an alternative way may be based on his negotiation and persuasion skills.

LEADERSHIP MIND-SETS

The decisions leaders make regarding work-life supports are driven by their mind-sets. These are easy to discern in the following comments. Consider the difference in the tones of these leaders, each of whom considers himself to be progressive and supportive of alternative working:

> You have to be sure employees don't take advantage of you. You have to hold them to clear accountabilities and be sure they're not goofing off. Then there is the perception that when they're home, they're probably not doing work. Working from home is a stigma. My employees work from the office in a traditional schedule.

Contrast that view with this one:

> I don't need to be a person that is controlling and managing things. I just want to hire really good people who will just go out and bust the world open. As a result, my team members work in many different ways. I've always been really open about how people work, when they work, and where they work.

These comments embody significant differences in underlying beliefs. Leaders may choose to embrace work-life supports to a greater or lesser degree based on how they will be perceived as leaders. Linda, general manager of her global technology company's software division, describes this factor.

> There are a lot of misconceptions about work-life integration— that it is accommodation and that I'm allowing weakness in the organization as opposed to being perceived as getting maximum

productivity from my employees and making sure I'm tapping the most diverse possible talent set in the organization.

Ross, a COO with an oil and gas organization, says that in his company many leaders believe they will be perceived as "weak" or as "softies" if they allow alternative working for their team members. He goes on to say, "It depends on the personality of the leader. If you're a slave driver versus a really sensitive, attuned person, you will make different decisions, letting employees have access to certain work-life supports."

Work team leader attitudes can be a barrier to the implementation or use of work-life supports, and this theme emerges consistently. Barbara, an executive leader of human resources for a global banking organization, says, "Some managers have antiquated mind-sets that we're still, even in this day and age, trying to work around." Some leaders continue to believe that effective working is defined by the number of hours an employee spends at his desk. Some leaders must see their team members in order to trust they are working and in order to manage effectively. Rick Wartzman, executive director of the Drucker Institute, agrees:

> You can have all the slogans and corporate guidelines you want, but at the end of the day, corporate policy plays out at the individual human level. And that's where power, control, ego, and insecurity can get injected into the equation—or not. Front-line managers are the key. You can lay out a whole bunch of wonderful policies, and even have a CEO who believes in them with all of his or her heart, but unless you have front-line managers who also believe in sharing responsibility and accountability and forging a clear sense of purpose, the best-laid plans will only amount to window dressing.[5]

The consistency of these statements is telling. What is also telling is the frequency of the comments. In my formal research, every single person I interviewed identified the attitudes of the leaders as the biggest factor—for better or for worse—in the provisions of work-life supports.

EVERYTHING COUNTS

Adding to the tone they set for their teams through their decisions and mind-sets, leaders also set a tone through their own behavior and approaches to work. Leaders who are themselves practicing flexible working arrangements send important messages to others in the organization concerning the acceptability of flexible work—and vice versa. Previously, I mentioned the leader who used to say, "You're behaving so loudly, I can barely hear what you're saying." Whether or not leaders intend to be role models, they are. Leaders' actions (theories in use) are windows to their deep-seated beliefs (espoused theories).

People are constantly observing leaders for cues concerning what is appropriate, what is rewarded, and what the future holds. Employees look to leaders from the moment the leader appears in the parking lot or enters the building. Every detail matters, including whether or not the leader wears a smile. The leader's actions affect what the subordinates conclude about the leader's attitude and even the health of the company. Everything has meaning and is interpreted—or misinterpreted. As a result, the tiniest details of a leader's day are actually decisions that matter: what time to arrive, whether to send e-mails before working hours, whether to work through lunch, with whom to eat lunch, when to ask for help, whether to share frustrations with others, and how transparent to be regarding personal challenges. A colleague has a rule of thumb: never vent down. By this she means that leaders must never share difficulties with those who report to them because team members will lose faith and confidence. If a leader must find an outlet for difficulties, she should vent across to peers or up to her own leader.

Every leader has informal influence simply by being in a position of leadership. Having a title says to members of the organization that a leader has been rewarded for her actions, so those actions are necessarily instructive to others. Bringing work to life involves a myriad of decisions pertaining to how organizations help employees meet work and life needs and integrate demands throughout through their life course. Leaders' behaviors are instructive to others in the organization about the extent to which work is supported and flexible work is acceptable.

NOTHING LEFT TO CHANCE

Many leaders say they are progressive and want to provide work-life supports to employees, but not all leaders actually behave in this way—making decisions that genuinely allow and support this type of work. Herein lies the importance of organizational systems to help ensure that work-life supports are available despite individual work team leader attitudes.

Organizations cannot leave work-life supports to chance—or entirely to the discretion of work team leaders. The following are recommendations to foster the attitudes and behaviors necessary to ensure success of work-life supports. Organizations should:

• Establish clear benefits, policies, and practices. The presence of formal benefits, policies, and practices sets boundaries and guidelines for work team leaders. These are a critical starting point for an organizational system that embraces work-life supports. Firm boundaries also help ensure equity among all employees. When leaders across the organization manage work-life supports too differently, a "have/have not" dynamic can emerge in the organization, where employees who work for some leaders perceive they receive less than employees who report to a different leader.

• Recruit the right leaders in the first place. Companies must select leaders based on a proven track record of managing in a way that is consistent with the culture it wants to promote.

• Hold leaders accountable for actions and behaviors that are in concert with work-life supports. This means providing feedback throughout the year, providing ratings on yearly performance reviews, and tying pay and promotion to performance that includes consideration for implementation of work-life supports. This accountability needs to start at the top. In a recent column in *Harvard Business Review*,[6] Kevin Sharer, former CEO of Amgen says, "As a CEO, you should realize that your greatest contribution is the behavior you cause or allow to thrive in the organization's upper ranks." This behavior in the upper ranks sets the tone for accountability throughout the organization.

• Create coalitions and communities of practice. Bring leaders together in regular forums to learn from one another, share ideas, and discuss challenges. Do this formally through "lunch and learns" or through the creation of mentorship programs. Do this informally through networking events in which leaders foster their own connections.

• Orient, train, and develop leaders.

Work-life supports succeed or fail based on leaders' behaviors and approaches, so these recommendations are important to consider. Leadership development is also a key ingredient for success in implementing work-life supports.

LEADERSHIP DEVELOPMENT

In addition to the considerations for development approaches and mentorship I discussed for employees, there are also important points regarding development of leaders. In order for work-life supports to be implemented and thrive in an organization, leaders must understand the benefits, policies, and practices pertaining to work-life supports, and possess the skills to implement them within the culture. They must also understand the expectations for their own leadership in this area. Very few companies offer this specific type of training. A handful do.

The companies that develop their leaders in this way offer training through a traditional classroom and through an online option, so leaders may choose how they prefer to learn. They also establish coaching groups, in which leaders meet with one another each month. Within these groups the leaders share ideas, lessons learned, and challenges. These groups are designed to provide ongoing value beyond the classroom/online opportunity and are designed to build a network of leaders learning together.

When companies offer training on the topic of work-life support, typical learning modules include the following:

- Why this is important for the company's business and culture
- How work is changing, third-party data on changing work, workforce, and connection to productivity
- Overview of the company's benefits, policies, and practices
- Leadership responsibilities
- How to work with employees to determine flexible work approaches (assessing needs, having the conversation with employees, working with the team, applying the policy)
- Checkpoints for accountability

ADJUSTING LEADERSHIP STYLE

Ultimately, leaders must meet employees where they are and adjust personal leadership styles based on the needs of employees. The most effective leaders are able to communicate empathy to their employees. Even when he may not have the answer, the leader must communicate that he understands the question and will be with the employee so they can work through it together. When employees are new or unsure, they typically need more direction for tasks and more emotional support from a leader. As the employee matures in the role and as a member of the team, he needs less of each of these.

The leader's challenge is to provide consistency across the team at the same time she is providing leadership that is unique to each team member. Ensuring that the leader is perceived as fair and not playing favorites at the same time she is able to provide leadership unique to each person on the team can be like walking on a razor's edge. Effective leaders are constantly shifting and adapting, and by meeting employees' unique needs, they are providing powerful work-life support.

IN SUM

The success of work-life supports is based largely on leaders, and the importance of leaders cannot be overstated. Their mind-sets, behaviors, decisions, and ability to adjust to employees' needs are critical. Organizations cannot leave leadership to chance. Selecting the right leaders, developing them, and holding them accountable for behaviors and decisions are required to bring work to life.

CHAPTER 14

Aligning with Teams

Organizations increase the chances of successfully implementing work-life supports when they consider teams in the process. As in all of the considerations for work-life supports, teams can be both a help and a hindrance to work-life supports. In fact, teamwork and collaboration are identified as one of the most important reasons for organizations to *avoid* allowing flexible working. While teamwork certainly isn't a reason to avoid flexible working altogether, it is a factor to consider, plan around, and for which to find solutions. This chapter discusses the importance of teams and the ways that teams fulfill both task-oriented and relationship-oriented needs. It discusses the requirements for openness, trust, well-managed conflict, and strong inter-team relationships.

TASK AND RELATIONSHIP

For the first half of my career, I was significantly focused on team development and leadership development. Through that work, I was reminded frequently that the most effective teams pay attention to both task and relationship requirements. The considerations for flexible work within teams also follow this guideline. When teams are most successful, they nurture relationships and build trust. In addition, they pay attention to task, cultivate excellence, and members follow through with one another. Teams are critical to work-life supports because they are the context for meaningful work and for strong connections. Allen, a director of finance and administration, from a banking and finance organization, has a perspective on the importance of these team relationships:

What I learned long, long, ago is that one person can't do it... you have to have a team. You have to empower that team... people don't have to sit in a particular place in an org chart to be a leader, but they do have to get up out of their chairs and go and talk to people and help explain what we're trying to do and to add value. The very concept of a team to me is that you have a diverse group of individuals to create an environment... where they get to grow and learn and be valuable. They can work anywhere, but you try to create a culture and an experience that they never want to leave. It's about enabling people to be themselves, and yet be part of a team.

Lee, a senior vice president in charge of real estate and facilities from a technology company says, "We're social creatures... and our most creative work occurs face to face... there's nothing better than a hallway conversation to increase productivity."

Recently, my team was conducting ethnographic studies (studies in which we observed workers in order to discover social dynamics in the work environment) at a well-known technology company in Silicon Valley. One of the dynamics we noticed was how powerful these hallway conversations were. In this particular company, the coffee bar was a magnet, a place where employees enjoyed snacks and drinks throughout the day. It was always a hive of activity and a place for cross-fertilization of ideas. During our study, every single conversation we observed started with a social connection ("How are your kids?" or "How was the ski weekend?") and ended with a conversation that solved a problem or met a customer need. These are conversations that add tremendous value to an organization. The social relationships form the fabric of strong bonds and they create the networks through which customer needs are met and problems are solved.

Gallup published a book recently called *Vital Friends*,[1] in which it shared its finding that the most important reason people stay with a company or a job is that they have at least one good friend with whom they work. Relationships help us thrive as individuals and as social creatures. They also help the organization thrive by retaining talent and getting good work done. In cases of remote work, technology can be used to bridge the gap. For workers who are always remote, connections through social networks, e-mail, or instant messaging can provide powerful connections. Virtual water coolers, as I mentioned previously, also help make connections as well. Some teams cannot ever choose to be face to face in real time. Their work is always virtual. In these cases, technology is a powerful enabler of teams and relationships.

OPENNESS AND TRUST

Openness and trust are among the factors in building a strong team that create abundance. The process of building trust is intricate and critically important to the overall health and performance of a team and the individuals on the team—and therefore to the successful provision of work-life supports. The Johari window, an exercise developed in 1955 by Joseph Luft and Harrington Ingham, is a useful model. It suggests there are elements of ourselves known to us and others (open), as well as elements of ourselves known only to us. These are aspects of ourselves that we keep hidden. Aspects of ourselves that are known to others and not to ourselves are our blind spots.

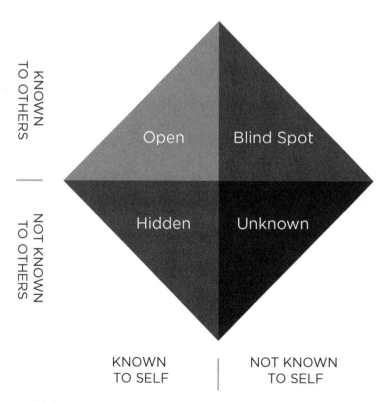

Figure 14-1 Johari Window

The model suggests that we can reduce our blind spots by asking for feedback and being open to input from others. This is the lifeblood of healthy teams. With this greater self-awareness, the individuals and the team tend to become stronger.

My colleague Jolie describes "have-your-back" levels of trust. In this type of relationship team members "have each other's backs," meaning they provide one another with feedback and suggest areas for improvement. Sometimes the feedback is tough, but it is preferable for a team member to point out a problem so it can be solved before it is visible to the world outside the team. In have-your-back relationships, team members also advocate for one another, stand up for one another, and generally help one another accomplish goals.

In another portion of the Johari model, moving more aspects of ourselves into the "open" by sharing with the team can help build relationships. Teams tend to build these relationships bit by bit. A team member shares and then observes how a colleague handles the information and whether she responds in kind. As individuals share more openly, and as others respond positively in a trustworthy manner, a virtuous cycle of sharing and relationship building is established. The opposite is also true. When individuals share less, others tend to do the same. Earlier, I made the point that proximity is the number one determinant of relationships. The concept applies here too. When team members share openly, they foster closeness and emotional proximity, which builds relationships.

Knowing more about the people with whom we work builds relationships. I consulted with an oil and gas company a few years ago. Its exploration division was run by a high-powered, tough leader named Carlos. He was perceived as a work-above-all leader. One day, school was cancelled for his children due to a power outage at the school building. Carlos had no child care that day because his wife was out of town and they didn't have backup child care. As a result, he took his children to work. They spent the day shadowing him, coloring on the whiteboard in his office, eating the candy out of the administrative assistant's bowl, and generally making friends in the office. After that day, Carlos was appreciated differently by his team. For the first time, team members were able to see more sides of him—not only the dictatorial leader but the kind father and committed family man. The people with whom he worked learned more about him and had a more complete perspective on what made him tick. This is the Johari window in action.

The starting point for trust must be an overall personal philosophy of respecting others, suspending judgment, and assuming good intentions on the part of others. Approaching the world with this perspective tends to influence the way the individuals behave, which in turn influences the way others behave. Positive reinforcing cycles are established when people work together on tasks, communicate and share openly, provide recognition, are honest and keep promises (both personal and task-oriented promises), and support others.

AVOIDING ASSUMPTIONS

Another key way to think of teams and team member relationships is to consider the Ladder of Inference, which was first conceived by Chris Argyris. The Ladder of Inference begins with the concept that there is a pool of objective data that is observable and irrefutable. This pool is at the bottom of the ladder. As humans, we tend to quickly select data, add meaning to the data, make assumptions, draw conclusions, adopt overall beliefs, and take action based on those beliefs. We "climb a Ladder of Inference" through this process.

Problems arise when we come to vastly different conclusions regarding motives and make assumptions that are not based on the pool of data. For example, if a team member comes in late for work (the fact/observable data is that she was twenty minutes late for the meeting), another team member could quickly come to the conclusion that she was slacking off. A conflict could arise when the team member confronts her colleague about her frustrations with her slacking. The alternative is to "stay low on the Ladder of Inference," asking more questions and focusing on the observable behaviors—in this case, the fact that the colleague was late for a meeting. By suspending judgment, assuming good intentions, and asking more questions, the colleague may discover that the team member was on a call that ran late with a customer. Conflict is averted and resolved more easily when team members avoid assumptions and focus more on facts and observable behaviors (staying low on the Ladder) and less on the conclusions they've drawn about others' motives.

The relationship between the Johari window and the Ladder of Inference is this: people will interpret others' actions through their own lens unless they know enough about others to guess at theirs. Carlos, whom I described earlier, is an example. Knowing more about his family and children provided

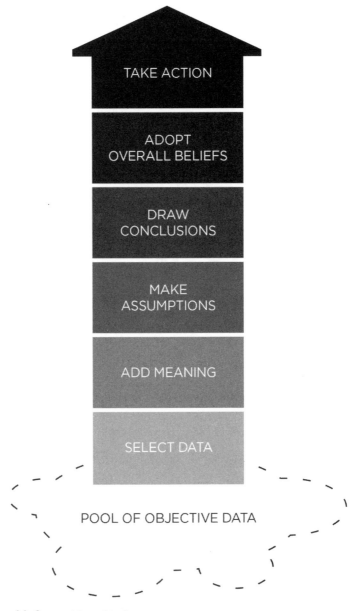

Figure 14-2 Ladder of Inference

a more nuanced lens through which others could view him. It is much easier to ascribe good intentions and bring accurate meaning when people know more about one other, and this allows them to interact at lower levels on the Ladder of Inference.

In addition, when people make inferences and draw conclusions, they can be more accurate in the conclusions they draw because they know more about each other. Now, when the team member is tardy for the meeting, other team members might also know that she has been working on closing a tough deal with a customer in Abu Dhabi and consider that she may be late because of that. Or, on a personal note, if she is tardy for the meeting, team members can recall that her daughter has been struggling with a recent brain injury and even though she had to take her daughter to the doctor this morning, she was online late last night getting work done. At a minimum, these models suggest that asking questions of one another to learn more and assuming good intentions contribute significantly toward a positive team environment in which people feel free to bring all of themselves to work. People don't trust what they don't understand. Sharing, asking questions, and communicating openly increase understanding and contribute toward trust.

SUCCEEDING BY FAILING

In addition to building trust and avoiding assumptions, teams also create positive conditions by sharing challenges and learning from them together. I once worked in a team that was very broken. One of its features was that you could never let another team member "see you sweat." Team members were in competition with each other for what they perceived to be scarce amounts of recognition and success. At meetings, team members would report on projects with a goal of presenting infallibility because they feared being perceived as weak or ineffective. They were regularly attempting to gain advantage over one another. In contrast, within my team today, we strive for the opposite type of culture. We share challenges and failures so we can learn from them, help each other, and boost each other up. When we share challenges and lessons learned, we provide feedback to one another, think together, and improve together.

A colleague said recently that she wants to have a team in which each person can "raise his hand and ask for help before things are a complete mess." This type of open sharing builds trust. When team members work in alternative or flexible manners, it is even more important to have strong relationships so they can help one another through difficulties. When relationships are strong, they reduce stress and demands on employees, and they boost the perceived capacity a worker feels. If an employee needs help, the team is there. If she is stumbling, she can trust her teammates to help her. These are critical elements to the success of work-life supports and to bringing work to life.

CONFLICT

Teams always face conflict. A healthy team is not characterized by an absence of conflict, but rather by well-managed conflict. Introducing work-life support options can stretch a team and its members in new ways. Some work-life supports change the typical ways of working and can therefore be the sources of dissonance or conflict. There is a proverb that says, "A boat that isn't going anywhere doesn't make any waves." A related proverb says, "When two heads think the same way, one is unnecessary." Conflict is necessary and helpful to progress, but when it isn't managed well, it can be very damaging.

Many years ago, our company utilized a personality profile for sales personnel in order to develop skills and drive performance. The expectation was that if employees better understood their personalities, they would be better team members and leaders. One of the indicators was the extent to which an individual created conflict. There were "grenade throwers" who would regularly initiate conflict. It was surprising to some that this was considered a significantly positive trait, correlated with team and leadership success. The catch? The "grenade throwing" employee had to have already created a safe, trusting dynamic within the team. When people on the team felt valued and safe, they were able to better work through disagreements and conflict with a learning perspective, building toward a common goal.

The majority of people are not very comfortable with conflict. They either lack the confidence or skills to work through conflict. However, conflict itself is not negative or damaging to a team. Conflict badly managed, or unmanaged, is damaging. In fact, conflict is a cue regarding passion since it only exists when workers care enough to feel passionately or disagree. In addition, every conflict situation features an ROI (return on investment) assessment. A person asks herself, consciously or not, whether the investment of energy in the conflict is worthwhile.

Teams that afford the opportunity for work-life supports may experience more conflict toward the beginning of the journey to establish work flexibility, as it is part of the process of adapting to change. It is helpful to start with a trusting team environment and to deal with issues as they occur. A friend in Texas says, "You need to lay the skunk on the table." In addition to getting issues out in the open, dealing with them face to face and staying low on the Ladder of Inference are a boon for solving problems quickly and growing from conflict situations.

Well-managed conflict asks tough questions and invites disagreement with the expectation that it will catalyze informed, effective decision making. Introducing dissonance—tension between where we are and where we'd rather be—interrupts the status quo and helps individuals and teams move forward. Deciding which work-life supports to enact for an organization can be controversial and have broad implications across the company and its employees. Well-managed debate and conflict produce the best decisions.

A COMMON ENEMY

Another way to manage conflict is through the classic sociological concept of the "common enemy phenomenon." This dynamic was (supposedly) discovered during a sociologist's Boy Scout expedition. During the trip, the scouts were having a difficult time getting along. There were some strong personalities in the group and they were arguing about everything from how many marshmallows to roast to how to set up the tent. On their first night in the woods, a terrible storm developed. The campers were suddenly forced to work together to secure tents, put supplies under dry wraps, and stay warm all night through the howling storm. The storm bonded the campers together against a common enemy. A similar phenomenon has occurred in cases where New Yorkers have been trapped in elevators. Twice in recent memory, New York City has sustained a fairly significant power outage in which people throughout the city have been stuck together in elevators. Those interviewed about the experience report having bonded with the others with whom they were trapped. Sometimes these bonds last many years.

A leader can create this same phenomenon for a team. Common enemies become mutual challenges. By clarifying the group's common goals and by pointing out shared obstacles—common enemies such as storms or power outages or figuring out how to stay connected when some team members work at home—the leader can create a situation in which members collaborate and connect in order to make new ways of working effective for the team. While it is counter-productive to identify another team within the organization as a common enemy, it is quite effective to identify situations as common challenges. For example, the need to learn a new technological platform or the need to respond to a unique customer requirement can be positive, mutual challenges around which a team can rally. The goal is to unite the team in a positive, mutual pursuit. Our team uses a "Team Playbook" as a vehicle to codify and continuously update the things that unite us. In it, we document our vision, purpose, and operating processes. We also document our interaction norms. These interaction norms, which we create collaboratively, identify how we work together and the protocols regarding how we will treat one another. Sharing openly, assuming good intentions, disagreeing constructively, and learning from one another are at the top of the list.

TEAM COMMITMENTS TO WORK-LIFE SUPPORTS

When team members are working together to accommodate work-life supports, they are well served to establish a mutual commitment among the employee, the work team leader, and the team itself. These, too, fit within a "Team Playbook." Companies that take this approach generally have a brief agreement that defines how often the employee will work away from the office and the schedule for this working time. The agreements also typically define the ways in which the employee and the team will stay in touch through meetings, phone calls, instant messaging, or the like. These agreements set explicit guidelines for the type of equipment the employee will have in order to stay connected.

For example, an employee sometimes has to commit to having reliable internet connectivity, a printer, or Skype. Sometimes these are company-provided and other times the employee is expected to provide them at his own expense in exchange for the privilege of working away from the office. In cases where an employee is working at home and has young children, these agreements often make an explicit reference to child care. For example, "The employee has appropriate child care, and working at home is not being used as a substitute for child care." While it is a rare employee who will use working at home as a substitute for child care, concern does exist and an explicit guideline to this end is helpful in putting minds at ease.

Guidelines typically also include formal checkpoints. Often, these are quarterly or biannual opportunities to formally review how the process is working and whether any alterations are necessary. Some of the most progressive companies expect that entire teams will sign a commitment. In cases of these agreements, all the team members commit to helping an individual employee succeed in alternative working and commit to certain protocols for communication. The advantage of this type of process and the transparency it fosters is that the whole team shares in a common goal and works toward mutual success. This reinforcement of shared objectives tends to increase the odds of success for the working model, for both the individual and the team as a whole.

INTER-TEAM RELATIONSHIPS

So far I've been focusing on intra-team relationships—relationships within the team. Inter-team relationships are those that form between teams. Like the trust that builds within teams, individuals and organizations are also served by trust and learning that occurs between and among teams. For example, the Johari window is relevant for teams as well as for individuals. A team can have information about itself that it shares openly with the world and also have blind spots in which it must seek feedback from the system in order to be more effective. As teams navigate work-life supports and as they learn what works and what doesn't, they are well served to communicate with other teams within the organization. One organization with which I consult accomplishes this cross-team interaction through quarterly "share outs," in which a few teams explain their recent projects, lessons learned, and challenges. Other teams leverage technology platforms such as SharePoint or a chatter feed on a sales management platform, on which they post questions or issues, help one another, and learn together.

IN SUM

Healthy teams that work well together and provide a positive overall experience for employees are themselves a support for team members who are navigating work and life demands. Teams are one of the most powerful work-life supports because they provide employees with fulfillment through connections and meaningful tasks shared with others. Trust and openness, well-managed conflict, and clear expectations for working together are context for strong task performance and strong relationships. Organizations create abundance and bring work to life through the strength of teams.

CHAPTER 15

Aligning with Culture

A final condition for the success of work-life supports is culture—this includes the culture outside and inside an organization. Everything I've covered so far affects and is affected by culture, which is the broader context outside an organization as well as the disposition within a company. Culture is important to the discussion of work-life supports because it can be an enabler, an obstacle, or both. Work-life supports can be effective in any organizational system. They must, however, be aligned with key features of the company and matched to where it wants to go.

Culture can be defined as the norms, beliefs, values, unwritten rules, and practices of a group (or a country, region, ethnic group, or organization). It is a disposition or an inherent quality of mood of the group. It is the natural inclination or tendency to think or act in a particular way. For an organization, culture is "the way things get done around here" and it shapes how an organization operates and how its employees behave. It is possible to see these patterns by observing what people do when they believe no one is looking. Culture will affect the choices people make and the decisions that guide their actions. Organizational culture is affected by a company's industry, competitive market, mission, business drivers, history, leadership, policies, measurement practices, HR practices, technology, and reward practices. These factors shape and are shaped by culture in a reciprocal relationship.

CULTURE OUTSIDE AN ORGANIZATION

First, let's briefly consider culture outside an organization. It is essentially the context within which an organization operates, and it is multifaceted. It describes the typical patterns of a country, an industry, an ethnic group, or even a family. Organizations function within this broader context. Because this external framework is part of a larger whole, companies have limited control over the culture within which they operate. Michelle, chief administration officer from a manufacturing company, puts it this way, "There are underlying cultural mores that go well beyond a company. I can do my damndest to have what I would call progressive, family-friendly policies, but the company still operates in a culture outside of ourselves and I can't change that."

A good friend, Bill, who has traveled extensively and has lived in several different countries across the world, used to say that all cultures have the same priorities. The only difference is the hierarchy of the priorities. For example, every culture would place family, work, religion, and group loyalty within their top ten values. However, the *order* in which group members place these priorities makes a significant difference in their actions. If a group prioritizes religion above life, its members may be more likely to fly suicide missions. If a group prioritizes family over career, its members may be more likely to miss the board meeting in favor of a daughter's concert. If the company values group loyalty over individual achievement, its employees may be less likely to speak up and disagree in a meeting. With decisions large and small, national culture, organizational culture, and personal values all have an impact on the actions we choose.

Culture outside an organization has a bearing on work-life supports because the organization and all its employees are part of this broader cultural experience. As a result, individual choice is a bit of an oxymoron since no choice occurs in a vacuum. "Personal choices are not always as personal as they appear. We are all influenced by social conventions, peer pressure, and familial expectations," says Sheryl Sandberg.[1] Organizations, and the conditions they create for employees' personal choices are part of a broader context. Richard Sheridan, CEO and cofounder of Menlo Innovations and author of *Joy, Inc.*, shares his perspectives on the importance of work-life supports and an organization's connections to the terroir[2] – the unique context, region or geography – in which it plants itself.

External Culture + Work-Life Supports: An Interview with Richard Sheridan, CEO and cofounder of Menlo Innovations and author of *Joy, Inc.*

Richard Sheridan is the CEO and cofounder of Menlo Innovations, which has won the Alfred P. Sloan Award for Business Excellence in Workplace Flexibility for six straight years and five revenue awards from Inc. Magazine. *He frequently speaks at business conferences and to major corporations such as Mercedes-Benz, Nike, and 3M. He lives in Ann Arbor, Michigan.*

To what extent do you believe culture is a mirror of a leader?

RS: When I think about culture, I think about alignment. When considering the alignment of a company's culture, I pick three data points. First, what is the world's outside perception of your company and your business and your approach? Some people might call that your brand but I think that's too narrowly focused on marketing. A truly authentic brand is one that encompasses so much more than your tag line and buzz phrases about your products. The question is "How would someone, who has never been to your company but knows about you, describe your organization?" The second data point is the inside reality. What does your own team believe about your organization and your business? What's it like on the inside? The third data point is the heart of the visionary leader(s) in the company. What do the leaders talk about, believe, and how do they behave? How do they treat team members? What do they tolerate as far as how the team treats itself? If you graphed those three points and tried to connect them with a straight line, you would probably have the typical organization in which those dots don't connect, but if you could get those all in alignment, that's where you get a culture that is incredibly powerful. You have a culture where all the stories align: inside, outside, up and down.

How do you think about navigating the organization in the broader culture that surrounds you? How do you go about affecting the world's perception of the company?

RS: I go back to a strong human tradition: *storytelling*. Think about how a society or a civilization or a community propelled itself forward over centuries of time. It was through storytelling with totems, songs, and at campfires. The culture itself has a storytelling component to it. This is the importance of alignment. You should be able to tell exactly the same story to your company and the world and your team. If those are in alignment, the team can tell stories without you there, the world can

(Continued)

tell stories, and it's all in alignment. This is a strong reinforcing system of alignment. It is also a system of accountability. For example, when I tell a story in my book or at a speaking engagement or on a tour, what would happen if I were lying? Imagine the cynicism and sarcasm that would result back at Menlo…so the storytelling component is incredibly important.

What are your perspectives on giving back to the community and how the organization connects to the broader community?

RS: Business must be integrated into the community as one whole. No business can stand alone. Every piece is part of the whole. It's like the saying, 'If a clod of dirt falls into the ocean, France is the lesser.' It's like this for a company. For example, the Burgundy region of France has a certain terroir to it. It literally refers to the earth of that place. If you plant a grape in that region, it will grow in a certain way based on the earth that exists there and the culture of that earth and how farmers have been taught to grow crops in that region, and to produce fine wines. Every community has a terroir to it – Boston, Detroit, New York City, Silicon Valley, Ann Arbor, Washington DC. When you plant your business in a community, you are part of the terroir of that community. You are planted in the earth of that community and must take responsibility for that. This all sounds pretty lofty. I don't think any of this is a zero-sum game. There are gains everywhere to be had when you create a system that allows your people to integrate their life and their work, when you create a system of storytelling, and when your business integrates with the community. All of this pays dividends in so many different directions you can't even count them all.

Tell me more about your perspectives on work-life flexibility.

RS: The first thing to talk about is sustainability. You can't have a flexibly available workforce unless that workforce itself is sustainable in the long term. As a society we spend a lot of time talking about sustainability of energy sources and climate and species and ecosystems and urban areas. But we need to start talking about the sustainability of humans. When we get to a certain point of tiredness and burning out people, we can't ask any more of them. You don't get the flexibility until you get the sustainability. For us, that's a core piece, to have a flexible team you have to first have a sustainable team. The question becomes—because that aspect of our culture is very important to us—how do we ensure a sustainable human pace to the work. We need to achieve flexibility in regards to the work we do for our clients. As much as my clients might love my culture, those customers have deadlines and requirements and things we have to do. Flexibility isn't the goal, it's the tool to get to sustainability. We need a sustainable workforce. Everything we created at Menlo is to create the flexibility so we get the sustainability. We pair people. We switch the pairs every five days so we're not building towers of knowledge. We have a flexible work space so we can bring more people to the project when we need more people so we can get more done. We've built this whole system to have the most flexible workforce possible so we can have the most sustainable workforce possible.[3]

DEFINING CULTURE INSIDE AN ORGANIZATION

Within an organization, clearly defining culture—current and desired—is the first step in managing it. A clear definition unites employees and leaders to pursue common goals, sets clear expectations, and provides a framework for accountability.

How does an organization define its desired culture? When we work with companies on the topic, we frequently assess it by asking people to list the attributes of the organizational patterns. This is straightforward, but then we continue the discussion by asking about what the culture is *not*. This type of is/is not analysis helps with definition because often when we try to define a concept, what it is *not* is as important as what it *is*. For example, an automotive organization was defining one norm in its culture as "process driven," which meant it was structured, documented, and efficient. However on the "is not" side of the equation, the employees clarified that "process driven" did *not* mean it was non-innovative, bureaucratic, or rigid. In another example, the organization defined a norm of "customer focused," which meant delivering value and solutions to customers. It did *not* mean giving customers exactly what they wanted, if what they wanted was not in their best interest. It did *not* mean committing to unrealistic schedules. The company also identified a norm of being "achievement oriented."

This meaning was connected to growth, clarity of goals, and hard work. "Achievement oriented" did *not* mean focusing on ends at the expense of means, achieving short-term goals at the expense of the long term, or burning people out in order to accomplish the goals.

From a work-life support standpoint, multiple organizations may value "work-life balance." In one company, this may mean that employees are encouraged *not* to work over weekends. In another company, the same cultural value may mean that employees are *not* required to come into the office, but *are* encouraged to work weekends at home to complete their work. The cultural aspiration of "work-life balance" is the same, but the companies have different ideas pertaining to how they accomplish it, which are visible in the way the attribute is put into practice. This is the value of understanding the "is not" side of the description as well as the "is" side of the description.

Another way to define organizational culture is to identify a person in the organization who is believed to embody the culture of the organization. Without necessarily sharing the person's name, it is possible to make a list of ways to describe her personality and characteristics. These are, by association, ways to describe the organization's culture. Another way to define culture is by having a group create a collage using images.

Figure 15-1   Defining Culture collage

When the team members select and post images of their desired culture, they capture why each image is indicative of the culture. This list of attributes will be descriptive of the desired culture. There are multiple methodologies to assess and define culture; these are merely examples.

Brand is also connected with culture. Culture is the "inside out" and brand is the "outside in" view of a similar set of attributes. Instead of thinking of brand and culture as separate factors for an organization, it is valuable to consider them together. First, describe the brand—the experience of the organization from the customer or consumer viewpoint. Then, describe the culture—the experience of the organization from an internal viewpoint. The attributes for each should be similar and in alignment.

Culture is a strategic advantage because it is the most difficult factor for competitors to replicate. Competitors may be able to copy products, mimic marketing strategies, or even hire away good people (steal talent), but because of the complexity of culture, it is almost impossible to reproduce.

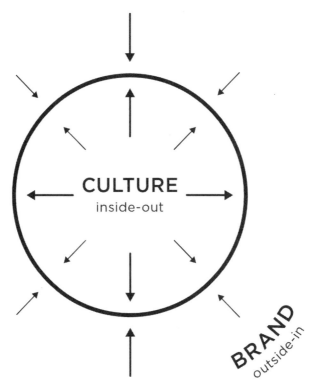

Figure 15-2   Brand and Culture

JOINING A CULTURE

When employees choose to join an organization, they are essentially choosing a culture and seeking a match. When our daughter was entering kindergarten, we worked diligently to select the best school system. We weren't simply choosing a teacher or a classroom. While those were important, they would only last a year. What would outlast the individual teacher or single year experience was the overall school system, including its philosophy, leadership, faculty, student assessment processes, facilities, and more. Employees who choose wisely are thinking in this same way. While a job or a particular work team leader may be attractive today, the typical employee is also looking for an organization within which he can grow, learn, and develop his career. Xavier Unkovic, global president for Mars Drinks, Inc., says:

> Mars has a unique DNA. If a company wants to be a Great Place to Work, it must be unique. We seek to attract people who are a match to our culture. We want them to join, not just because we're a well-known company or we have great brands, but because of our unique DNA. It goes beyond the product you produce. It's about the culture you create.[4]

Culture is the broader determining factor of the overall career experience that an employee will have.

SYMBIOTIC RELATIONSHIPS

Work-life supports tend to be a *product* of an organization's overall culture. The extent to which a company values employees and the extent to which the company communicates this to employees through the provisioning of work-life supports is instructive. Work-life supports are also mechanisms for culture change. They send messages about how workers are trusted and valued. They shape the culture. When workers are provided with tuition reimbursement and the opportunity to attend a class during working hours, it sends a message. When an employee is allowed to take longer-than-usual lunch breaks on Wednesdays in order to visit her aunt at the hospital nearby, it also sends a message. Additionally, the extent to which employees feel they can take advantage of the support available is culturally based. There is a symbiotic relationship between culture and work-life supports. They drive and reflect each other.

CULTURAL IMMUNE SYSTEMS

A culture is a living system comprised of people and practices. As with any system, it has an immune response. It is easiest to discern this immune response when people who are foreign to its constitution enter the culture. A company with which I consulted was seeking to renew its culture. It perceived that it had become stagnant and was not open enough to innovative ideas, risk taking, or new business ventures. As a solution to the problem, senior leaders brought in a handful of additional leaders who were countercultural. One leader in particular is an example. Whereas the pattern of behavior within this company was generally cautious and risk averse, she was aggressive and risk taking. Whereas the norm was friendliness and conflict avoidance, she was confrontational and tended to incite conflict. Whereas the organization had allowed less-than-stellar performance to be maintained, she was a stickler for results.

The culture and the people within the organization struggled. Similar to an immune response, they tended to isolate this newer leader. She wasn't invited to meetings. Because they feared her, employees tended to agree with her publicly and then disagree and talk behind her back later. For a while she was successful in spite of the immune response. She had the sponsorship of senior leaders and was catalyzing change as they'd intended. She fired some people. She started some new ventures. She achieved positive financial results. However, she wasn't happy, and the organization fatigued her. After a few years, she left in search of a company with a better match to her disposition and her approach to leadership. The organization's culture had resisted her style.

WORK-LIFE SUPPORTS WITHIN A CULTURE

Cultural immune systems and the leaders and practices cultures will accept or reject have a bearing on the work-life supports that are available to employees. Some cultures may embrace work-life supports to a greater extent than others, providing more benefits, having more policies, and allowing more practices that support work-life integration. No matter what types of work-life supports the company provides, culture is at the heart of these decisions.

Isaiah, head of real estate, facilities, finance, and information technology from a global technology company, says, "People are free to work in remote locations, work at hours that are flexible to accommodate their personal situation, and free to pursue their own interests within the context of their work. This is engrained and accepted in their culture." Ross, chief operating officer at a leading oil and gas organization, describes his company in terms of its values. He says that his company's culture of integrity and respect for employees is the foundation for its work-life practices.

Allen, director of finance and administration, with a finance company, shares a story of an employee who had knee replacement surgery. After his initial recovery period, when he wanted to work but couldn't be at the office in person, he regularly phoned in from bed for meetings. The culture was accustomed to having meetings via phone, so his time recuperating was easily facilitated by this approach, which was already the norm. These are all examples in which the organization's culture is context for work-life supports.

When implementing work-life supports, one element of culture that can be problematic is a preference for face-to-face interactions. Frank, an executive in charge of engineering, real estate, facilities, and quality, discusses the cultural reality within his manufacturing organization: if an employee is out of sight, she may be out of mind. Some cultures prefer face-to-face interaction and are less apt to include team members who are not physically present.

Sometimes, even when a culture officially offers work flexibility, employees do not feel free to take advantage of it. Herein lies perhaps one of the greatest challenges to the success of work-life supports. This reality is frequently due to leader behaviors, as we discussed in an earlier chapter, but it is also frequently due to the organization's culture. Brent, vice president of optimization, from a manufacturing organization, cites "cultural hurdles" as reasons that there are fewer people who take advantage of flexible working arrangements. Rita, chief diversity officer for a global consumer brand, shares that she knows team members who will commonly leave a jacket on the back of their chair in order to send a message that they are in the office. She knows a gentleman who would regularly wear two jackets on days he wanted to attend his Habitat for Humanity board meetings. He would wear one and leave the other on his chair so that it appeared that he was still in the office when he was gone for the meeting.

LEVERAGE POINTS FOR CHANGING CULTURE

How do leaders influence culture? How do they create cultures in which work-life supports can flourish? Dr. Dan Denison, author of *Leading Culture Change in Global Organizations: Aligning Culture and Strategy,*[5] has originated a model for culture change. In his approach, organizations must find a balance of external and internal focus. They must also find a balance of flexibility and stability. The relationship of these dynamics results in twelve leverage points that will drive culture change and result in better organizational performance:

- Mission consists of *strategic direction and intent, goals and objectives,* and *vision.*
- Consistency consists of *coordination and integration, agreement,* and *core values.*
- Involvement consists of *capability development, team orientation,* and *empowerment.*
- Adaptability consists of *creating change, customer focus,* and *organizational learning.*

Through his research, Dan has proven that appropriate focus on these variables results in corporate growth and performance, profitability, quality, employee satisfaction, innovation, and customer satisfaction.

Gallup reports another perspective on the variables that affect culture. Its researchers studied 3,477 managers from companies in the oil and gas, banking and finance, property development, tourism, automotive, and telecommunications sectors. They found that clear expectations, role definition, trust in the environment, and employee growth and development most significantly impacted culture.[6] These are leverage points for the priorities through which companies develop their cultures.

Often, cultural shifts are evident from the vantage point of mergers, acquisitions, or new leadership. When I started my career, I worked for a company—we'll call it BestCo—that was one of *Fortune's* "100 Best" for many years. It was successful and profitable. Its mission was to serve both customers and employees. BestCo offered development programs, a generous benefits package, employee choice in projects and career paths, flexible working options, and abundant recognition.

After I left, BestCo was purchased by a much larger organization, KingCo, and everything changed. The mission shifted to focus exclusively on customers. The processes became more hard driving. Educational benefits and some medical benefits were retracted. Educational development was still available for employees but the company only offered learning opportunities related to technical skills. Team skills, interaction skills, and diversity classes were suspended. KingCo fired significant numbers of leaders and employees from BestCo in order for new talent to enter and manage differently.

Remaining BestCo employees feared they would soon be asked to leave. In one meeting, a leader of KingCo, Rex, asked that all employees of BestCo raise their hands. A quick-thinking leader of BestCo, Jake, spoke up and said, "We're all employees of KingCo now." No one raised his hand and the meeting went on with a sigh of relief. Today, Jake is one of the few leaders who remains as part of KingCo. This is an example of how cultures can change and how the leverage points for culture such as mission, expectations, leadership, policies, and work-life supports are part of that experience.

THE IMPORTANCE OF EXPECTATIONS

Like so many features of work-life supports, culture is also affected by alignment between what people expect and what they experience. People are more satisfied when there is a match—alignment—between their expectations and the reality of their experiences. Years ago, an experiment was conducted in a call center. At the time, call centers were known as the sweatshops of white-collar work. The job wasn't fun. In fact, it could be grueling to talk with angry customers and be tethered to the phone for hours at a time. The call center in the experiment was facing 80 percent turnover and spending inordinate amounts on recruitment and training at the same time employees were unsatisfied and burning out. As a result of an assessment of their challenges, the company changed its recruiting and hiring practices. Instead of selling candidates on the job, they were honest about the challenges of the job—the attitudes of the customers, the fact that the employees were largely tethered to their desks, and the often thankless character of the work itself. An interesting thing happened. The company's retention levels actually increased. The difference was that expectations and reality matched. Workers took the job knowing what they were getting into. The reality of the job hadn't changed, but employees' expectations of the job had. Now, the expectations of the job matched the experience of the job, and this made all the difference.

Sociologically, people are more satisfied when their expectations are met. People are less satisfied when they expect something great and they're disappointed. The situation itself can be exactly the same. The difference is whether the situation is matching or falling below the expectations—coming up short.

In some ways, companies that have cultures that are well known and well respected have a greater challenge than companies without such renown. The challenge of the companies with positively perceived cultures is in meeting the expectations of those who are joining the organization. Depending on how high the pedestal, it may be difficult or impossible to meet the expectation. Companies with cultures that are expected to be perfect are set up to fail in some ways because they can't possibly measure up.

Every company has flaws. Honesty in the hiring and selection process is critical. When organizations are authentic with people regarding what

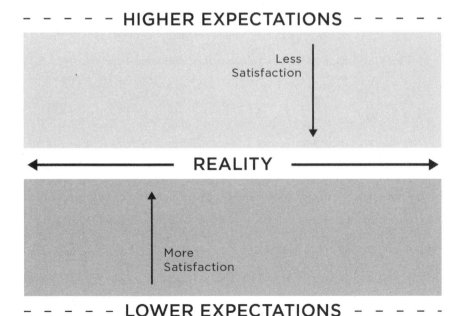

Figure 15-3 Expectation / Satisfaction Gap

to expect, and whether they can meet those expectations, workers will be more satisfied overall. As it relates to work-life supports, leaders must give employees a realistic sense of the culture as well as a realistic sense of the job. They must give employees an accurate expectation about the work-life supports that are available and those that aren't. Armed with realistic expectations, employees can make choices on whether to join a company or whether to shift to that next job within the company.

The Power of Culture for Work-Life Supports: An Interview with Dr. Dan Denison

Dan Denison, PhD, founder of Denison Consulting, and professor at the University of Michigan, has created a model for organizational culture. He has demonstrated a link between organizational culture and business performance—elements such as innovation, customer satisfaction, employee satisfaction, growth, profitability, and ROI. These are affected through four main channels of an organization's culture: creating a sense of direction and mission; ensuring both flexibility and adaptability; fostering employee participation; and providing consistency through core values. He comments here on the relationship between culture and work-life supports.

What is the relationship between culture and work-life supports?

DD: Well, what goes around comes around, and you definitely see lots of cases where the culture of an organization determines whether employees are valued for their whole selves or just their billable hours. The character of an organization determines the way employees will be supported—or not supported. Once you support employees, you've turned something loose that has a lot of positive impacts. Focusing on supporting employees has significant influence on the broader organization.

In what ways does the culture support or not support work and life?

DD: The ways that an organization provides work-life supports makes a powerful statement about what the organization values. It tends to snowball and you can't treat it in isolation. A culture is a combination of many factors and many aspects of the system. Does an organization require employees to punch a clock? Or to work over the holidays? What are the systems to provide support? You have to think about where the greatest leverage will be. That is, what aspects of the culture will provide the greatest return for the organization and the employee? What is the point where you can intervene that has the biggest and best impact? You can look at both sides of that cycle. What are the places that culture influences the support you provide, and once you define that support, what influence do those have on culture?

Say more about those leverage points.

DD: Well, the culture has to perform across many different variables. If you're going to compete in a triathlon, you can't excel at swimming only, because you'll lose in the biking and the running. Or, think of it this way, what part of an airplane is the most important in flight? The answer? None of them independently. They have to work together in order to fly. The ability to coordinate and focus is essential to performance. It is in this way that a culture needs to attend to all its variables. When the different parts of an organization aren't in alignment, the organization doesn't get leverage, synergy, or momentum. It really limits the impact the organization can have and the results it can achieve.

What is an example of this?

DD: The best example is consulting firms. The leaders recognize that half their talent base is made up of men and half their talent base is made up of women. If they don't appeal to the whole person through work-life supports, they can't compete. They have to have a system and a culture that is in alignment and allows them to compete for talent. Otherwise, they will only be drawing on part of the workforce.

What about leadership?

DD: Leadership is also a key leverage point. Leaders need to calibrate their perspective to the bigger picture of the organization. Their approach as leaders needs to be calibrated and aligned to the organization. Leaders need to focus on what comes next.

(Continued)

In other contexts you've referred to the importance of focusing on the "whole person." Can you say more about that?

DD: You have to think of how much of the organization appeals to the individual. Sometimes organizations are narrow in their focus. For example, in the case of a contract salesperson, they only care about how much he sells, but a long-term play means you pay attention to the broader piece of an individual's life and you support and integrate that. We used to joke that sometimes in life, the opportunity to focus on work provides us with the chance to set aside the complexity of the rest of our lives for a few minutes. The other side of the coin is that even family relationships are not 100 percent inclusive, you have a life outside your role in the family. The whole person has multiple dimensions that we need to support overall through the organization's culture.[7]

WORTH THE EFFORT

Attending to culture is worth the effort. John Kotter and James Heskett, both from Harvard, studied 207 companies in twenty-two industries over eleven years. They compared key variables in companies that managed and nurtured their cultures compared with those that didn't. They found that when companies nurtured their cultures, revenue grew 682 percent (compared with 166 percent in unmanaged cultures), stock price rose 901 percent (compared to 74 percent), job growth increased 282 percent (compared with 36 percent), and net income grew 756 percent (compared with 1 percent).[8]

IN SUM

Culture—both inside and outside the organization—is critical to work-life supports and whether they will take root. An organization that knows where it wants to go with its culture in the future and can accurately assess its culture in the present can close the gap. By considering the leverage points for change and ensuring that expectations are clear, an organization takes control and can use culture to its advantage. Work-life supports grow out of the culture and in turn contribute to it. They require attention, careful planning, and implementation. The next chapter will address factors related to implementation.

PART III

Leading for Adaptation: Implementing Work-Life Supports

CHAPTER 16

Leading for the Business Case

Work-life supports are good business. They are good for employees and employers, and the process of adopting work-life supports requires adaptation. Organizations often require a strong business case before they implement work-life supports. When creating one, it is advantageous to consider the stakeholders to whom the business case will be sold and the decision-making approaches the organization will embrace. This chapter covers these topics.

HERE TO STAY

Will work-life integration and navigation really matter as organizations move into the future? Is this a short-lived trend? Or is it a longer-term reality? Leaders in my research agree resoundingly that work-life supports are a long-term reality. They attribute this continued and increasing demand for work-life supports to global work, technology, speed of information, and employees who need to provide elder care to family members. Isaiah, global head of real estate, facilities, finance, and information technology at a global technology company, says about work-life supports:

> This is more than just a trend. It's reality now and it's the way work is done. The barriers and walls that prevent work-life supports will continue to come down. Individuals and companies who are not familiar with working this way will become obsolete.

Rita, chief diversity officer, from a global consumer brand, says, "Demand for work-life supports will only grow. People will demand it and they will vote with their feet if we don't give it to them."

MAKING THE BUSINESS CASE

When organizations embrace work-life supports for their journey into the future, leaders must frequently sell the idea to executive leadership teams and to boards of directors through a business case. The business case serves to justify recommendations, secure funding, and build consensus among leaders concerning the value of work-life supports.

The elements of an effective business case include:

1. Background and problem statement—this provides information on the situation and creates tension by describing a problem. Fodder for this section of the business case could include the time poverty people face as well as the pressure organizations are under to perform.

2. Goals and objectives—this section articulates the vision and describes the ideal future state that will be created if the business case is adopted.

3. Criteria—in this section, the business case identifies the criteria for a solution. Elements such as cost, ease of implementation, and alignment with mission, culture, and values are examples.

4. Options and analysis—the business case includes multiple options for consideration. Each is analyzed against a set of criteria. There are multiple frameworks for judging the options. Examples include financial analysis (cost and expected benefit/return), market/competitive analysis (sometimes this includes competitive market for talent), SWOT analysis (strengths, weaknesses, opportunities, threats), or balanced scorecard analysis. Most important is that some rigorous analytical method is completed, and that it facilitates sound decision making about the work-life supports being considered. Typically, business cases take an objective approach to these options by providing data without any judgment.

5. Recommendation and rationale—this section of the business case articulates the recommendation being made and describes it in detail. It also justifies the recommendation with a rationale and additional detail on why it is the best option.

6. Risks—in the business case, the "risks" section provides additional information on the potential hazards of adopting the recommendation as well as the hazards of *not* adopting the recommendation. For the potential negative ramifications associated with adopting the recommendation, this section also includes information on how the risks will be mitigated.

7. Outcomes—the "outcomes" section promises results based on proceeding with the recommendation. It demonstrates the positive effects that will emerge from the successful implementation of the recommendation.

8. Action plan—the business case enumerates a plan for implementing the recommendation.

9. Summary—the summary recaps the previous sections, focusing on the recommendation and the outcomes.

ASSESSING STAKEHOLDERS

Successfully selling the idea of work-life supports and obtaining buy-in from those who must be on board with a change requires attention to stakeholders. Stakeholders are those people who have a stake and some level of connection with an action or its outcome. Stakeholders exist at all levels of the organization and are both inside and outside an organization. Understanding various stakeholder points of view is important to honing and customizing a message that is unique to each. It is necessary to assess the extent to which stakeholders are already on board with the change. They may be staunch supporters or entrenched detractors, or they may be somewhere in between. Next, assess the extent to which stakeholders are taking action on their positions. Are they vocal about their position? Are they actively seeking to influence others? Are they visibly acting on their position?

These two types of assessments (whether people are on board and whether people are actively advocating for their position) result in four different types of approaches. When stakeholders are actively supportive, enlist their support in order to set tone and influence others toward positive reactions and receptivity. Leverage their involvement as liberally as possible. For stakeholders who are supportive of adopting work-life supports but are less active in their approach, it is most effective to simply keep them informed and involve them as needed.

Some stakeholders will be less enthusiastic about the change, but not very active in advocating for their opinion. For this group, it is necessary to proactively address areas of concern that may be unique. Communication efforts should keep this group informed as necessary and should monitor and respond to any additional issues that arise. The stakeholders who evoke the most concern are those who are less supportive of work-life efforts and are active in expressing their concern, dissent, or objection. This group of stakeholders is critically important since they potentially introduce dissent among others. Stakeholders who fall into this set require communication that provides them with a sense of ownership and engagement. It is important to gain buy-in and support from this group. Overall, it is necessary to address concerns that arise in order to gain their confidence. While it is not a good idea to capitulate to this group, it is usually important to invest time with them to listen and quell concerns.

The importance of broad support for a change effort related to work-life supports cannot be exaggerated. Without adequate leadership buy-in, the change effort can be derailed. Recently, I consulted with a multinational engineering services company. One of the company's senior leaders was in the process of making a case to his executive leadership team in order to convince them of the value of alternative working approaches and persuade them to allocate budget dollars to his program. Together, he and I and our teams worked over a Christmas holiday to build a business case. It was an airtight case with all the right components. He had received the necessary approvals to move forward and thought his leadership team was on board. He was moving through the process of vendor selection and even beginning to sign contracts. It was at this point that he was stopped. The company implemented a merger and his job was in jeopardy. Unfortunately, the support for his project was deeply felt only by him and his immediate boss. Because the support was not shared widely enough, his efforts were put on hold and he was never able to regain momentum. The lesson is that broad stakeholder support is necessary in order to ensure decisions will have residual value. In cases where decisions are not deeply supported, they can become derailed by other variables that affect the business.

MAKING GOOD DECISIONS

No matter how solid the business case or how many stakeholders are on board, complete certainty is virtually impossible. With any decision pertaining to work-life supports and the extent to which an organization will change benefits, policies, practices, or their culture, some judgment is necessary. Curt Pullen, president of Herman Miller North America, describes a 70/7 rule for decision making:

> I subscribe to a 70/7 rule of decision making. We can't always be 100 percent sure before we make a decision and if we are, it can cause us to make decisions too slowly. Instead of striving for 100

Figure 16-1   Rule of Decision Making

percent certainty before making a decision, when I'm 70 percent sure, I'll go ahead and make the decision. I'll be wrong in perhaps three out of the ten decisions, but I'll be right in seven of the ten and we'll keep moving forward. The times I'm wrong are an opportunity for learning. Of course the 70/7 rule applies in a lot of situations, but it doesn't apply to *all* decisions. It's really the manager's job to know which decisions apply, and to make their best choices and judgments in all situations. But when we empower people to make decisions and be supported through those, we send a signal that we're constantly learning as an organization.[1]

Testing a decision is important. Companies must thoroughly assess potential risks, implications, and unintended consequences. "Regardless of how much you test decisions, uncertainty is a fact of life."[2] Decision making is one of the fundamental tasks of leadership, and specifically, the decisions regarding work-life supports are critical. They bring work to life and enable employees to perform at their best so that organizations may in turn perform at theirs.

TESTING THE WATERS

In addition to making good decisions based on a business case, organizations must also consider their readiness for change. To what extent is the organization prepared to embrace work-life supports? A change readiness assessment is often completed in the form of a formal survey, but even more often it is completed as a thought experiment in which the decision makers consider key tenets of change readiness. As an example, if the organization is generally risk averse, the change process will be more difficult. In addition, if the organization has recently been through change efforts that did not succeed, there may be resistance. The opposite is also true. An organization's readiness is partially dependent on its successful completion of other changes that have come before. Also related to readiness is the extent to which the organization has planned for measuring outcomes of the approach it implements. Planning for these ahead of time, rather than after the work-life supports have been implemented, is most beneficial.

Often, an organization's readiness to change is enhanced by the use of a pilot. A pilot can be an effective way to begin a process of implementation and to build a cadre of supporters and advocates. Beginning on a small scale with a team, work group, or business unit means that there is an opportunity for learning and adaptation before a change is rolled out to the whole organization. If a pilot has already occurred and its lessons have been integrated, the organization will be more ready for the overall change.

It is also valuable to consider whether the change will be implemented in a single swoop—a revolutionary change—or whether the change will be implemented incrementally—in a more evolutionary approach. For example, some organizations choose to start with benefits. They offer greater support for parental leaves, increased opportunities for education, or improved benefits for part-time workers. Once these are implemented successfully, the company may add a policy allowing flexibility in working hours but not yet offer flexibility in working locations. Ultimately, the organization may offer flexibility in working locations as well. As I've mentioned, there are myriad approaches and solutions, all of which may be part of an overall evolutionary process to test, implement, and evolve.

IN SUM

Making the case for work-life supports and effectively selling stakeholders requires a solid business case with clear recommendations and rationale. It will be impossible to know everything with certainty, so the ability to test for the organization's readiness, to make decisions with *most*—if not all—of the information, and move forward with conviction are key to successfully creating the conditions of abundance that come through work-life supports.

CHAPTER 17

Leading for Change and Impact

Once stakeholders are sold on the value of work-life supports, how should leaders implement them and lead the process of adaptation and change management within the organization? The companies that are having the most success with work-life supports are those that are taking proactive steps to implement them. They are managing to a formula for change and are seeking to win over employees and leaders in terms of both hearts and minds. Success comes from providing ample information to help people move through a process to adapt to and adopt changes. Finally, success depends on measuring the effects of work-life support in order to prove return on the investment and continuously improve the process. This chapter addresses these requirements and approaches.

A FORMULA FOR CHANGE

Successfully managing change comes down to a formula. Few things in life fit neatly into a formula but these elements of change management actually do. In order to achieve successful change with people and organizations, attention to four elements is necessary. They include vision, dissatisfaction, knowledge, and perceived costs.

VISION

The first element of the formula for change is a vision of the future state. The vision must be clear, compelling, and, most importantly, it must be shared. In *Breakpoint and Beyond*[1] George Land and Beth Jarman discuss how a clear vision is true north for individuals, teams, and organizations. Decisions shape the vision to the extent that they point the way toward the direction the

Figure 17-1   Formula for Change

organization is going. The concept of "hologram thinking" applies here. With puzzle-piece thinking, everyone brings an element of a vision (or piece of the puzzle) and each piece is necessary in order to visualize the whole. A hologram is different. It contains the entire scene on every point of the image. Whereas a photograph shows light from a single point onto a single point, in a hologram, each point is showing the light reflected from every other point in the scene. Vision in an organization is like this. The goal is that each person possesses a sense of the whole future, not a partial view.

The best leaders provide a complete and compelling vision of the future that is deeply shared by every member of the organization. The vision should address the organization's aspirational, bigger-picture future, and also how the employee herself fits in and benefits personally.[2] If the leader has done her job well, each member of an organization has the entire future scene fully represented. Every decision for work-life support sheds light on future direction and on what's important.

DISSATISFACTION

For change to coalesce, people need a healthy sense of dissatisfaction with the present. This condition, which is necessary for change, is the most forgotten and misunderstood condition. It is the burning platform. It is the articulation of how the present is no longer working. It is necessary to be sensitive when sharing this element of a message. People are invested in the present. Many of them have built their careers by creating the present reality, so it is important that the present be validated at the same time that changes are being advocated. Usually, the most effective approach is discussing how the present situation was built for all the right reasons with the best of intentions and the best knowledge at the time. Now that the company knows more and the context has changed, the current solution is no longer serving it.

In establishing the burning platform, companies must articulate what *isn't* working today and what is a problem or a point of difficulty. Sometimes this seems counterintuitive—to point out the negative—but success lies in how it's done. Earlier, I described Nick, a wise and long-term employee at a company with which I worked. Sometimes when sticky issues came up with employees, we would consult Nick. He always had his finger on the pulse of the organization and could give us an accurate read on what was really happening. One time, we were discussing a problem and Nick was asking questions to discover more and to brainstorm how we should resolve it. Nick asked whether the problem was real or whether people were simply engaging in "recreational bitching." His point? The problem wasn't genuine. The concerns had turned into excessive whining rather than articulation of real concerns about real issues. This perspective was a reality check on which issues really needed solving and which needed to be simply refocused.

When pointing out problems or challenges, leaders are not encouraging "recreational bitching" but rather identifying substantive ways that the present situation is no longer serving the organization. Leaders should explain that while past solutions may have served the organization, as the situation changes the solutions must change as well. For example, previous ways of managing—by supervising a staff that was in the office from 8 a.m. to 5p.m., Monday through Friday—worked in the past, but as companies move toward a more global workforce and must accommodate different working hours, that way of managing is no longer possible. Companies must manage differently.

KNOWLEDGE

Once stakeholders have a vision of where the organization is going (vision) and a sense of why it can't stay where it is (dissatisfaction), people need knowledge of how to close the gap. They must know the practical first steps to make a change. They must have a sense of the actions necessary to move forward through the change (for example, research policies at other companies, create proposal for new policy, present the proposal to executive committee and get approval, add the new policy to policy manual, distribute and communicate the new policy to employees, train work team leaders). Much of this may feel mundane, but these stepping-stones will create the conditions for successful change.

PERCEIVED COSTS

These factors—vision, dissatisfaction, and knowledge—must be greater than the perceived costs that go with the change the organization is seeking. The costs may be time, money, people, or political influence. There are costs to every change so the goal is not to minimize or "spin" them, but rather to be honest with people about the investment (costs) that will be necessary. It's a trade-off. The investment an organization makes will result in a better future (vision) as well as the relief of problems (dissatisfaction) when the organization's leaders have the understanding and skills (knowledge) to implement successfully.

THE FORMULA

This approach can be expressed in the formula:

$$\text{Vision} \times \text{Dissatisfaction} \times \text{Knowledge} > \text{Perceived Costs}$$

For change to occur, vision times dissatisfaction times knowledge must be greater than perceived costs. For those who remember algebra, all of the factors on the left of the equation—vision, dissatisfaction, and knowledge—must be in place. None of them can be ignored (zero) because anything multiplied by zero is zero. If any one of the factors is missing, the perceived costs of a change will be too great for the change to occur. When managing the change and implementing work-life supports, it won't be enough to attend to any one part of the formula. Success will be achieved when leaders attend to all the necessary elements of managing the change.

ENGAGING HEARTS AND MINDS

Previously, I discussed the importance of winning both hearts and minds. This "hearts and minds" approach is evident here as well. In general, on the emotional side of change, people progress through a fairly predictable pattern of moving from denial to resistance to exploration to acceptance and then to commitment. On the cognitive side, people move predictably from awareness to understanding to translation to action and finally to ownership.[3] Most models of change conflate—that is, mix together—the emotional and cognitive side of change. To decouple them—to take them apart—is useful in building understanding of the process and helping people move through it. The effective management of change helps people progress through this process by providing direction and support as well as vision, dissatisfaction, knowledge, and truth about costs and investments.

Managing change through the process of implementing work-life supports builds organizational competencies. When organizations go through change related to work-life supports successfully, they enhance capability for the next change. Competence in dealing with change is a transferable skill that tends to increase overall agility. Author and former *Time* magazine editor Joshua Cooper Ramo says, "Resilience will be the defining concept of the twenty-first century."[4]

Earlier I mentioned the concept of "future proofing," in which organizations seek to ensure success into the future. The skill of future proofing is the ability to continually adapt and respond to changes both inside and outside the organization. The metaphor of a boiled frog is apt. It is actually possible to boil a frog[5] without the frog jumping out of the pot. When the temperature of the water is turned up quickly, the frog will jump out of the water, but when the temperature of the water is turned up slowly, the frog continually adapts its body temperature until it is critically hot and beyond the point of recovery. The lesson is that leaders must continually assess situations and determine what type of response is necessary, especially as different employees have unique and varying "boiling points." To simply adapt without thought, planning, or knowledge of the situation is to become critically incapacitated. This is the skill of future proofing: continually listening to the situation and environment and making conscious decisions regarding when and how to adapt and adopt change.

PROGRESSING THROUGH THE PROCESS

People progress through a relatively predictable set of concerns in a situation of change. The Hersey-Blanchard Situational Leadership model suggests they start with contextual concerns ("Where is this coming from? What's the context or big picture?"). They quickly move to personal concerns ("How will this affect me? Will this be good or bad for me?") and from there, they move onto procedural concerns ("How will this work?"). After these concerns are resolved, they tend to bring up concerns regarding impact ("Will this matter? What will be the payoff of this effort?"), as well as concerns pertaining to collaboration ("How will we involve others and how will we get others on board?"). Finally, they concern themselves with refinement ("How will we improve this on an ongoing basis?").

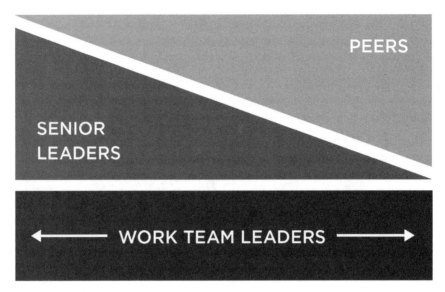

Figure 17-2   Change Management Influence

People also look for sponsors when they are going through change. These are the people who are promoting or supporting a change. At the beginning of the change, employees focus more on the messages and sponsorship from senior leaders, and this reliance on senior leaders tends to wane over time. In an opposite fashion, at the beginning of a change process, people tend to rely less on peers. Over time, the peer influence expands. Throughout the change process, the immediate work team leader's involvement is crucial.

One company has made use of this knowledge by leveraging town hall meetings and MBWA (management by walking around). These venues give senior leaders the opportunity to speak with groups through "walk-abouts" in order to share the vision for the change, discuss the reasons for the change, present how the employees will be supported, listen to reactions, and discuss the trade-offs. At the same time, the company sets up "coaching groups" in which peers can connect regarding the change and share what they've learned.

Leaders must share information in such a way that people accept the change. When there is a dearth of information, people will fill in the blanks, and spend unnecessary time wondering, postulating, and exchanging rumors about the future. I had a boss who used to say the rumor mill is always right because it is an immense brainstorming session. Eventually, every possibility is represented in the rumor mill. One of those possibilities is always the actual decision that is made. To quell rumors, it is generally best to communicate more and to communicate early. Even when decisions aren't finalized, it can be productive to share as much information as possible with employees. Share what is known. Be open regarding the decisions that are not yet complete. Be transparent about how decisions are being made. Sharing information is always a judgment call, but in general, more information flowing through the system creates a situation with more trust and openness,[6] and fewer distractions from rumors.

What are the implications for work-life supports? As leaders and organizations implement work-life support programs they must work through peoples' concerns and respond to multiple questions through "lunch and learns," website question submittals, FAQ documents, and the like. In addition, it is valuable for senior leaders to carry a strong message and invest time at the outset to get people on board and engaged with the change. Time is well spent in town hall meetings and in connecting formally and informally with people online and in person. Building peer support through communities of practice—groups learning together—and committee structures sets up work team members who will be strong peer supporters as the change process matures. First-line work team leaders have perhaps the most difficult jobs. They are frequently in a position in which they must adapt to the change personally—by shifting their leadership style or by developing their understanding of work-life policies, for example—at the same time they must lead and champion the change, sending a strong message of support. Due to the challenge of their roles, they also require support through the changes.

SUPPORTING THE CHANGE THROUGH ACTIONS

As in all aspects of work-life supports, leadership actions are essential for success. If leaders are supporting a change, what are they doing and saying? If an organization wants to hold a leader accountable for implementing and effectively executing work-life supports, what behaviors should it target? Here is a starting list. Leaders can use it as a self-assessment for their own progress in leading and managing the change.

- I am taking appropriate actions to be an overall sponsor for the change.
- I am personally acting in new ways (not remaining the same and simply insisting *others* change).

- I am clearly communicating and regularly reinforcing the change.
- I am staying aware of the obstacles and risks and managing them appropriately.
- I am paying attention to unique concerns and responding appropriately.
- I am setting and reinforcing clear expectations, including providing clarity on how decisions will be made.
- I am handling objections appropriately.
- I am obtaining feedback throughout the process.
- I am keeping people informed in order to reduce surprise or ambiguity.
- I have provided appropriate choice, involvement, and ownership to my team members.
- I am providing positive reinforcement of behavior that is helpful to a successful change.
- I am demonstrating patience in providing people with time to digest and accept the changes.
- I have provided clarity on why the change is occurring and "what's in it for me" for individual stakeholders.
- I have provided support for employees who may need to build their skills or knowledge in advance of the change.
- I am providing opportunities for celebration.
- I am supporting my team members who are part of the change project team by allowing them time for that involvement.

MEASURING THE IMPACT

As work-life supports are implemented, it is critical to measure the impact and determine the extent to which they are operating effectively. Measuring successfully provides the opportunity to demonstrate ROI (return on investment), which is critical to maintaining funding for programs and support for policies and practices. The feedback and data obtained through measurement is infused into the system in order to continuously learn and improve processes. How do companies measure work-life supports?

- Some companies are using survey data. They implement work-life supports and then ask people whether the supports matter in terms of the employees' satisfaction, productivity, and intention to stay with the company. Companies may poll employees through a special, dedicated survey.

Occasionally, they poll using a few questions that are incorporated into the company's overall annual survey.

• Other companies are measuring the impact of work-life supports by examining related data such as turnover rates. While turnover is admittedly affected by a multitude of other variables, companies that use this data believe that work-life supports are one important variable, and that turnover is a metric worth tracking.

• There are organizations that are using data from performance systems. They are tracking which groups in an organization are using work-life supports to a greater or lesser degree and then overlaying data from performance management systems in order to determine whether performance scores are higher in the groups with greater or lesser use of work-life supports. They are also implementing 360-degree feedback approaches in order to ensure that leaders and employees receive feedback and are accountable to multiple stakeholders.

• Another way that companies are tracking the effectiveness of work-life supports is through work team leader data. This is also a survey, but it focuses on the qualities of leadership. Companies are tracking the areas in which work-life supports are more deeply applied and then comparing these to leaders' performance review scores in order to determine whether the provision of greater work-life supports is correlated with perceptions of improved leadership performance and behavior.

• Organizations are also leveraging exit interviews—the conversation a departing employee has with a company leader—to obtain feedback about the company and its policies, practices, leadership, and the effects of those on the employee.

• There may also be a connection to corporate boards, which are increasingly measuring their own performance. The Conference Board, a global business membership and research association, has conducted research that discovered that 90 percent of large organizations in the United States have boards that evaluate their own performance.[7] It would be a coup to have this overall effectiveness measure include some aspect of employee satisfaction with work-life supports.

Organizations are also ensuring flexibility in measurement systems. They implement and then monitor in order to determine what changes should be made. Any measurement process is limited by current knowledge. The headlights on a car are not bright enough to shine to a final destination, but they will successfully carry its passengers any number of miles by illuminating one hundred feet at a time. Implementation is like this. Companies must begin measuring based on what they know today and based on their overall goals, connected to their desired business outcomes. As they progress, they may need to make adjustments. This is to be expected, and success will be accomplished through this incremental journey.

Measuring results of work-life supports is invaluable in cementing programs. In one example, a law firm had implemented a broad array of work-life supports, and within two years the firm was acquired. The acquiring firm was preparing to retract almost all the work-life supports. Fortunately, the law firm had kept impeccable records and data on employee satisfaction, client satisfaction, and billable hours. Because the data was so positive, the acquiring firm decided to keep the work-life supports in place. The data ensured the sustainability of the program.

Measurement approaches must make deposits into an organization's "patience bank." Similar to a bank balance, organizations have limited resources of time, money, and human capital. Organizations make withdrawals of these resources when they invest in new ventures, policies, or practices. Returns on these investments are important so that the organizational patience bank remains solvent—and it's important to maintain a balance long enough that there is time for payback.

Organizations can be very impatient. Leaders make decisions or investments and they want to see results. Often, they want to see results almost immediately, especially if the companies are publicly held. If results don't come quickly enough, organizations run the risk of removing investments too quickly. However, it is usually the bigger investments in more systemic changes that have the longest-term returns. Organizations must ensure that measurement systems make enough of a deposit into the patience bank to maintain a balance. With a greater balance in the patience bank, companies ensure that investments into programs or processes won't be removed prematurely, before payoffs can be recognized. It will be necessary to invest time, money, and human resources for a work-life support program to be successful. Most of all, it is critical that the entire senior team understands the level of long-term commitment that is necessary.

ALIGNING FOR IMPACT

In order to create abundance, leaders must ensure that work-life supports—the benefits, policies, practices, and cultural norms—they provide are in sync with where the organization is going. When a leader or an organization considers selecting and implementing work-life supports, it is wise to consider a range of options. Some options will be a match to the current culture. Some will stretch the organization in new directions. Some will be too extreme and might interfere with the organization accomplishing its goals.

Alignment means selecting the right work-life supports that appropriately stretch an organization but don't take it to the breaking point or create problems. For example, offering tuition reimbursement might be a match for where an organization is today. Offering time off work to attend classes may stretch an organization appropriately. Providing the opportunity for an employee to conduct research for his class during work hours may take an organization beyond its level of comfort with the current or the desired culture. Each organization needs to make its own choices and stretch toward a culture of work-life support and flexibility but stop short of reaching so far that the work-life support negatively influences the desired culture or gets in the way of a positive work environment.

An organization that pushes too far too fast will know it. Resistance or negativity will emerge, potentially overshadowing the benefits the organization receives in the form of engagement and enthusiastic commitment on the part of employees. To go back to the example, offering time off for an employee to attend class may meet with some questions from other employees but these may be easily handled if the school-attending employee is able to complete his work after hours. On the other hand, if the student-employee is conducting class-related research during work hours, this may become so distracting and take so much time away from the work of multiple employees that it becomes problematic. This may be pushing too far.

In addition, work-life supports must be integrated into the business. Rather than a program-of-the-month or a short-term solution, they will be most successful when they are part of the fabric of the organization and when they are fully integrated into existing processes. For example, integrate the training for leaders on work-life support options and their implementation into the existing leadership development curriculum. Or, rather than conducting a separate assessment for a worker who wants to take advantage of work-life flexibility options, integrate this assessment into the existing framework of performance reviews. Rather than launching a separate education or communication approach on work-life supports, include the education in the existing processes for communication such as monthly business updates or town halls. In other words, make the work-life supports part of the processes that are already woven into the way the organization does business. This will help work-life supports to take hold.

IN SUM

The goal of any change management or measurement approach is for work-life supports to become ingrained in the organizational processes and systems as well as in the actions, behaviors, and beliefs of leaders and employees. Following the change formula, engaging hearts and minds, managing to the predictable progression of concerns, and demonstrating tangible support for work-life supports will increase the likelihood of success. When work-life supports are viewed as common practice rather than as programs, success is close. When the implementation of work-life supports is habitual and taken for granted, success is also at hand. When work-life supports take hold, the organization is bringing work to life.

CONCLUSION

Planting Trees

The best time to plant a tree is twenty years ago. The second best time is today. This is never more true than as it relates to work-life supports. Some organizations will say that they wish they'd implemented work-life supports long ago, but in lieu of previous implementation, there is no time like the present.

Employees must integrate—not balance—all the demands they face with work and life. When leaders and organizations support them in this effort by creating the conditions for abundance and joy throughout their lives, the investment will pay significant dividends in employee engagement, satisfaction, productivity, attraction and retention, and overall business results. Organizations must select work-life supports that are exactly right for them. The work-life supports must align with work, workplace, workers, performance systems, and the organization's culture. In addition, organizations must pay attention to work team leaders and teams who are pivotal to the success of work-life supports.

There are multiple right answers when it comes to how leaders and organizations can implement work-life supports, so the considerations I suggest don't point to a formulaic approach or one right answer. Instead, there are various approaches for organizations and leaders to consider. The right answer for any organization is a cocktail—the right mixture of work-life supports across areas of the business and customized for teams and individuals. To implement work-life supports that aren't aligned with the organization's values and direction would be folly and a waste of time because they wouldn't work. Effectiveness of work-life supports is dependent on alignment to the business.

In establishing the right cocktail, it will be important to strive for "simplicity on the other side of complexity." By this, I mean working through complexities as part of a process that should ultimately lead to simplicity. It is frequently messy in the middle of the process, but elegant simplicity is the goal. The simplicity does not mean "dumbing down" or simplifying. Instead, it means culling information so it is digestible and usable. "Simplicating" is finding the appropriate elegance after working through the complexity. Mark Twain is often (incorrectly) credited with the phrase "If I'd had more time, I'd have written a shorter letter."[1] The considerations presented in this book are designed to be the shorter letter—or the elegance in simplicity. It is a summary of what's necessary to consider in the process of implementing work-life supports successfully.

The work-life solutions will need to be both systemic and systematic. For the solutions to be systemic, they will need to be integrated with multiple processes within the organization—financial processes, measurement processes, HR processes, training and development processes, and more. Additionally, they must be thorough and comprehensive in the parts of the organization they touch. At the same time, the solutions will need to be systematic. They must be well planned, organized, efficient, and logical in their sequential implementation.

Both agency and structure must be considered if work-life supports are to succeed, and their implementation is a matter of importance for individuals, leaders, and organizations. Individuals have a responsibility to be knowledgeable about work-life supports and to advocate for these supports in their organization. Leaders, too, have a level of individual accountability in making work-life supports successful. They should model the way through their own behaviors and decisions and they should continually set direction for the work-life supports that will most positively impact their area of the business. In these ways, both individuals and leaders have agency—personal choice and responsibility toward persuading organizations to implement greater work-life supports.

At the same time, organizations have responsibilities to create the conditions in which work-life integration and navigation can flourish. This is structure. Individuals—whether they are workers or leaders—will have a difficult time without structural supports for work-life integration. Finding the right solutions to work-life supports is not an either-or situation in which either individuals have responsibility *or* organizations have responsibility. The best solutions require both individual responsibility—agency— as well as organizational responsibility—structure.

In addition to addressing both agency and structure, organizations must be clear and explicit in describing how work-life supports fit into the overall framework through which the organization operates. Work-life supports must serve both people and the organization. If these are out of sync, the process won't be sustainable. When people's needs are maximized and the organization isn't served, the benefits, policies, or practices won't last because they won't be profitable or advantageous to the organization. They may work in the short term, but they will be overturned in the long term, when the organization goes through cost reductions or when the economy cycles downward. Likewise, if organizational needs are maximized at the expense of worker needs, work-life supports will also be ineffective because attraction, retention, and engagement will suffer. Work-life supports are quickly becoming differentiators among companies, and those companies that don't offer them will lose or fail to attract the best employees. The answers that any one company embraces for its cocktail of work-life supports must serve both individuals and the organization.

Finally, testing new approaches is rarely wrong. The best answer is positive action and forthright efforts toward a holistic solution. Companies will need to implement and execute repeatedly over time. Work will change, workers will change, the broader context will change, and companies will need to shift as well. Companies must implement, monitor, adjust, revise, and repeat. Even more than selecting the right work-life supports at the outset, success lies in renewal and adaptation so that work-life supports are responding to the realities of work and life on a continual basis.

Implementing work-life supports will be a lot of work. It will be worth it. It will benefit individuals and it will benefit organizations. It will create abundance and it will bring work to life.

Appendix

Some readers will be interested in my research methods and additional background on my studies. This section is for them.

STUDYING WHO WE ARE

Bring Work to Life focuses on white-collar professional work. Not because it's the only work or the most important work, but because it is what I know. It's the people and data to which I have access. During my PhD program, there was a student who sported extensive tattoos. What was his subject of study? It was the sociological reasons for body art. He studied who he was and what he knew. We're all like that. We're studying who we are. As a working wife and mother with a penchant for learning, working, and family, I study work-life issues.

Before my husband and I had children, I earned my first Master's degree in management and organizational behavior. It was challenging, but with a supportive husband and no children, it was easy by my current standards. When the time was right to go back and seek my PhD, I set a goal to start my program at the same time my son started kindergarten, and it worked out well for the whole family. My daughter was in third grade and my son was in kindergarten. Like most families, we take a photo of the children at the beginning of each school year. That year, I was in the photo along with them.

As a 1986 *Crowded House* song says, it's like "trying to catch the deluge in a paper cup." As life became increasingly full, I was deluged with demands, and I needed more than a paper cup to hold them all. It also became clear to me that *balance* wasn't the ideal, or even the right end game. I wanted it all and I wasn't willing to trade off one part of my life for another. I had work and family and education and self and community and much more. Balance was the wrong metaphor altogether. It felt more like charting a course and navigating my way through the flow of life. I integrated work into the whole that was my life. This integration and navigation—not balance—became the concepts on which I would base my dissertation research.

At the same time I was a wife, mother, student, and community member, I was also a leader in my own organization. I was curious about how leaders could create a context within which workers could thrive. I began my career in human resources, learning, and organizational development within an automotive company. My organization touted "Scanlon Principles," named after Joe Scanlon, a steelworker who got attention with his idea that workers needed equity, participation, identity, and competence to succeed and contribute to the success of the organization. Despite how long it's been since the principles were articulated, I believe they still have value today. Later, when I moved on to a leadership position with a contract furniture company, I wondered how work and life could come together. If it was necessary to successfully navigate and integrate, how could workers accomplish that? What could leaders and organizations do to create the conditions for fulfilled employees and positive bottom line results?

THE RESEARCH AND THE EVIDENCE

Early in my career, I spent a fair amount of time leading process redesign efforts. Between Quality Circles, Theory of Constraints, Toyota Production Systems, and Kaizen processes, I was indoctrinated into a process improvement mind-set. Working hand in hand with the Japanese through translators, I learned an acronym that has stayed with me. "If you want to achieve your GOAL, you have to Go Out And Look." In other words, go and see. Get the evidence. Take action after learning the facts. As a result, a fundamental premise of this book is that we are well served by looking at evidence—studying, interviewing, and exploring real situations in order to draw conclusions and take action. We are well served by knowing more about context—what surrounds our own situation—and we are also well served by learning from others.

SPILLOVER

In 2008, while working on my PhD at Michigan State University, I researched the effect of spillover from work to family and from family to work. My quantitative study examined the relationships among sociodemographic data in the General Social Survey (GSS). I found that women experience interference (spillover) from work to family more than men. In addition, those with higher incomes experience less interference from work to family. My study also found that age was not significantly correlated with work/family interference. Instead, what mattered most to spillover were gender and income level.

LEADERS' SOLUTIONS

As a follow-up to that first quantitative research, I wanted to dive more deeply. In 2009 and 2010, I studied the ways that senior executives integrated their work and families. I interviewed various executives within two very different companies—one oil and gas company and one manufacturing company—and identified how key senior executives made it all work. I studied both men and women, targeting senior executives who had children in middle school or younger. The work-life supports within their companies were critical factors in their success.

EXECUTIVE VIEWPOINTS

I became increasingly curious about these work-life supports, so in 2010 and 2011, I launched another study of senior executives and their views of work-life supports. I spoke with executives from multiple for-profit U.S. companies. They were Fortune 100 and 500 companies and the number of employees at each company ranged from 6,000 to 426,000. At the time of the study, the total number of employees represented among all the companies was 1,243,703. The companies were in banking and finance as well as manufacturing. I also included media companies, technology companies, and oil and gas organizations. I chose the companies and the sectors because I thought they would be significantly different from one another. I also wanted to be sure that this study covered multiple locations, so I ensured that the companies I studied were in different parts of the country. They were evenly divided across the west, east, and central portions of the United States.

In my research, I interviewed senior leaders concerning work-life supports and the effects of these for the organization. I didn't select this group because it was representative of the overall U.S. population, and I wasn't seeking to generalize from my data to the broader population. Rather, I interviewed the senior leaders because they strategically influence company practices based on their broad chains of command. I interviewed senior leaders because they make the rules with which the majority of workers live. Leaders' views drive

their companies' decision making. I was interested in how they were thinking and therefore how work-life supports were provided to employees in their
companies. These leaders also influence other senior executives through personal and professional networks. Due to their visibility, status, and spans
of control, others may look to them for clues pertaining to organizational
norms. This has broad implications for work and family because, through
their actions, these men and women influence others regarding behavior
within organizations. Senior leaders were an influential group to study.

The executives I researched (all within three levels of the C-suite) had
responsibility for an array of areas within their companies. Their breadth of
responsibility covered general management, key business units, and lines
of business. Some of them had responsibility for functions such as human
resources, corporate communications, and employee health/wellness areas.
These were key positions in organizations. These were the groups that were
influencing policy, hiring, and practices. I also had the benefit of speaking
with leaders who had responsibility for administration, risk management,
and engineering. No matter their role, I asked the leaders about work-life
supports, and whether they believed that work-life supports had any bearing
on the bottom line.

Finally, it mattered to me whether the executives had children because I
believed their points of view would be affected by their personal life experience. As it turned out, most of them were either empty nesters or had older
children still living at home.

MY OWN NETWORK

A final type of data that I present and synthesize within this book is the
data I've derived from hundreds of executives with whom I have worked
throughout my career. I'm a regular full-time employee, leading a business
unit that works with customers. Through this work, I've been humbled
to connect with a who's who list of clients. Executives have shared details
regarding their perspectives, including those derived from situations of difficulty or adversity, where the most significant learning occurs.

HONEST OPINIONS

A reader should also be aware of the hidden agendas and assumptions the
writer brings to the table. Let me be explicit and honest about my opinions.

One assumption underlying my research is that work and family are interconnected and inseparable. Hence, they should be treated this way for the purposes of study. This approach and the emphasis on relationships between the worlds of work and family are rather new. Often, we've regarded work and family as separate. Some have regarded them as having their own "containers," and researchers have often considered them separately, but profound social change has occurred over the last decades. The boundaries between work and family have become permeable, and spillover has become the norm. Work and family are intertwined at individual, collective, and societal levels. We cannot separate them and have a full picture of reality. Instead, it is necessary that we connect them to understand them fully.

A second assumption behind this study is that work is fundamentally social and reciprocal. I'm a trained sociologist, and from that vantage point, it is clear that individuals shape their work and in turn, work shapes individuals, groups, and society. Organizations are social systems, and they are in a complex, symbiotic relationship with the environments in which they function. They influence each other. Not all work is the same, and different work and workplaces have a range of effects on individuals and families. Here, I focus on corporate, white-collar work. Race and class biases also matter in the way work is distributed, but those are topics for another book.[2]

A third assumption underlying my research is that work provides a critical context for family members. Work affects what men and women earn and in turn, their access to resources. Work also has implications for social networks, including who people know and the friends people have. It affects the support networks they can access and the leisure activities in which they engage. Work also has important effects on physical, emotional, and mental health. It affects the ways people define themselves, the way they are defined by others, and the level of prestige they are afforded. The work-life supports that companies offer have an influence over the work experience of employees, and carry over into the nonwork and family situations they face.

IN SUM

I hold a personal belief that work-life supports are important and valuable to individuals, families, and companies. I believe they help employees more effectively navigate and integrate the numerous demands they face both from work and from personal obligations. I also believe they result in increased engagement and productivity, which is a benefit for companies. In short, I believe that *more* work-life supports, and the appropriate work-life supports, are better for individuals, families, and organizations. They bring work to life and this is a worthwhile endeavor.

MAKING CONTACT

I would love to hear from you. Connect with me via e-mail at tracybrower@ tracybrower.com or via LinkedIn at Tracy Brower, PhD or on Twitter at TracyBrower108. You may also visit my website www.tracybrower.com.

Acknowledgments

If you want to go fast, go alone. If you want to go far, go together.
AFRICAN PROVERB

I've been blessed to have some of the very best companions as we journey far together. To my husband, Terry, thank you for always believing in me and supporting my work and life. I appreciate you every day and we've grown something good. Alexa (Alex to us) and Dylan, you are each a unique treasure and an exquisite gift. We could not be more fortunate than to be a family with you. I admire each of you, and I love you immeasurably. Terry, Alex, and Dylan, thanks for letting me occasionally skate out of my share of the dishes, laundry, and grocery shopping. You made space for my crazy sleep schedule with the 2 a.m. weekend alarm clock, and picked up KFC to feed the unusual craving that the birth of this book provoked. Thanks to my mom for the very best editing, ever. Your precise reading, care-full recommendations, and loving support have contributed hugely to this effort. May we always bifurcate our efforts, keep machines running, and pay attention to culture. If I can provide even a thimble-full of the inspired parenting to Alex and Dylan that you've provided to me, they will be fortunate indeed. As Shinichi Suzuki said, "Where love is deep, all things are possible." My family makes this true.

Thanks to the professionals who believed in this project: John Willig for your brilliant Sherpa guidance on this journey, and Jill Friedlander and Erika Heilman for your professionalism, expertise, and the innovative community of which I am fortunate to be a part. Thanks to Margot Atwell, for your fast turnaround, substantive suggestions, and thinking with me about issues big and small. Thanks to Susan Lauzau for your attention to detail and the quality you've ensured, and to Jill Schoenhaut and Shevaun Betzler for your expertise in shepherding the process. Thanks to those who supported my formal research, allowing me interviews and access during my master's degree and dissertation efforts. Thank you to those at Michigan State University who contributed to my dissertation committee: Dr.

Maryhelen MacInnes, Dr. Barbara Ames, Dr. Cathy Liu, Dr. Nan Johnson, and Dr. Maxine Baca Zinn. Thanks to Rebecca Van Singel for visualizing these concepts, giving them texture and life, even in their pre-book infancy. Thanks to Lisanne for valuable input and perspectives.

Thanks to all the people at Herman Miller with whom I work, think, and conspire every day. Thanks to Brian, Curt, and Greg for the terrific support. Thank you to my team for the hard work, ingenuity, creativity, and dedication. I'm humbled to work with such rock stars. Thanks to you, Holly. We've been at this a long time. Thanks for having my back, teaching me about the best time to plant a tree, and reminding me about the value of critical thinking (If you're not outraged, you're not paying attention!). Thank you to my friend John in Texas, and all the other customers with whom I've been privileged to work. I have a grass-is-always-greener job since I'm always in the place the grass is greener, working with so many tremendous companies and their employees.

Thank you to the experts with whom I share these pages: Brian Walker, Curt Pullen, Greg Parsons, Rick Wartzman, Lisa Brummel, Frank LaRusso, Xavier Unkovic, K.H. Moon, Dr. Dan Denison, Kevin Knebl, Quentin Hardy, Richard Sheridan, and Dr. Paul Zak. Your contributions to this project have brought depth and richness. Thanks to Clark and Kurt. Thanks to Kim, Diane, Rick, and Cynthia who helped me make valuable connections.

In 1997's *As Good as It Gets* (starring Jack Nicholson and Helen Hunt), the characters Melvin and Carol ponder whether this life is indeed as good as it gets. I believe it is. In fact, it couldn't be better, and I am profoundly grateful.

Notes

Foreword

1. Brian Walker was named president and CEO of Herman Miller, Inc., in July 2004. He had served as COO, CFO, and president of Herman Miller North America, overseeing the company's core business operations for the U.S., Canada, and Mexico. He also held various financial management positions in Herman Miller's international operations. Brian was instrumental in the adoption of the Economic Value Added (EVA) financial and performance metric at Herman Miller. He has also strengthened the company's commitment to design and operational excellence. Brian serves on various for-profit and nonprofit boards of directors. His interests include biking, skiing, and the martial arts. He lives with his wife, Colleen, and three children in Holland, Michigan.

Introduction

1. Lauren Sandler, "None Is Enough," *Time,* August 2013, 38–45.
2. Peter Drucker (1909–2005) was an author, consultant, and educator on the topic of management. He is commonly known as the father of modern management and contributed to philosophy and practice of management in Japan, the United States, and worldwide.
3. James T. Bond, Cindy Thompson, Ellen Galinsky, and David Prottas, "Highlights of the National Study of the Changing Workforce Executive Summary," No. 3, Families and Work Institute (2002), http://familiesandwork.org/site/research/summary/nscw2002summ.pdf, 3.
4. Steve Crabtree and Jennifer Robison, "Engaged Workplaces Are Engines of Job Creation," *Gallup Business Journal,* October 8, 2013, accessed December 10, 2013, http://business journal.gallup.com/content/165233/engaged-workplaces-engines-job-creation.aspx? utm_source=WWW&utm_medium=csm&utm_campaign=syndication.
5. Crabtree and Robison, "Engaged Workplaces Are Engines of Job Creation."
6. "Video produced for the Focus on Flexibility Conference," Alfred Sloan Foundation, accessed December 1, 2013, www.youtube.com/watch?v=dgz879Oqnos#t=308.
7. The Family and Medical Insurance Leave Act seeks to make more of this leave paid. See http://www.nationalpartnership.org/issues/work-family/family-act.html for more details.
8. Updates to FMLA include reduction of required forms, inclusion of veterans, inclusion of adult children, and modification of rules for use by airline staff and crew (Allen Smith, "Family Leave Turns 20; DOL Modifies Rules," *HR Magazine,* March 2013, 11).
9. Susan J. Wells, "Benefits Strategies Grow and HR Leads the Way," *HR Magazine,* March 2013, 25–34.
10. While I have worked with multiple executives in diverse countries, this book focuses only on U.S. companies and their practices.

Chapter 1

1. The Carl Frost Center for Social Science Research of Hope College in Holland, Michigan, seeks to provide its clients, faculty, and students with diverse research and analysis capabilities that are accurate, accessible, and practical for the shaping of informed decisions.

2. Patricia Voydanoff, "Toward a Conceptualization of Perceived Work-Family Fit and Balance: A Demands and Resources Approach," *Journal of Marriage and Family* 67 (2005): 822-836.

3. "The All-Out War for Good Jobs," *Gallup Business Journal*, accessed December 8, 2013, http://businessjournal.gallup.com/content/151856/War-Good-Jobs.aspx#2.

4. Ellen Galinsky et al.,"Workplace Flexibility: From Research to Action," *The Future of Children*, vol. 21, no. 2 (2011): 141–181.

Chapter 2

1. "Stress in America," American Psychological Association, accessed July 16, 2013, www.apa.org/pubs/info/reports/2007-stress.doc.

2. Catherine Albiston, "Flexibility for Families that Work," *The San Francisco Chronicle*, July 18, 2013, http://www.sfchronicle.com/opinion/openforum/article/Flexibility-for-families-that-work-4673786.php?t=f4af459dcbcefdcb88&utm_source=Members&utm_campaign=bb97031780-RSS_EMAIL_CAMPAIGN&utm_medium=email&utm_term=0_a79b9ce96e-bb97031780-22098421.

3. "Our Story," Herman Miller, http://www.hermanmiller.com/about-us/who-is-herman-miller/our-story.html

4. Karl Marx and Friedrich Engels, "Economic and Philosophic Manuscripts of 1844," in *Collected Works, Volume 3* (New York: International Publishers, 1884).

5. "American Psychological Association Press Releases," American Psychological Association, accessed August 9, 2013, http://www.apa.org/news/press/releases/stress-exec-summary.pdf.

6. "American Psychological Association Press Releases."

7. "American Psychological Association Press Releases."

8. "American Psychological Association Press Releases."

9. P.J. Rosch, "The Quandry of Job Stress Compensation," *Health and Stress*, March (2001): 1–4.

10. Crabtree and Robison, "Engaged Workplaces Are Engines of Job Creation," *Gallup Business Journal,* October 8, 2013, accessed December 10, 2013, http://businessjournal.gallup.com/content/165233/engaged-workplaces-engines-job-creation.aspx?utm_source=WWW&utm_medium=csm&utm_campaign=syndication.

11. Jim Clifton, "High Energy Workplaces Can Save America," *Gallup Business Journal*, December 14 (2011), accessed December 8, 2013, http://businessjournal.gallup.com/content/150710/High-Energy-Workplaces-Save-America.aspx.

12. Jay Deragon, "Being Human Creates Higher Returns," *The Relationship Economy*, October 29, 2013, accessed December 8, 2013, http://www.relationship-economy.com/2013/10/being-human-creates-higher-returns/.

13. "The How Report," LRN.com, accessed December 20, 2013, http://www.lrn.com/how metrics/data/LRNHowReport2012.pdf.

14. Rick Wartzman is the executive director of Claremont Graduate University's Drucker Institute, a social enterprise with the mission of "strengthening organizations to strengthen society." It does this, in large part, by turning the ideas and ideals of the late Peter F. Drucker into tools that are both practical and inspiring. Wartzman is a former reporter and editor at the *Wall Street Journal* and *Los Angeles Times*. He is columnist for *Time* magazine online; author of three books, including two narrative histories and a collection of his columns called *What Would Drucker Do Now?*; and the editor of *The Drucker Lectures: Essential Lessons in Management, Society, and Economy.* He lives in Los Angeles, CA.

15. Rick Wartzman, interview by the author, December 18, 2013.

16. Peter Fleming, "The Birth of Biocracy," in *Reinventing Hierarchy and Bureaucracy: From the Bureau to Network Organizations*, by Thomas Diefenbach and Rune Todnem (Bingley, UK: Emerald Group Publishing, 2012), 205-227.

Chapter 3

1. According to an HBR study in 2011 examining 180 firms over eighteen years, those which focused most on sustainability and environmental efforts returned the greatest share prices and earnings to their shareholders. ("A Green Light," *The Economist*, March 29, 2014.)
2. Ellen Galinsky et al., "Overwork in America: When the Way We Work Becomes Too Much," Families and Work Institute (2005), accessed August 10, 2013, http://familiesandwork.org/site/research/summary/overwork2005summ.pdf.
3. J.T Bond et al., "Executive Summary of the National Study of the Changing Workforce, 2002," Families and Work Institute, accessed September 8, 2013, http://familiesandwork.org/site/research/summary/nscw2002summ.pdf.
4. Christina Passariello, "The Hand Embroiderer's Tale," *The Wall Street Journal Magazine*, October 2013: 114-117.
5. In Singapore, it takes people an average of 10.5 seconds to traverse 60 feet. In Bahrain, it takes 18 seconds. In Malawi, it takes 31 seconds. People walk faster in developed versus developing cultures and people walk fastest in the biggest cities. ("Fairy Creatures," *The Economist*, April 5, 2014.)
6. Jamie Lee Curtis and Laura Cornell, *Is There Really a Human Race?* (New York: Harper Collins, 2006)
7. Jessi Hempel, "IBM's Massive Bet on Watson," *Fortune*, October 7, 2013, 82.
8. Chris Gile and Kate Allen, "Southeastern Shift: The New Leaders of Global Economic Growth," *Financial Times*, June 4, 2013.
9. "Yellowstone Park Foundation," Herman Miller, January 2, 2012, accessed January 3, 2012. http://www.hermanmiller.com/research/case-studies/yellowstone-park-foundation.html.
10. This book is admittedly focused on the higher skilled, white-collar world of work.
11. "Class in America: Mobility Measured," *The Economist*, February 1, 2014, 23.
12. "Is College Worth It?," *The Economist*, April 5, 2014.
13. "How to Look Into the Future," *Fast Company*, November 2013, 22.

Chapter 4

1. Third places are locations such as coffee shops that are frequently used for off-site work but are not specifically designed for that purpose. Fourth places are locations that are specifically designed for offsite work such as work clubs or business centers.
2. Milton Moskowitz and Robert Levering, "The 100 Best Companies to Work For," *Fortune*, February 3, 2014, 118.
3. George F. Dreher "Breaking the Glass Ceiling: The Effects of Sex Ratios and Work-Life Programs on Female Leadership at the Top," *Human Relations*, vol. 56, no. 5 (2003): 541-562.

Chapter 5

1. Ellen Galinsky et al., "Workplace Flexibility: From Research to Action," *The Future of Children*, vol. 21, no. 2 (2011): 141–181.
2. Greg Parsons is vice president, New Landscape of Work at Herman Miller and leads the team developing Living Office: new product, knowledge, and service strategies. Greg also leads the effort to build an offer of products and solutions to enrich users' experiences with technology. At Herman Miller, Greg is pursuing his interest in people and work and the greatest potential of both. Previously, Greg was a principal with Stone Yamashita Partners leading business, brand, and innovation efforts for a variety of Fortune 500 clients. Greg also ran his own consultancy where he helped clients create transformative brands and customer offerings. Greg holds an MBA in strategic management from the University of Chicago, and a BA and BFA from Cornell University.
3. Greg Parsons, interview by the author, April 18, 2014.

4. I will use terms like business "outcomes," "results," and "benefits" interchangeably.

5. K.H. Moon is president of the New Paradigm Institute of Korea, a former member of the Korean National Assembly, a member of the Drucker Institute Advisory Board, and past chairman and CEO of Yuhan-Kimberly. Under Moon's leadership, Yuhan-Kimberly, a consumer products company and joint venture between Yuhan Corporation and Kimberly-Clark, became widely known for product innovation, a commitment to lifelong learning opportunities, a family-friendly corporate culture, considerate care of employees, and a flexible working environment. Moon was lauded for avoiding worker layoffs during the Asian financial crisis of the mid-1990s. As a result of Moon's leadership, Yuhan-Kimberly has won many accolades, including in 2011 being named a "Great Place to Work in Korea" by the Great Places to Work Institute and one of "Korea's Most Admired Companies" by *Fortune Magazine*. In addition, Moon himself was voted the most admired CEO of Korea by *Fortune*. Moon is also known for his environmental leadership, through which he has led efforts to plant fifty million trees in Korea and throughout Asia. Moon formed the Creative Korea Party in 2007 and was elected to the Korean National Assembly in 2008.

6. K.H. Moon, interview by the author, January 6, 2014.

7. Scott Leibs and Alessandra Petlin, "You Can Buy Happiness," *Inc.* magazine, December 2013–January 2014, 109–112.

8. Lisa Brummel is the chief people officer at Microsoft and has led human resources since May 2005. Before leading HR, Brummel held a number of leadership roles across the company, including management, marketing, and leadership of the Home & Retail Division. Brummel is the co-owner of the WNBA Seattle Storm franchise and is active in charitable ventures such as Homelink. Brummel earned her bachelor's degree in sociology from Yale University and her MBA from the University of California.

9. Lisa Brummel, interview by the author, January 21, 2014.

10. Brummel, interview by the author.

11. "Video produced for the Focus on Flexibility Conference," Alfred Sloan Foundation, accessed December 1, 2013, www.youtube.com/watch?v=dgz879Oqnos#t=308.

12. "Video produced for the Focus on Flexibility Conference."

13. Rick Wartzman, interview by the author, December 18, 2013.

14. Shawn Achor, *The Happiness Advantage* (New York: Random House, 2010).

15. Naomi Simson, "Productivity Hacks: Happy People are Productive People," LinkedIn, January 21, 2014, accessed January 22, 2014, http://www.linkedin.com/today/post/article/20140121000342-1291685-productivity-hacks-happy-people-are-productive-people?trk=eml-mktg-inf-m-productivity-0121-p5.

16. Simson, "Productivity Hacks."

17. Adam Waytz and Malia Mason, "Your Brain at Work: What a New Approach to Neuroscience Can Teach Us About Management," *Harvard Business Review*, July–August 2013, 103–111.

18. Paul J. Zak, *The Moral Molecule: The Source of Love and Prosperity* (New York: Penguin, 2012).

19. Paul J. Zak, professor, Claremont Graduate University, interview by the author, December 13, 2013.

20. Xavier Unkovic is the global president for Mars Drinks, a Mars, Inc. company. Based out of the global headquarters in West Chester, PA, Xavier develops and drives the Drinks business strategy, delivering key commitments to Mars, Inc., and providing leadership around associate engagement.

21. Xavier Unkovic, interview by the author, January 3, 2014.

22. Unkovic, interview by the author.

23. Milton Moskowitz and Robert Levering, "The 100 Best Companies to Work For," *Fortune*, February 3, 2014, 118.

24. Unkovic, interview by the author.
25. "American Psychological Association Press Releases," American Psychological Association, accessed August 9, 2013, http://www.apa.org/news/press/releases/stress-exec-summary.pdf.
26. Jacob Morgan, *Forbes*, October 1, 2013, accessed October 12, 2013, http://www.forbes.com/sites/jacobmorgan/2013/10/01/8-indisputable-reasons-for-why-we-dont-need-offices/.
27. Martin Jacknis, "The Art of Hiring '10s,'" *Inc.* magazine, October 1, 1987.
28. Darren Hardy, "Your Hiring Goal: 'To Be the Dumbest One in the Room,'" Monster, accessed October 1, 2013, http://hiring.monster.com/hr/hr-best-practices/recruiting-hiring-advice/attracting-job-candidates/recruiting-hiring.aspx.
29. "The How Report," LRN.com, accessed December 20, 2013, http://www.lrn.com/howmetrics/data/LRNHowReport2012.pdf.
30. Wartzman, interview by the author.
31. Galinsky et al., "2008 National Study of Employers," Families and Work Institute, http://familiesandwork.org/site/research/reports/2008nse.pdf.
32. Brummel, interview by the author.

Chapter 7

1. Yoni Assia, "MIT research shows that eToro can beat the Market with Social Trading," yoniassia.com, May 14, 2012, accessed January 11, 2014, http://yoniassia.com/mit-research-shows-that-etoro-can-beat-the-market-with-social-trading/.
2. Kevin Knebl, author and professional speaker, interview by the author, December 18, 2013.

Chapter 8

1. There is a similar quote typically attributed to William Gibson: "The future has already arrived, it's just not evenly distributed yet," (Quote Investigator, January 24, 2012, accessed January 11, 2014, http://quoteinvestigator.com/2012/01/24/future-has-arrived/).
2. https://www.youtube.com/watch?v=HeqEDHBBXRg
3. "No Workaholics Allowed," *Inc.* magazine, February 2014, 54.
4. For more on the Internet of things and the security concerns it raises see "Spam in the Fridge," *The Economist*, January 25, 2014.
5. "Sex and Brains: Vive la Difference!" *The Economist*, December 7, 2013, 81–82.
6. Matt McFarland, "How iBeacons Could Change the World Forever," *The Washington Post*, January 7, 2014, http://www.washingtonpost.com/blogs/innovations/wp/2014/01/07/how-ibeacons-could-change-the-world-forever/.
7. Parking assist on cars is another example. As cars begin to do our parallel parking for us, we will likely lose this skill.
8. Quentin Hardy, deputy technology editor, the *New York Times*, interview by the author, December 24, 2013.

Chapter 9

1. Xavier Unkovic, interview by the author, January 3, 2014.
2. For more on this topic, see Rob Kirkbride, "Screen Time," *Monday Morning Quarterback*, March 5–11, 2012.
3. Tracy Brower, "Workplace Environments That Improve Business Outcomes: Re-Thinking the Traditional Office Layout," *The Voice*, July 2012, 14.
4. Frank LaRusso is the vice president of business development at Mars Drinks. During his twenty-three-year career with Mars, Frank held positions in sales and marketing and led the research which resulted in the launch of FLAVIA® Beverage Systems business unit (now Mars Drinks). He helps cultivate the B2B national account distributor network and leads commercial real estate for North America.

5. Lawrence E. Williams and John A. Bargh. "Experiencing Physical Warmth Promotes Interpersonal Warmth," *Science*, vol. 322, no. 5901 (2008): 606-607.

6. Sally Augustin, "Coffee and Tea Stations—They're Not Amenities But Necessities," *officeinsight*, December 9, 2013, 15.

7. Veronica Roth, *Allegiant* (New York: HarperCollins, 2013).

8. David Sokol, "Let's Move!" *GreenSource*, July 2013, accessed July 30, 2013, http://green source.construction.com/features/currents/2013/1307-lets-move.asp.

9. Phil Mobley, "Designed to Be Effective," *BOMA Magazine*, November/December 2013, 24–27.

10. For more on this topic, see James R. Hagety and Ben Kesling, "Say Goodbye to the Office Cubicle: Walls Come Down as Many Companies Switch to Layouts Designed to Foster Collaboration," *The Wall Street Journal*, April 2, 2013.

11. For more on this topic, see Rob Kirkbride, "Is Teleworking Over?" *Monday Morning Quarterback*, March 11–17, 2013.

12. Rachel Emma Silverman, "Tracking Sensors Invade the Workplace: Devices on Workers, Furniture Offer Clues for Boosting Productivity," *The Wall Street Journal*, March 7, 2013.

13. Tracy Brower, "Reality Check: Making Data-Driven Decisions to Optimize Your Workplace," *Area Development*, June 25, 2013, accessed June 26, 2013, http://www.areadevelop ment.com/siteSelection/Q3-2013/data-driven-decisions-optimize-workspace-152242413.shtml.

14. The research term for this is "face validity."

15. Edward Ross, "The Mob Mind," *Popular Science Monthly,* vol. 51 (1897): 390–398.

16. Tracy Brower, "Executive Viewpoints: Work-Life Supports = Organizational Results," *The Leader*, May/June 2012, 12–16.

Chapter 10

1. Lisa Brummel, interview by the author, January 21, 2014.

2. Robert Cialdini, *Influence: The Psychology of Persuasion* (New York: William Morrow and Company, 1984).

Chapter 11

1. "Moving Mindsets on Gender Diversity: McKinsey Global Survey Results," McKinsey & Company, January 2014, accessed January 22, 2014, http://www.mckinsey.com/Insights/ Organization/Moving_mind-sets_on_gender_diversity_McKinsey_Global_Survey_ results?cid=other-eml-alt-mip-mck-oth-1401.

2. Sangeeta Badal, "The Business Benefits of Gender Diversity," Gallup Business Journal, January 20, 2014, accessed January 22, 2014, http://businessjournal.gallup.com/content/ 166220/business-benefits-gender-diversity.aspx?utm_source=WWW&utm_medium= csm&utm_campaign=syndication.

3. "Women Matter 2013—Gender diversity in top management: Moving corporate culture, moving boundaries," McKinsey & Company, http://www.mckinsey.com/~/media/McKinsey/ dotcom/homepage/2012_March_Women_Matter/PDF/WomenMatter%202013%20 Report.ashx.

4. The practices included: 1) measure diversity and inclusion, 2) hold managers accountable, 3) support flexible work arrangements, 4) recruit and promote from diverse pools of candidates, 5) provide leadership education, 6) sponsor employee resource groups and mentoring programs, 7) offer quality role models, 8) make chief diversity officer position count (Boris Groysberg and Katherine Connelly, "Great Leaders Who Make the Mix Work," *Harvard Business Review*, September 2013, 68–76.).

5. Groysberg and Connelly, "Great Leaders."

6. "Moving Mindsets on Gender Diversity."

7. "Moving Mindsets on Gender Diversity."

8. Ellen Galinsky, *Ask the Children: The Breakthrough Study That Reveals How to Succeed at Work and Parenting* (New York: William Morrow and Company, Inc., 1999).

9. "Sex and Brains: Vive la Difference!," *The Economist*, December 7, 2013, 81–82.

10. Arlie Hochschild, *The Second Shift* (New York: Viking, 1989).

11. "Video produced for the Focus on Flexibility Conference," Alfred Sloan Foundation, accessed December 1, 2013, www.youtube.com/watch?v=dgz879Oqnos#t=308.

12. Herminia Ibarra, Robin Ely, and Deborah Kolb, "Women Rising: The Unseen Barriers," *Harvard Business Review*, September 2013, 61–66.

13. Sheryl Sandberg, *Lean In: Women, Work, and the Will to Lead* (New York: Alfred A. Knopf, 2013).

14. Adil Ignatius, "Where Are the Female Leaders?" *Harvard Business Review*, September 2013, 12.

15. Christine Silva, Nancy Carter, and Anna Beninger, "And the Plumb Assignment Goes To ..." *Harvard Business Review*, September, 2013, 87.

16. Lauren Sandler, "None Is Enough," *Time*, August 12, 2013, 38–45.

17. Kathleen Gerson, *No Man's Land: Men's Changing Commitments to Family and Work* (New York: Basic Books, 1993).

18. Gerson, *No Man's Land*.

19. Nicholas W. Townsend, *The Package Deal: Marriage, Work, anf Fatherhood in Men's Lives* (Philadelphia: Temple University Press, 2002).

Chapter 12

1. "The All-Out War for Good Jobs," *Gallup Business Journal*, accessed December 8, 2013, http://businessjournal.gallup.com/content/151856/War-Good-Jobs.aspx#2.

2. Nicholas Bloom, "To Raise Productivity, Let More Employees Work from Home," *Harvard Business Review*, January/February 2014, 28–29.

3. Martha Sinetar, *Do What You Love, the Money Will Follow: Discovering Your Right Livelihood* (New York: Dell, 1987).

4. Rick Wartzman, interview by the author, December 18, 2013.

5. K.H. Moon, interview by the author, January 6, 2014.

6. Moon, interview by the author.

7. Xavier Unkovic, interview by the author, January 3, 2014.

8. Curt Pullen is president of Herman Miller North America, and prior to this role he was the executive vice president and chief financial officer for Herman Miller. Previously, Curt served in various executive roles at the company including SVP of dealer distribution and SVP of finance. Curt has been with Herman Miller since 1991. He is a CPA and practiced at BDO Seidman before joining Herman Miller. Curt is also a veteran of the U.S. Air Force and is a pilot. Curt is also chairman of the board for the Drucker Institute.

9. Curt Pullen, interview by the author, January 16, 2014.

10. Unkovic, interview by the author.

11. Jessi Hempel, "How to Craft an Artsy, Homegrown Culture," *Fortune*, September 19, 2013, 27.

Chapter 13

1. I'm using the terms "work team leader," "manager," and "supervisor" synonymously.

2. Curt Pullen, interview by the author, January 16, 2014.

3. K.H. Moon, interview by the author, January 6, 2014.

4. Moon, interview by the author.

5. Rick Wartzman, interview by the author, December 18, 2013.

6. Kevin Sharer, "How Should Your Leaders Behave," *Harvard Business Review*, October 2013, 40.

Chapter 14

1. Tom Rath, *Vital Friends: The People You Can't Afford to Live Without* (New York: Gallup Press, 2006).

Chapter 15

1. Sheryl Sandberg, *Lean In: Women, Work, and the Will to Lead* (New York: Alfred A. Knopf, 2013), 100.
2. *Terroir* is the set of special characteristics that uniquely define the geography, geology and climate of a certain place.
3. Richard Sheridan, CEO and cofounder of Menlo Innovations, interview by the author, March 27, 2014.
4. Xavier Unkovic, interview by the author, January 3, 2014.
5. Daniel Denison, Robert Hooijberg, Nancy Lane, and Colleen Lief, *Leading Culture Change in Global Organizations: Aligning Culture and Strategy* (San Francisco: Jossey-Bass, 2012).
6. Ehssan Abdallah and Ashish Ahluwalia. "The Keys to Building a High Performance Culture," *Gallup Business Journal*, December 12, 2012, accessed December 11, 2013, http://businessjournal.gallup.com/content/166208/keys-building-high-performance-culture.aspx?utm_source=WWW&utm_medium=csm&utm_campaign=syndication.
7. Daniel Denison, founder, Denison Consulting, interview by the author, December 10, 2013.
8. John P. Kotter and James L. Heskett, *Corporate Culture and Performance* (New York: The Free Press, 1992).

Chapter 16

1. Curt Pullen, interview by the author, January 16, 2014.
2. Ram Charan, "You Can't Be a Wimp—Make the Tough Calls," interview by Melinda Merino, *Harvard Business Review*, November 2013, 73–78.

Chapter 17

1. Beth Jarman and George Land, *Breakpoint and Beyond* (New York: Harpercollins, 1992).
2. Some people refer to this as the WIFM (What's In It For Me).
3. While similar, this model is not to be confused with Kubler-Ross's model, which includes the process for grief including stages of denial, anger, bargaining, depression, and acceptance.
4. Joshua Cooper Ramo, *The Age of the Unthinkable: Why the New World Disorder Constantly Surprises Us and What We Can Do About It* (New York: Back Bay Books, 2010).
5. Not that any but the most sadistic would try this.
6. Tracy Brower, "The Transparent Office," *The Drucker Institute Blog*, May 16, 2013, accessed May 17, 2013, http://thedx.druckerinstitute.com/2013/05/the-transparent-office/.
7. "From Cuckolds to Captains," *The Economist*, December 7, 2013, 72.

Conclusion

1. While Twain is often credited with the pithy phrase, it is actually from French mathematician and theologian Blaise Pascal who said, "I would have written a shorter letter, but I did not have the time."

Appendix

1. For more on this topic, see Brower, "How Single Mothers Survive in Poverty," in *Diversity in Families*, by Maxine Baca Zinn, D. Stanley Eitzen and Barbara Wells (Boston: Allyn & Bacon, 2011), 147.

References

Abdallah, Ehssan and Ashish Ahluwalia. "The Keys to Building a High Performance Culture." *Gallup Business Journal*, December 12, 2012. Accessed December 11, 2013. http://businessjournal.gallup.com/content/166208/keys-building-high-performance-culture.aspx?utm_source=WWW&utm_medium=csm&utm_campaign=syndication.

Achor, Shawn. *The Happiness Advantage*. New York: Random House, 2010.

"A Green Light." *The Economist*, March 29, 2014.

Albiston, Catherine. "Flexibility for Families that Work." *The San Francisco Chronicle*, July 18, 2013. http://www.sfchronicle.com/opinion/openforum/article/Flexibility-for-families-that-work-4673786.php?t=f4af459dcbcefdcb88&utm_source=Members&utm_campaign=bb97031780-RSS_EMAIL_CAMPAIGN&utm_medium=email&utm_term=0_a79b9ce96e-bb97031780-22098421.

Alfred Sloan Foundation. "Video produced for the Focus on Flexibility Conference." Accessed December 1, 2013, www.youtube.com/watch?v=dgz879Oqnos#t=308.

American Psychological Association. "American Psychological Association Press Releases." Accessed August 9, 2013. http://www.apa.org/news/press/releases/stress-exec-summary.pdf.

―――. "APA Announces 2013 Psychologically Healthy Workplace Award Winners." March 6, 2013. Accessed January 10, 2014. http://www.apaexcellence.org/resources/goodcompany/newsletter/article/423.

―――. "Stress in America." Accessed July 16, 2013. www.apa.org/pubs/info/reports/2007-stress.doc 2007.

Assia, Yoni. "MIT research shows that eToro can beat the Market with Social Trading." yoniassia.com, May 14, 2012. Accessed January 11, 2014. http://yoniassia.com/mit-research-shows-that-etoro-can-beat-the-market-with-social-trading/.

Augustin, Sally. "Coffee and Tea Stations—They're Not Amenities But Necessities." officeinsight, December 9, 2013.

Badal, Sangeeta. "The Business Benefits of Gender Diversity." *Gallup Business Journal*, January 20, 2014. Accessed January 22, 2014. http://businessjournal.gallup.com/content/166220/business-benefits-gender-diversity.aspx?utm_source=WWW&utm_medium=csm&utm_campaign=syndication.

Bloom, Nicholas. "To Raise Productivity, Let More Employees Work from Home," *Harvard Business Review*, January/February 2014.

Bond, J.T., C. Thompson, E. Galinsky, and D. Prottas. "Executive Summary of the National Study of the Changing Workforce, 2002," Families and Work Institute. Accessed September 8, 2013. http://familiesandwork.org/site/research/summary/nscw2002summ.pdf.

Brower, Tracy. "Executive Viewpoints: Work-Life Supports = Organizational Results," *The Leader*, May/June 2012.

―――. "How Single Mothers Survive in Poverty," in *Diversity in Families*, by Maxine Baca Zinn, D. Stanley Eitzen and Barbara Wells (Boston: Allyn & Bacon, 2011).

―――. "Reality Check: Making Data-Driven Decisions to Optimize Your Workplace," Area Development, June 25, 2013. Accessed June 26, 2013, http://www.areadevelopment.com/siteSelection/Q3-2013/data-driven-decisions-optimize-workspace-152242413.shtml.

―――. "The Transparent Office." *The Drucker Institute Blog*, May 16, 2013. Accessed May 17, 2013, http://thedx.druckerinstitute.com/2013/05/the-transparent-office/.

————. "Workplace Environments That Improve Business Outcomes: Re-Thinking the Traditional Office Layout," *The Voice*, July 2012.

Brummel, Lisa (chief people officer, Microsoft), interview by the author, January 21, 2014.

"CEO Succession: Making the right choices." Spencer Stuart. May 2011. Accessed December 10, 2013. https://www.spencerstuart.com/research-and-insight/ceo-succession-making-the-right-choices-uk.

Charan, Ram. "You Can't Be a Wimp—Make the Tough Calls." Interview by Melinda Merino. *Harvard Business Review*, November 2013.

Cialdini, Robert. *Influence: The Psychology of Persuasion*. New York: William Morrow and Company, 1984.

Clifton, Jim. "High Energy Workplaces Can Save America." *Gallup Business Journal*, December 14, 2011. Accessed December 8, 2013, http://businessjournal.gallup.com/content/150710/High-Energy-Workplaces-Save-America.aspx.

"Class in America: Mobility Measured." *The Economist*, February 1, 2014.

Crabtree, Steve, and Jennifer Robison. "Engaged Workplaces Are Engines of Job Creation." *Gallup Business Journal*, October 8, 2013. Accessed December 10, 2013, http://businessjournal.gallup.com/content/165233/engaged-workplaces-engines-job-creation.aspx?utm_source=WWW&utm_medium=csm&utm_campaign=syndication.

Curtis, Jamie Lee, and Laura Cornell. *Is There Really a Human Race?* New York: Harper Collins, 2006.

Denison, Daniel (founder, Denison Consulting), interview by the author, December 10, 2013.

Denison, Daniel, Robert Hooijberg, Nancy Lane, and Colleen Lief. 2012. *Leading Culture Change in Global Organizations: Aligning Culture and Strategy*. San Francisco: Jossey-Bass, 2012.

Deragon, Jay. "Being Human Creates Higher Returns." *The Relationship Economy*, October 29, 2013. Accessed December 8, 2013, http://www.relationship-economy.com/2013/10/being-human-creates-higher-returns/.

Dreher, George F. "Breaking the Glass Ceiling: The Effects of Sex Ratios and Work-Life Programs on Female Leadership at the Top." *Human Relations*, vol. 56, no. 5 (2003): 541-562.

"How to Look Into the Future," *Fast Company*, November 2013.

"Fairy Creatures." *The Economist*, April 5, 2014.

Fleming, Peter. "The Birth of Biocracy." In *Reinventing Hierarchy and Bureaucracy: From the Bureau to Network Organizations*, by Thomas Diefenbach and Rune Todnem (Bingley, UK: Emerald Group Publishing, 2012).

"From Cuckolds to Captains." *The Economist*, December 7, 2013.

Galinsky, Ellen. *Ask the Children: The Breakthrough Study That Reveals How to Succeed at Work and Parenting*. New York: William Morrow and Company, Inc., 1999.

Galinsky, Ellen, James T. Bond, Kelly Sakai, Stacy S. Kim, and Nicole Giuntoli. "2008 National Study of Employers." Families and Work Institute. http://familiesandwork.org/site/research/reports/2008nse.pdf.

Galinsky, Ellen, James T. Bond, S.S. Kim, L. Backon, E. Brownfield, and K. Sakai. 2005. "Overwork in America: When the Way We Work Becomes Too Much." Families and Work. Accessed August 10, 2013. http://familiesandwork.org/site/research/summary/overwork2005summ.pdf.

Galinsky, Ellen, Kelly Sakai, and Tyler Wigton. "Workplace Flexibility: From Research to Action," *The Future of Children*, vol. 21, no. 2 (2011): 141-181.

Gerson, Kathleen. *No Man's Land: Men's Changing Commitments to Family and Work*. New York: Basic Books, 1993.

Giles, Chris, and Kate Allen. "Southeastern Shift: The New Leaders of Global Economic Growth." *Financial Times*, June 4, 2013.

Groysberg, Boris, and Katherine Connelly. "Great Leaders Who Make the Mix Work." *Harvard Business Review*, September 2013.

Hagerty, James R., and Ben Kesling. "Say Goodbye to the Office Cubicle: Walls Come Down as Many Companies Switch to Layouts Designed to Foster Collaboration." *The Wall Street Journal*, April 2, 2013.

Hardy, Darren. "Your Hiring Goal: 'To Be the Dumbest One in the Room,'" Monster. Accessed October 1, 2013. http://hiring.monster.com/hr/hr-best-practices/recruiting-hiring-advice/attracting-job-candidates/recruiting-hiring.aspx.

Hardy, Quentin (deputy technology editor, the *New York Times*), interview by the author, December 24, 2013.

Heller, Steven. "Reputations: Bruce Mau." *Eye Magazine*. Winter 2000. Accessed September 10, 2013. http://www.eyemagazine.com/feature/article/reputations-bruce-mau.

Hempel, Jessi. "How to Craft an Artsy, Homegrown Culture." *Fortune*, September 19, 2013.

———. "IBM's Massive Bet on Watson." *Fortune*, October 7, 2013.

Hochschild, Arlie. *The Second Shift*. New York: Viking, 1989.

Ibarra, Herminia, Robin Ely, and Deborah Kolb. "Women Rising: The Unseen Barriers." *Harvard Business Review*, September 2013.

Ignatius, Adil. "Where Are the Female Leaders?" *Harvard Business Review*, September 2013.

Inc. magazine. 2014. "No Workaholics Allowed." *Inc.*, February: 54.

"Is College Worth It?" *The Economist*, April 5, 2014.

Jacknis, Martin. "The Art of Hiring '10s,'" *Inc.* magazine, October 1, 1987.

Kirkbride, Rob. "Is Teleworking Over?" *Monday Morning Quarterback*, March 11–17, 2013.

———. "Screen Time." *Monday Morning Quarterback*, March 5–11, 2012.

Knebl, Kevin (author and professional speaker), interview by the author, December 18, 2013.

Kotter, John P., and James L. Heskett. *Corporate Culture and Performance*. New York: The Free Press, 1992.

Land, George and Beth Jarman. *Breakpoint and Beyond: Mastering the Future Today*. New York: Harpercollins, 1992.

LaRusso, Frank (senior business development director), interview by the author, January 3, 2014.

Leibs, Scott, and Alessandra Petlin. "You Can Buy Happiness." *Inc.* magazine, December 2013–January 2014.

Marx, Karl, and Friedrich Engels. "Economic and Philosophic Manuscripts of 1844." In *Collected Works, Volume 3*, by Karl Marx and Friedrich Engels. New York: International Publishers, 1884.

McCracken, Grant (research affiliate, MIT), interview by the author, January 3, 2014.

McFarland, Matt. "How iBeacons Could Change the World Forever" *The Washington Post*, January 7, 2014. http://www.washingtonpost.com/blogs/innovations/wp/2014/01/07/how-ibeacons-could-change-the-world-forever/.

Mobley, Phil. "Designed to Be Effective." *BOMA Magazine*, November/December 2013.

Moon, K.H. (president, New Paradigm Institute of Korea), interview by the author, January 6, 2014.

Morgan, Jacob. 2013. *Forbes*. October 1. Accessed October 12, 2013. http://www.forbes.com/sites/jacobmorgan/2013/10/01/8-indisputable-reasons-for-why-we-dont-need-offices/.

Moskowitz, Milton, and Robert Levering. "The 100 Best Companies to Work For." *Fortune*, February 3, 2014.

"Moving Mindsets on Gender Diversity: McKinsey Global Survey Results." McKinsey & Company, January 2014. Accessed January 22, 2014. http://www.mckinsey.com/Insights/Organization/Moving_mind-sets_on_gender_diversity_McKinsey_Global_Survey_results?cid=other-eml-alt-mip-mck-oth-1401.

"Move Over, Siri." *The Economist Technology Quarterly*, November 30, 2013.

Parsons, Greg (vice president of Landscape Environments and Living office), interview by the author, April 18, 2014.

Passariello, Christina. "The Hand Embroiderer's Tale." *The Wall Street Journal Magazine*, October 2013.

Pullen, Curt (President, Herman Miller North America and chairman of the board for the Drucker Institute), interview by the author, January 16, 2014.

Ramo, Joshua Cooper. *The Age of the Unthinkable: Why the New World Disorder Constantly Surprises Us And What We Can Do About It*. New York: Back Bay Books, 2010.

Rath, Tom. *Vital Friends: The People You Can't Afford to Live Without*. New York: Gallup Press, 2006.

"Remote Workers Log More Hours and Are Slightly More Engaged." *The Gallup Blog*, July 12, 2013. Accessed January 19, 2014. http://thegallupblog.gallup.com/2013/07/remote-workers-log-more-hours-and-are.html.

Rosch, P.J. "The Quandry of Job Stress Compensation." *Health and Stress*, March (2001): 1-4.

Ross, Edward. "The Mob Mind," *Popular Science Monthly*, vol. 51 (1897): 390–398.

Roth, Veronica. *Allegiant*. New York: HarperCollins, 2013.

Sandberg, Sheryl. *Lean In: Women, Work, and the Will to Lead*. New York: Alfred A. Knopf, 2013.

Sandler, Lauren. "None Is Enough." *Time*, August 12, 2013.

"Sex and Brains: Vive la Difference!" *The Economist*, December 7, 2013.

Sharer, Kevin. "How Should Your Leaders Behave." *Harvard Business Review*, October 2013.

Sheridan, Richard (CEO and cofounder, Menlo Innovations), interview by the author, March 27, 2014.

Silva, Christine, Nancy Carter, and Anna Beninger. "And the Plumb Assignment Goes To..." *Harvard Business Review*, September 2013.

Silverman, Rachel Emma. "Tracking Sensors Invade the Workplace: Devices on Workers, Furniture Offer Clues for Boosting Productivity." *The Wall Street Journal*, March 7, 2013.

Simmel, Georg. "The Metropolis of Modern Life." In *Simmel: On Individuality and Social Forms*, edited by David Levine. Chicago: Chicago University Press, 1971.

Simson, Naomi. "Productivity Hacks: Happy People are Productive People," LinkedIn, January 21, 2014. Accessed January 22, 2014. http://www.linkedin.com/today/post/article/20140121000342-1291685-productivity-hacks-happy-people-are-productive-people?trk=eml-mktg-inf-m-productivity-0121-p5

Sinetar, Martha. *Do What You Love, the Money Will Follow: Discovering Your Right Livelihood*. New York: Dell, 1987.

Smith, Allen. "Family Leave Turns 20; DOL Modifies Rules." *HR Magazine*, March 2013.

Sokol, David. "Let's Move!" *GreenSource*, July 2013. Accessed July 30, 2013. http://greensource.construction.com/features/currents/2013/1307-lets-move.asp.

"Spam in the Fridge." *The Economist*, January 25, 2014.

"The All-Out War for Good Jobs," *Gallup Business Journal*. Accessed December 8, 2013. http://businessjournal.gallup.com/content/151856/War-Good-Jobs.aspx#2.

"The How Report." LRN.com. Accessed December 20, 2013. http://www.lrn.com/howmetrics/data/LRNHowReport2012.pdf.

Townsend, Nicholas W. 2002. *The Package Deal: Marriage, Work, anf Fatherhood in Men's Lives*. Philadelphia: Temple University Press.

Unkovic, Xavier (global president, Mars Drinks, Inc.), interview by the author, January 3, 2014.

Voydanoff, Patricia. 2005. "Toward a Conceptualization of Perceived Work-Family Fit and Balance: A Demands and Resources Approach." *Journal of Marriage and Family* 67 (2005): 822-836.

Wartzman, Rick (executive director of the Drucker Institute), interview by the author, December 18, 2013.

Waytz, Adam, and Malia Mason. "Your Brain at Work: What a New Approach to Neuroscience Can Teach Us About Management." *Harvard Business Review*, July-August 2013.

Wells, Susan J. "Benefits Strategies Grow and HR Leads the Way." *HR Magazine*, March 2013.

Wikipedia contributors. "Amplitude." Wikipedia, The Free Encyclopedia. Accessed August 10, 2013. http://en.wikipedia.org/wiki/Amplitude.

Williams, Lawrence E., and John A. Bargh. "Experiencing Physical Warmth Promotes Interpersonal Warmth." *Science*, vol. 322, no. 5901 (2008): 606-607.

"Women Matter 2013—Gender diversity in top management: Moving corporate culture, moving boundaries." McKinsey & Company. http://www.mckinsey.com/~/media/McKinsey/dotcom/homepage/2012_March_Women_Matter/PDF/WomenMatter%202013%20Report.ashx.

"Yellowstone Park Foundation." Herman Miller, January 2, 2012. Accessed January 3, 2012. http://www.hermanmiller.com/research/case-studies/yellowstone-park-foundation.html

Zak, Paul J. *The Moral Molecule: The Source of Love and Prosperity.* New York: Penguin, 2012.

Zak, Paul J. (professor, Claremont Graduate University), interview by the author, December 13, 2013.

Index

About the Author

Dr. Tracy Brower is a work environment sociologist studying how humans affect their work-life and how their work-life affects them back. Throughout her career Tracy has had the opportunity to engage with hundreds of organizations, including many of the Fortune 500. Tracy is an award-winning speaker and seeks constant learning and new insights in connection with her network.

Professionally, Tracy is the Director of Performance Environments + Living Office Placemaking at Herman Miller, Inc. Tracy has experience in a wide range of industries including for-profit, not-for-profit, higher education, and healthcare. Her expertise spans work environments, HR/OD, organizational effectiveness and culture, change management, alternative working, business process improvement, and evaluation systems. Tracy has also taught university courses in management and organizational effectiveness.

Tracy received her PhD in sociology from Michigan State University. Prior to that, she received her Master's of Management in organizational effectiveness from Aquinas College, and her Bachelor of Arts in English literature, communication, and business from Hope College. She holds a Master of Corporate Real Estate from CoreNet. In addition, her work has been referenced and published in multiple sources.

Tracy lives in Michigan with her husband and their two children. You can find Tracy at www.tracybrower.com.